PAUL MARTIN

PAUL MARTIN

The Power of Ambition

John Gray

KEY PORTER  BOOKS

National Library of Canada Cataloguing in Publication

Gray, John, 1937–
    Paul Martin : the power of ambition / John Gray.

Includes index.
ISBN 1-55263-217-2

1. Martin, Paul, 1938–. 2. Canada—Politics and government—1993–. 3. Cabinet ministers—Canada—Biography. 4. Politicians—Canada—Biography. 5. Businessmen—Canada—
Biography. I. Title.

FC636.M37G73 2003   971.064'8'092   C2003-903656-1

The Canada Council | Le Conseil des Arts
for the arts | du Canada
since 1957 | depuis 1957

ONTARIO ARTS COUNCIL
CONSEIL DES ARTS DE L'ONTARIO

The publisher gratefully acknowledges the support of the Canada Council for the Arts and
the Ontario Arts Council for its publishing program. We acknowledge the support of the
Government of Ontario through the Ontario Media Development Corporation's Ontario
Book Initiative.

We acknowledge the financial support of the Government of Canada through the Book
Publishing Industry Development Program (BPIDP) for our publishing activities.

Key Porter Books Limited
70 The Esplanade
Toronto, Ontario
Canada M5E 1R2

www.keyporter.com

Cover design: Peter Maher
Electronic formatting: Jean Lightfoot Peters

Printed and bound in Canada

03 04 05 06 07 08 6 5 4 3 2 1

For Elizabeth Gray

Contents

Author's Note

URING THE ANXIOUS WINTER after Paul Martin was fired from Jean Chrétien's government, John Godfrey, the Toronto MP, talked of the perils that travel in the wake of ambition. He was not concerned with the performance of Prime Minister Chrétien or of his former finance minister but of his Liberal colleagues who were—and always are—pathetically eager to ingratiate themselves with a man of power or a man of potential power. Their affliction is that most of them are not content with the existence and duties of a mere member of Parliament; they feel they must become a cabinet minister if they are to be accounted a success in politics, even a success in life. The folklore of politics is replete with the stories of politicians who live beside their telephones when there is a rumour in the Ottawa air of a cabinet shuffle. John Godfrey: "My own feeling is that you have to tell yourself intellectually that this is a very foolish thing to aspire to, simply because if you don't tell yourself that, then you are always in a mode of self-censorship and sucking up. You keep second-guessing yourself because it might possibly have some impact on the likelihood of your being chosen."

Self-censorship and sucking up. They are the inescapable associates of political ambition. You're doing a book on Paul Martin, the man who wants to be prime minister? Love to talk to you. But please don't use my name. In some measure they are eager to help, in some measure they are eager to prove how well they know the man, how much they are insiders in the process of power. But, no, they do not want it recorded that this paradigm of political brilliance and virtue is perhaps modestly flawed—not at least with their name attached to such a judgment.

This is not to blame but to explain: why should they talk if their candour might in any way jeopardize their own future? It is an old journalistic conundrum: candour and no names, or names and limited candour? Everyone has hesitations—old friends, old enemies, advisers, fellow parliamentarians, fellow cabinet colleagues, public servants, former business associates, and those who might hope for the beneficence of a Martin government. I have opted for candour without names, which will explain a number of long quotations that are unattributed. But even that proviso was not sufficient for some: I'll call you by Wednesday and we'll talk, they said, but Wednesday never came. But there were many more who gave me a lot of time and many insights, and to them I am deeply indebted.

The story of Paul Martin Sr. is profoundly important, both in himself, as the political beacon for his son's politics, and as the symbol of a defeat his son was determined never to suffer himself. As a young reporter for the now defunct *Montreal Star*, I covered Paul Martin Sr. in his last years of active politics, at the United Nations, campaigning for the Liberal leadership in Montreal and in small-town Quebec, and occasionally later in Ottawa, during his bitter days as a senator after he had lost the Liberal leadership to Pierre Trudeau. I have drawn on those memories and, more especially, the quite wonderful three volumes of memoirs that he wrote after his withdrawal from public life. Aside from a thousand newspaper clippings, the other printed record of immense value was *Double Vision*, the definitive story of the first years of the Chrétien government by Edward Greenspon and Anthony Wilson-Smith. There is also the more narrowly focused *Paul Martin: A Political Biography* by Robert Chodos, Rae Murphy and Eric Hamovitch.

Mention should be made also of Sheila Martin, who has little patience with any aspect of politics, especially interviews with the wife of. She was candid and she provided me with ham sandwiches, and for both I am grateful.

Paul Martin was more generous with interview time than might be expected of a front-runner who has nothing to gain by talking. Those interviews are an important part of the book. The various quotations from Martin come from three long interviews in the winter of 2002–2003 and from an earlier interview for the *Globe and Mail* in the autumn of 2001, long before this book was ever contemplated.

When Anna Porter phoned in September of 2002 and asked whether I would like to write a book on Paul Martin, it seemed, I admit, improbable. Moreover, in the course of the following winter there were moments when I wished that the wonderful Ms. Porter and I had never met; but we both persisted and I am grateful. My thanks also to Meg Taylor, who deftly saved me from bursts of factual and stylistic foolishness to which even careful writers are prone.

John Godfrey, one of those who was prepared to be quoted and be damned, is fond of citing an aspiring politician in one of the novels of Arnold Bennett, of whom it is asked: "With what great cause is he associated?" A good question. Paul Martin has already had one great cause: he is the man who eliminated the budget deficit—by fair means and foul, perhaps—a challenge at which his predecessors had failed pathetically. In doing so he set a standard for governments in his own country and elsewhere. But what will be Paul Martin's next great cause? That is the central question in Canadian politics today. The answer lies somewhere in the conflict between the quite conservative instincts of the son and the quite radical instincts of the father who remains his inspiration. As to how that conflict will be resolved, there is as yet no knowing.

John Gray
July 2003

Introduction

IN THE SUMMER OF 1977, Paul Martin Sr. was back in Canada for a summer holiday. He had just flown in from London, where he was Canada's High Commissioner to the court of St. James. Clever tongues would dismiss the posting as one of those gifts that is bestowed on one politician by another, a grace and favour gesture to absolve a political embarrassment. But in the case of Paul Martin Sr., such a judgment would sully a man who had devoted his life to public service and who had helped to change the face of Canada. Improbably in the world of political favours, Martin was a man particularly well suited to the court of St. James. He had long been a serious student of international affairs; for five years he was Canada's secretary of state for External Affairs; and he had served as head of the Canadian delegation to the United Nations back in the days of the founding of the world organization. At the end of a long career, frustrated in his ultimate dream of becoming Canada's prime minister, he was consoled with the appointment to London. He was well into his seventies, but he was not a man suited to leisure. He had been a witness and a participant in the great sweep of world events after the Second World War; he seemed to have seen everything, and he seemed to know everyone. Nobody who knew Paul Martin would have expected him to sit back and enjoy a well-deserved rest, and, of course, he did not. He entertained members of the royal family, the British government and the British government's sternest critics. In Ottawa, members of the department of External Affairs were astonished by his energy and awed by the range of his acquaintances.

In midsummer by a lake, Paul Martin Sr. was interested not in the world of diplomacy so much as the inner world of his only son, like him named Paul. Paul Junior was an impressive figure in his own right. In the dozen years since he had graduated from law school in Toronto he had become a remarkably successful businessman. He had turned his back on his earlier dream of doing good works in the Third World; instead, he was proving himself as a firefighter in the jungles of Canadian capitalism. Not yet 40, Paul Junior was already a vice president of Power Corp. and the president of Canada Steamship Lines.

In the diaries Paul Martin Sr. kept of the years he served as High Commissioner in London, the tracking of his son's ambitions creates a fascinating counterpoint to the chronicling of British politics and the subtleties of world diplomacy. On July 31, 1977, father and son were at a fishing camp that belonged to Canada Steamship Lines, on a lake carved deep in the granite of the Saguenay region of Quebec. The Saguenay is at the heart of Quebec mythology, a region of breathtaking lakes and rivers and trees, brutally harsh winters and the isolation of farmers who were sent north to create colonies where they could bring forth children to sustain their faith and their language. Canada Steamship Lines was not central to that Quebec mythology, but Lac Laurin was good fishing, and the fishing camp was one of those little baubles that accompanies corporate success.

Father and son had matters of import to consider. The elderly diarist recorded the day and a discussion they had had before:

With his head on a seat cushion, he opened the "old question": Why should he not run in the next election, if he was assured of a cabinet post? He has the bug, I am afraid. I have, of course, suspected this all along—in fact I have known it. He has told me. Likewise he has confided his desire to Nell. My reply has been, "Wait until you are older."... "You are doing so well as a businessman. Become firmly established as a man of commerce. They will come after you instead of you pursuing them. You will be treated by some prime minister, perhaps Trudeau, as St. Laurent and Trudeau himself was. They were called to the cabinet and became ministers forthwith.... When you are forty-five years of age might be a good time to take the plunge. No one, of course, can foresee the future that clearly. In six or seven years you will likely be a tower of a man. You can do then what I failed to do. If you are still bent on politics, you could be where Trudeau is." There are, of course, many imponderables but now is clearly, in my mind, not the time.

There are two things to note. The first is the father's dream of the son's future: "You can do then what I failed to do. If you are still bent on politics, you could be where Trudeau is." The second is the father's postscript to that conversation, a recollection of a recent visit to London by Canada's then prime minister, Pierre Trudeau. Paul Sr. had mentioned to Trudeau that his son "had the bug" for politics, and he recorded the prime minister's response: "My view is that Paul should wait until he is ready. Waiting around as so many do (like me, he was saying) is such a waste."

Whatever the dreams he had for his son, Paul Martin Sr. was confronted by that stark judgment that his own life, measured in terms of the dream that had sustained him since he was a young man, was a waste. That was the judgment of the very man, Pierre Trudeau, who had beaten him for the prize he treasured beyond all else in life. So the pursuit of that prize would now be the mission of the son, as father and son both understood.

CHAPTER 1

Paul Martin Senior

I F JOSEPH JAMES GUILLAUME PAUL MARTIN had ever become prime minister of Canada, his would have been one of those extraordinary stories of improbable triumph over tremendous disadvantage. A Canadian Horatio Alger story, people would have said. As a child he had survived a brush with death that left him partly disabled for the rest of his life. His family had little money; he managed an education only through the kindness of benefactors and by the scrimping, saving, and sacrifice of his parents and his brothers and sisters. He launched himself into a life of politics, self-consciously styling himself as a reformer, a liberal, even a radical, in a party that was not eager for such adventures. When he left Parliament 40 years later, the face of the country had changed and a new Canada had been born. In those 40 years the Canadian state itself had blossomed into a usually benign and comforting presence in the lives of its citizens. At home and abroad there was a new consciousness of what was to be expected of Canada. Paul Martin Sr. had been central to the shaping of that consciousness. In the end, he achieved most of his dreams, and those dreams were the social programs that are the texture of modern Canada. But one dream—the grandest dream—eluded him. He never did get to be prime minister, and that disappointment clouded his life and remained a bitter legacy.

NOT LONG AFTER THEIR NEW BABY was born in Ottawa in the early summer of 1903, Philippe and Lumina Martin bundled up their infant son and their few possessions and moved to Pembroke, a lumber town 100 miles upriver from the nation's capital. For the Martin family, the trip to Pembroke was a search for a better life. They soon discovered that there was prosperity for the mill and factory owners and managers who lived in the east end of town and up the hill, but that prosperity was not for everyone. In the good times young Paul's father got work as a store clerk, a bill collector, and later in a factory warehouse, carrying steel desks and cabinets on his back, but there were also times when there was no work and no money. Even in the forgiveness of many years, there was little romance in that penury: "Our family was never well off; I doubt whether my father earned more than twenty dollars a week in his whole life." One of the problems was that Paul's father was devoted to sports more than anything else in the world; his wife occasionally nagged him about it, but everyone understood that umpiring a baseball game was infinitely more important to him than working in the evening. To help make ends meet, it was young Paul who began doing odd jobs after school; he delivered shoes and later sold Pembroke's weekly newspaper, occasionally invading the dining room of the local hotel to read the editorials aloud in the hope that he could persuade the diners to buy the paper and read the rest of it for themselves. But odd jobs did not make the family rich. The two bedrooms in their house had to accommodate the two parents and the seven surviving children. When a Martin boy died in infancy at the home of an aunt, Martin's mother wheeled the body home through the streets of Pembroke in a baby carriage.

When he was just four years old Paul was afflicted by spinal meningitis, a disease that at the time was frequently fatal. For a number of years he had to be pulled around town on a wagon by his father and then by his younger brother Emile. His mother first sought a cure from local doctors; when the effects of the illness persisted, she took the boy, then eight or nine, to visit Brother André, the Montreal priest who was renowned for his miraculous cures through faith, later the inspiration behind the founding of St. Joseph's Oratory on Mount Royal. Mother and son also visited the shrine at Ste. Anne de Beaupré, and Mrs. Martin came to believe that the boy's recovery was the result of divine intervention. Indeed, he achieved an almost complete recovery, except for a lingering weakness in his left leg and his shoulders.

In later life he would swim every day to build up the strength in his weakened shoulders. As a youth he played sports as best he could, which was not particularly well, and for one summer after he had finished secondary school he managed to get a job at the Pembroke Lumber Company. It was a painful test for his weak muscles, and it was no great satisfaction that for an 11-hour workday he made just $1.50. As he recalled in his memoirs years later, it was an experience that shaped his view of the world:

> It was here that I learned about the lot of the working man and the value of trade unions. I supposed that our one dollar fifty a day was standard, but it was nevertheless a pittance for such a long shift and contrasted starkly with what went into the owners' pockets.
>
> One of the vice-presidents of the lumber company used to walk through the mill every morning, immaculately dressed in a wing collar and sporting a carnation in his lapel. I grew to form a keen dislike of what his appearance represented. Pembroke really belonged to five or six men who lived beside one another, sat on each other's boards, and called all the tunes. I became acutely aware that the town was essentially a closed society, providing limited opportunities for young men like me. To my parents' chagrin, I even attended a meeting called to test Pembroke's reaction to the One Big Union, for I knew there had to be a better way.

Paul Martin could not have grown up without suffering some of the pressures that afflicted Canada in the early days of the 20th century, for his family was caught right in the middle of the tensions that divided English and French. The Martin family had originally come from County Mayo in Ireland, but after years in Quebec had become French-speaking. Then, when the family arrived in Pembroke with its English-speaking majority, Joseph Philippe Ernest became simply Philip. In his memoirs written many years later, Paul

Martin skated around and past Pembroke's communal tensions with the smooth skill that was long the hallmark of his politics. Because both French and Irish had gone to the town in search of work in the mills, and there were always more people than jobs, he wrote, "this led to a certain lack of amity between them." That certain lack of amity fractured the town during the bitter First World War conscription crisis and during the equally bitter debate over French schooling. The Martins, as French-speaking Liberals, supported the war but found themselves at odds with most of their neighbours when they opposed conscription. Almost half of Martin's classmates were of French descent, but they were taught only in English at the local separate school. It was a delicate understatement when he observed that Franco-Ontarians were "very upset" that they could not get schooling in their own language. The grief extended even to the Pembroke Cathedral, when Bishop Patrick Ryan was appointed to succeed a French-speaking bishop; the popular new bishop did not really help matters when he delivered his entire Sunday sermon in English and then repeated the whole thing word for word in French. As Martin wrote years later of that terribly Canadian tension surrounding English and French, "The undercurrent that began in those years seems to have persisted throughout my life."

Not everyone succumbed to that corrosive undercurrent. The same Irish bishop changed Martin's life just after he had finished public school at the age of 15. With money provided by a lumber baron from Renfrew, Bishop Ryan got him enrolled in Ironside, a French-language classical college at St. Alexandre, just up the Gatineau River from Ottawa. The harsh regimen at Ironside was designed to prepare boys for the priesthood. While he seems to have accepted the assumption that he was destined to be a priest, Martin acknowledged at the same time that he was struggling between his desire to be a priest and his longing to be like Wilfrid Laurier, the former Liberal prime minister who was revered by the entire Martin family. Such was the youngster's adoration that when Laurier died in February 1919, he broke all the rules by leaving the school without permission and walking the

10 miles to Ottawa so that he could watch the great man's funeral, which he did from the branches of a tree along the funeral route. So moved was he by the event that he walked to Ottawa's main post office, asked for paper, and wrote a long and effusive letter to Laurier's widow. Of Laurier, he wrote later, "His life had become my beacon and in a mysterious way had influenced what I wanted to do." At the end of his third year at Ironside he announced that he would not become a priest; instead, like Laurier, he would become a lawyer and eventually he would enter public life.

The first step towards that dream of public service was St. Michael's College at the University of Toronto. The boy from a very small town suddenly found himself in a very big world. He threw himself into reading, debating, theatre, and the exchange of ideas. His friends and acquaintances would be among the major figures in the generation to come: Lester Pearson, Vincent Massey, Sidney Smith, Morley Callaghan, Lionel Chevrier, Donald Fleming, Wishart Spence. Fifty years later his memoirs lovingly evoked his excitement at discovering philosophers from Plato and Plotinus to Spinoza and Leibnitz. Rather unnecessarily he explained that "the 'rah rah' aspect of college life—football hoopla and pennants festooned on one's walls—was not my style." After he had finished his undergraduate work he launched himself into law at Osgoode Hall; at the same time he undertook a master's degree in philosophy at St. Michael's College because he found Osgoode Hall "a little dull." In a line that should give pause to future generations of lawyers he wrote of Osgoode that "the professors were stimulating, but it was not a community with the university's intellectual animation." So, in pursuit of that stimulation, he wrote his master's thesis on Cardinal Newman's "An Essay in Aid of a Grammar of Assent."

He cannot have had much spare time. His first shock at university had been his second day at St. Mike's. He was told that he would need $275 to pay his room and board for the year and another $70 for university fees. After his summer of working at the Pembroke Lumber yard, his total savings amounted to just $40. So a few days later he began work as a part-time cashier at the Blue Bird Cafe, a Chinese restaurant near the university. His summers were spent at Thorncliffe racetrack, selling parimutuel tickets and pocketing $12 a day. Later he also got work at Woodbine racetrack, and every summer he spent at least six weeks at three tracks in the Windsor area. While he was in Windsor he also managed night work at the Ford plant as a cleaner and odd job man.

Paul Martin would return to Windsor and in time would become its most famous citizen, but that was in the future. In the meantime there were other concerns, academic and political. The political concern was one of those experiences that is sent by the gods—or should be—to teach a modicum of humility to those who aspire to a life of politics. In the early summer of 1928, as Martin was finishing his law examination in Toronto, a deputation of Liberal worthies travelled from Pembroke to invite him to contest the Liberal nomination in the provincial riding of Renfrew North where there would shortly be a by-election. His parents were unhappy at the idea, not least because the Conservative candidate was E.A. Dunlop, owner of the office equipment factory where Martin's father worked. At the age of 25, Martin was bathed in rectitude: "Dad, you don't understand these things. Anyone who stands in the way of desirable change must be challenged." The eager Liberal candidate was defiantly urging a universal minimum wage for the workers of Ontario, only to discover that his leader, W.E.N. Sinclair, was not prepared to make the same commitment. Also, Martin was opposing Prohibition but Sinclair was in favour. Martin emerged from the campaign with at least his rectitude intact. As he confided to an election diary: "I feel particularly happy in the thought that my fight was sincere and that I was not playing politics in the cheap sense of the word. I would sooner be right and be a defeated candidate than be wrong and be the member for Renfrew North."

On election night Martin was thoroughly thumped. Dunlop won the largest majority ever in Renfrew North, but Martin managed to steal a small consolation. When Dunlop was in the full flight of his victor's speech in the Pembroke Armouries Martin strode into the hall and onto the platform to shake his hand; with Dunlop's speech suddenly eclipsed, the assembled Conservatives cheered Martin's sportsmanship and decency. The astonished Dunlop accepted the handshake and growled quietly at Martin: "You little son of a bitch."

For the next two years Martin devoted his efforts to postgraduate studies at the Harvard Law School; at Trinity College, Cambridge; and at the Geneva School of International Studies. After that it was time to earn a living. He managed to get home to Pembroke but then had to borrow money from a friend who had also worked at the racetracks. He needed $65 for the train ride to Windsor and some modest purchases to set himself up in a rented room. Windsor is a long way from Pembroke and a few months of working at a racetrack would seem to be a slender introduction to a new home, but Martin had been thinking about Windsor's politics for a long time. Certainly the drubbing he had suffered in the by-election did not make Pembroke a particularly appealing choice for young Liberals, and he had the promise of a job in Windsor. Besides, he recalled, "the sizable French Canadian and immigrant population in Essex County could be helpful to me if and when I ventured into politics." If and when, indeed. For Paul Martin and politics, there was no if, and the when was as soon as seemed reasonable.

He had hardly arrived in Windsor before he set out to make himself known nationally and locally. He had survived his one brief and disastrous by-election campaign and had disappeared abroad for two years of study. But within months, among the powers of the Liberal Party, Paul Martin was a name people began to recognize. He courted Mackenzie King, then the recently defeated prime minister and soon to be re-elected prime minister; he and Vincent Massey set up a summer school to explore new ideas for the Liberal Party; he searched out prominent Liberals wherever they were to be found in the hope that they would eventually be helpful; he made speeches to whatever audience would listen; he was active in Windsor's League of Nations Society and almost immediately seemed to know everyone in the city who had ever worn a Liberal button. He made sure that the local newspaper, the *Border Cities Star*, was aware of his activities and he noted with obvious satisfaction that in the pages of the *Star* he had "made the transition from 'Liberal lawyer' to 'Liberal stalwart' with ease." It was less than an entirely edifying campaign, but when the Liberal electors of Essex East met in June of 1935 to choose a candidate for the coming federal election, the easy winner was Paul Martin. A few months later, in the federal election that returned Mackenzie King and his Liberal Party to power, the new MP for Essex East was Paul Martin. It was the beginning of a long and loyal relationship. When his daughter Mary Anne asked him what he could tell her about heaven, the wise father replied, "Heaven, darling, is Essex East."

Reflecting many years later on 10 consecutive election victories in 33 years, Martin insisted that he never really enjoyed campaigning. But campaigning became second nature to him. "It is said that I knew everyone, that I was a good door-to-door, store-to-store, supermarket-to-supermarket canvasser, and that I never forgot a face; in short that I was a politician's politician. There were other designations that pleased me more." There must have been some part of him that enjoyed being a politician's politician because he did it so instinctively and so determinedly. He was scornful of his colleagues who neglected their ridings, who were content to let the fate of the riding rise and fall with the party's broad support. There was no doubt about his view of his own riding: "I tended mine like a garden." If the House of Commons was in session he got home to Windsor every weekend—the 4 o'clock train from Ottawa on Friday afternoon, change trains in Toronto, overnight to Windsor, arriving at about 7 o'clock on Saturday morning. It was a routine that did not change much over more than three decades. He would meet constituents on Saturday morning to discuss their problems, whether it was about getting their pension or getting a job. Whenever he was in Windsor he tried to have lunch at the counter in the downtown Kresge's. On Saturday evenings he and his wife, Nell, would go to a church supper, a concert by one of Windsor's immigrant groups, a meeting, or a local sports event. He went to mass at a different church every Sunday. His secretary scanned the local newspapers for the names of people to whom he should write about a birth, a death, a graduation, or a marriage. Wherever he went in Canada or around the world, sooner or later he would say, "Is there anyone here from Windsor?" He used to ask the same question when he walked into Canada House in London, where he was Canada's High Commissioner, and, of course, quite often there was.

In his later years this avid pursuit of votes was mocked. People would tell of his boast that he could put a name to 50,000 people on the streets of Windsor. Nobody quite believed it, but nobody was quite prepared to deny it. The pity of it was that in his later years he seemed to be almost a parody of a politician, and when politicians get to be elder statesmen, there is not much dignity in the scramble for votes. So people loved to tell the story of how Martin arrived in a small town during an election campaign and made the customary round of Liberal dignitaries at the airport, with the usual greetings that are effortlessly suitable for friends old and new and half-remembered.

"Hello, how are you?"

"Good to see you again, Mr. Martin."

"Glad to be here. And how's your mother?"

"Actually, she died just before Christmas."

"I'm terribly sorry to hear that. I was always very fond of her."

Depending on who told the story and where it was told, that particular exchange between Martin and a young man occurred on three occasions on the same day as Martin made the round of old Liberal friends at various gatherings. Martin's half-memory of the young man was as uncertain on the third meeting as it had been on the first. But on the third occasion, in response to the same solicitous question about his mother, the young man simply replied, "Still dead, Mr. Martin." The story fit the Paul Martin mythology, so there were reporters who would swear they were actually there and overheard the exchange; it happened in Shawinigan and it happened in Lindsay, it happened last spring or it happened three years ago. The best evidence for the story is that Martin recorded his own version in his memoirs, telling the story on himself with obvious amusement. He too understood that it fit the Martin legend.

The curse of his later years was that the reputation of the Constant Politician threatened to obscure the rest of the Martin legend. More significant to the history of the country in mid-century was the effort of the MP from Essex East to remind the Liberal Party of its ostensible commitment to reform. While Martin was still a teenager, at the same 1919 convention that chose Mackenzie King to be its leader, the Liberal Party committed itself to a sweeping program of social reform that would include "an adequate system of insurance against unemployment, sickness, dependence in old age, and other disability, which would include old age pensions, widows' pensions, and maternity benefits." By the time Martin arrived in Ottawa as a new MP, 16 years after the 1919 convention, none of those commitments had been met. A few weeks after he got there, Mackenzie King took him aside and offered some encouraging words, including the solemn injunction that "a Liberal must always be a reformer." That said, Martin could see little evidence of reform in King's new cabinet. The minister of finance was the voice of big business and economic orthodoxy; heavyweights like C.D. Howe shared that conservative outlook; the minister of mines and immigration was a defender of 19th century laissez-faire capitalism and was blind to the problems of industrial society, and so it went.

In the Liberal Party of the 1930s, Paul Martin was an uneasy fit. The genius of the Liberal Party has usually been that it is able to spread itself sufficiently to left and right so that it occupies a broad swath of the political centre to the exclusion of rivals. In the wake of the 1935 election, the Liberals were virtually unchallenged so King was content to allow the party to drift to the right. Even with the country still sorely suffering from the effects of the Depression, King was unwilling to recognize a role for government in economic affairs. When the National Employment Commission finally produced a report after two years that recommended a large public works program and youth training programs to help overcome unemployment, the government worried about provincial consent. All this meant that the new MP from Essex East was pretty much alone on the Liberal left. He was a strong supporter of organized labour, which made him friends among the auto workers in Windsor but caused unhappiness among his fellow Liberals when he advocated collective bargaining for industries controlled or owned by the government. He intervened personally in the explosive 1945 Ford strike and persuaded the cabinet and the auto workers to accept Mr. Justice Ivan Rand as an arbitrator. The result was the Rand formula, which allowed workers to remain outside the union but enforced the collection of dues from them. The formula became the cornerstone of labour relations in the country and Martin continued to march at the head of Windsor's Labour Day parade, but he was profoundly hurt that the auto workers pledged their political support to the left-wing Co-operative Commonwealth Federation. At the time most Liberals made little distinction between the CCF and the Communists: they were all hovering dangerously close to revolution. Martin was much more restrained; he saw the CCF as his natural political rivals in Windsor, yet he found them seductive. He knew that some senior Liberals distrusted him for his left-wing views, but he thought he had the support of the unpredictable prime minister. "Sometimes I perhaps went too far even for Mackenzie King, but I believe he saw my views as an asset to the party—certainly the CCF would have made more gains in Windsor and in other industrial cities if I had not taken the positions that I did." Another consideration, as he admitted, was that "perhaps I got a certain thrill out of considering myself more modern than most of my colleagues."

Along with his self-satisfaction as a Liberal rebel, Martin was possessed from the start with a driving ambition. As soon as he got to Ottawa he wanted to be in the cabinet. That took 10 years; then, once in the cabinet, he wanted to be prime minister. When Mackenzie King announced in January 1948 that he would be stepping down, Martin was enraged that King stage-managed the whole succession process so that Louis St. Laurent would move smoothly into the job, virtually without opposition. He inveighed against "Mackenzie King's fine Italian hand," but as he did so he wondered whether the cards might be stacked against him in any case because of his politics. At the dinner in the Chateau Laurier hotel when King announced his impending departure, Martin made a speech in which he outlined an agenda of reform—work for those willing to work; adequate nutrition and housing; insurance for unemployment, disability, age, and loss of income; and health insurance to cover medical, dental, surgical, and hospital services. Such reforms had been on the Liberal Party platform for 30 years but Martin immediately began to fret whether "my speech was closing doors and convincing some in the party that I was far too progressive ever to be considered a Liberal leader." He admitted the speech was designed to stop the party from drifting further to the right, but pondered the cost: "I am sure that it confirmed the party moguls' belief that I was too much of a firebrand ever to get close to the leadership."

It was not helped that King's designated successor was Louis St. Laurent, the unbending and conservative Quebec City corporate lawyer. Whatever might be his virtues, St. Laurent was not a Paul Martin Liberal: "Many accepted his laissez-faire approach but I felt it was not enough for a complex industrial society. My more interventionist bias hinged on using the power of government to allow individuals to develop to their fullest capacity; it encompassed more than St. Laurent might readily countenance.... To him, I was always the scourge, agitating for reform."

In fact, in the months before St. Laurent became prime minister, Martin was responsible for one of those relatively minor events that change the course of history. It was a story he loved to tell in his later years, after he had been shunted off to the peaceful pastures of the Senate, because it was a sweet reminder of those days when he was a "scourge, agitating for reform." When Martin was minister of health, Dr. Wilder Penfield, the Montreal neurosurgeon, arrived in Martin's office to announce that his Neurological Institute needed an annual sustaining grant of $40,000; if the grant was not forthcoming, the institute would have to move to the United States. At the time, the minister of health was a creature of few powers and virtually no budget. As Martin was fond of saying, the authority of the federal government in matters of health did not go much further than inspecting the state of drinking water on trains. Martin had already been chastised for his inclination towards government extravagance a year before when he had tried to organize a conference in Ottawa of Canada's leading cancer specialists; the cabinet bluntly refused to pay their travelling expenses. However, even then Penfield and his institute had achieved a measure of renown and Martin knew that nobody in the cabinet, certainly not King, would lightly see the institute closing its doors in Montreal. King was easy to convince, and eventually even C.D. Howe, one of the recalcitrant and powerful right-wingers of the cabinet, agreed. As a contribution to medical research, the $40,000 was little enough, but as Martin wrote, "This precedent helped break the ground for an extension of the government's activities." Ten years later the still reluctant cabinet approved a plan for hospital insurance, and 10 years after that the country would be embarked on a medical care program that was at once the most expensive and the most cherished of Canadian governmental endeavours.

In his first cabinet job, as secretary of state in 1945, Martin stirred some controversy with his introduction of the Citizenship Act. Until then there had been no such animal as a Canadian citizen, and those who took pride in their identification as "British" did not appreciate their change in status. The debate was rancorous, but as far as the cabinet was concerned at least it cost no money. Eighteen months after he first entered the cabinet, he became minister of health and welfare, the portfolio from which he most successfully led the fight for a more liberal Liberalism. The battleground was hospital and medical care, and pensions for the elderly, the blind, and the disabled. He was not inclined to rest on his laurels. When Mitchell Sharp, then a senior public servant and later a cabinet colleague, congratulated him on winning approval for his Old Age Security reforms, Martin brushed off his kind words and replied that his priority was medical care insurance. None of it was easy because it all involved far more government spending than his cabinet colleagues wanted even to consider, and the spending of Health and Welfare always seemed a particular extravagance: "There are few more lonely assignments for a cabinet minister than to tilt against his colleagues' opposition. I have watched my successors in the department of health and welfare going through the same agony."

As always, Martin was sustained by a conviction of his own rightness that must have driven his colleagues to distraction: "Government health services would eventually bring returns not only in human happiness but in productivity and wealth, which would more than offset the dollars expended. I was no out-and-out radical, but rather saw myself as a tenacious small 'l' liberal. Our party had to move steadily to the goal of social justice. If it stood still, it would perish ... Yet most of St. Laurent's cabinet, including the prime minister, prized soundness of administration and budgetary surpluses as much as popularity. ... I kept reminding the finance minister of the budgetary surplus, imploring him to move quickly to help our older citizens."

Throughout his long public life, Paul Martin was alternately blessed and cursed by timing. In his pursuit of social legislation, Martin was undoubtedly helped by a change in public attitudes in the years after the Second World War. The Liberals caught up with the Canadian public and in the process laid the groundwork for one of the most comprehensive social systems in the Western world. In that, Martin was the beneficiary. However, in the pursuit of his ultimate dream, the prime ministership, Martin kept discovering that he was the wrong man at the wrong time.

As the Liberals prepared to choose a successor for Louis St. Laurent in 1958, Paul Martin thought his time had come. He had invested more than two decades in the business of Parliament and politics, and he had been at the centre of the transformation of Canada's social policies. But two months before the Liberals chose a successor, Lester Pearson won the Nobel Peace Prize for his work at the United Nations in ending the 1956 Suez crisis and in the formation of an international UN peacekeeping force. This was big time; this was world class; no Canadian had ever won such recognition. As Martin recalled bitterly, "The party establishment wanted a leader with glamour, and Mike certainly had that after the Nobel Peace Prize."

There was another aspect of timing. Since Laurier, the Liberal Party had been careful to alternate their leaders between English and French, and within a couple of generations this principle had become holy writ within the councils of the party. After the St. Laurent years, the Liberals of Quebec recognized that it was the turn of the other guys, and almost all Quebec delegates turned their back on the bilingual Martin and swung their support to the perfectly unilingual Pearson. If Martin were to have any chance he had to have Quebec, and Quebec was not for the having.

Besides all that, by 1958 Martin had been around for more than two decades, and for some at least he seemed a man from a different era of politics. Christina McCall-Newman put it most bluntly: "Martin, who had a better record of service to the party as an MP for twenty-three years and as an effective minister of health and welfare, besides an outstanding academic background in law and international studies, was seen as a ward-heeling pol. He *wanted* power, curious creature, and he let people see this base desire." It was hardly a contest. When they counted the votes, Lester Pearson became the leader of the Liberal Party by 1,074 votes to 305 for Paul Martin.

There would be other disappointments in his life, but that was the defeat from which perhaps he never fully recovered. If there was ever a time that was right for Paul Martin it was 1958. He was still in his mid-fifties, with intellectual and physical energy that awed his colleagues. Almost 20 years later, well out of politics and happily ensconced in London as Canada's High Commissioner, as he watched the struggle for the leadership of Britain's Conservative Party, it was his defeat by Lester Pearson that stirred a lingering regret: "I cannot help but recall my own disappointment in the leadership races, but that is life and some would say, all for the best. Pearson was a good Prime Minister and I have the greatest love for him, but I am still not convinced that I could not have done a better job. . . ."

Whatever the regret or the bitterness, Martin and Pearson were inseparable colleagues for the next 10 years. At first, after the landslide victory of John Diefenbaker's Conservatives in 1958, Martin and Pearson, along with Jack Pickersgill and Lionel Chevrier, were virtually the only opposition the Liberals could muster against the Tories. For all of them, after more than 20 years of Liberal rule, their arrival on the opposition benches was an unsettling shock, but to the distress of the Diefenbaker government they learned their new roles quickly and were relentless in their attacks on the prime minister and his hapless supporters.

When the Conservatives collapsed and the Liberals returned to power as a minority government in 1963, Martin became minister of external affairs. It was a role for which, in some ways, he had been preparing himself for most of his political life. From his earliest days as an MP, while the League of Nations was regarded as the last best hope of peace, he had been chosen to sit on Canadian delegations abroad. He was a Canadian delegate at the first meeting of the United Nations General Assembly in London in 1946 and then at the first meeting of the General Assembly in New York. His signal success at the UN was in 1955 when, as chairman of the Canadian delegation, he took a leading role in negotiating an end to a nine-year deadlock on new memberships in the world body. After months of difficult and sometimes ugly negotiations, 16 new members were admitted to what an emotional Martin described to the Assembly as "the only existing parliament of man." The principal roadblocks had been the United States, Britain, and France, and Martin described the process as "some of the most difficult and disagreeable negotiations ever undertaken between Canada and its major allies." The end of that deadlock was instrumental in transforming the UN into a genuinely world body. That probably accounted for some of the proprietary air that Martin exuded whenever he was at the UN, even in his final days as minister of external affairs. He was constantly greeting fellow veterans of the diplomatic wars, whether they were aging ambassadors or waitresses in the delegates' lounge who had been at the General Assembly when it first met in New York. And with his shrewd political memory, of course, he could put a name to all of them.

Sadly, by the time he got to be minister of external affairs, Martin was past his prime. Even the consummate oratory that had dazzled his friends and dumbfounded his foes, seemed to have degenerated into an exercise in verbosity. Someone described his performance in the Commons as "stoning his critics to death with marshmallows." One wonders whether Lester Pearson was being entirely candid when he said, "How I envied Paul his parliamentary debating skill—never using one simple word when fifty were needed to confuse and frustrate our political foes...."

Martin certainly began his years at External with his dreams high. He wanted Canada to grant diplomatic recognition to Mainland China; he wanted Canada to open its world to the south by seeking membership in the Organization of American States; and, above all, he wanted Canada to help seek an end to the war in Vietnam. Other critics were more harsh, but his own cabinet colleague Walter Gordon was not far off the mark when he wrote that "he had difficulty making up his mind on hard issues; he usually seemed to seek a mild-mannered and non-controversial solution which, in the long run, weakened his position." In Martin's five years at External, Gordon said, "no changes in policy were made or any new initiative of any consequence taken."

The reason lay either in the caution that comes of age or the caution that comes of concern for political pitfalls. In 1967, when the same Walter Gordon made a speech criticizing the United States for its role in Vietnam, for becoming involved in a civil war "which cannot be justified on moral or strategic grounds," the country cheered loudly—at last, Canada had a voice—but Martin tried to line up support to have Gordon fired from the cabinet. As others came to see the war in moral terms, Martin was forever at pains to tread the narrowing path of credibility between the United States and the North Vietnamese, and you couldn't do that if people like Walter Gordon were going to engage in noisy rhetoric. A few months later, when President Charles de Gaulle gave his cry of *Vive le Québec libre!*" the country and most of the cabinet yelled for his head, but Martin cautiously "recommended that cabinet give the president an opportunity to explain himself before we issued any statement that might force his hand." Whatever may have been the reason for his hesitation about upsetting the Americans on Vietnam, it was assumed that Martin did not want to support harsh words towards de Gaulle lest this upset any nationalists in Quebec who might be delegates to the next Liberal leadership convention. To an earlier generation, a much earlier generation, Paul Martin had been the voice of small-l liberalism and he took pride in that reputation as a progressive, as a reformer. By the end of his career he had come to be seen as very much the image of the old politics. In 1968 the defining conflict between young and old was the Vietnam War, and it was the war and the United States for which Martin seemed to be a hapless apologist.

The Liberal leadership convention came soon enough. When Lester Pearson announced in December that he would be stepping down, the first name that came up in all speculation was that of Martin. And why not? After all, he had been around Ottawa for more than 30 years. As he himself wrote, "Besides being the most senior cabinet minister in point of service, I was also the eldest, and this I knew highlighted both my assets and my liabilities." At the time, nobody understood the extent of those liabilities. Martin, however, must have had at least an uneasy feeling because before the press conference to announce his candidacy he dyed his hair black. It was painfully obvious. Asked about the fact that he was 64, Martin airily dismissed the concern: "Age is not a question of years, but of health, vitality and ideas." Anyway, he was ahead in all the polls, and he had shaken more hands than any of the other candidates had ever even seen.

The ascent of Pierre Trudeau to the leadership of the Liberal Party has become a familiar chapter in the folklore of Canadian politics. With the help of the retiring Lester Pearson, who pushed him into the national spotlight, Trudeau and a relatively small band of friends took the party by storm. He was the logical response to the aspirations that had been excited by Expo 67, and after a decade of Pearson and Diefenbaker, he redefined what politics and politicians should be. His warts were discovered soon enough in power, but those who watched the process of Trudeaumania would not soon forget their own astonishment.

Martin stayed ahead in the polls for another six weeks, and he clutched at every straw that came within the range of his vision, but his collapse was only a question of time. That collapse came on the first ballot of the Liberal convention. Of the 2,366 votes cast, Paul Martin got just 277, an embarrassing 11 per cent. When the result was read out in the Ottawa Civic Centre, there was a pause and then a collective noise that was halfway between a groan and a sigh. So much for a lifetime in politics. A few days later the new prime minister, Pierre Trudeau, made Martin an offer he could not refuse, and the Member of Parliament for Essex East became the new government leader in the Senate.

When he came to write his political memoirs, the chapter on his humiliation in the 1968 leadership was called "Paradise Lost." In that chapter he recalled the words of John Buchan: "Politics is still the greatest and most honourable adventure." The sentiment is noble enough, but if Martin or Buchan had been entirely candid about the matter, one of them would have added the corollary that, even for the greatest of its practitioners, politics is bound to end in cruel disappointment.

CHAPTER 2

Paul Junior

OR PAUL MARTIN SR., A NOVICE POLITICIAN whose ambition knew no bounds, the pregnancy of his wife, Nell, was a serious dilemma. In the late summer of 1938, just three years after his first election to the House of Commons, Martin got a call from the prime minister, Mackenzie King. Would he be part of the Canadian delegation to the League of Nations Assembly that would be meeting in Geneva in mid-September? It was the kind of mission for which inexperienced MPs were rarely chosen. The head of the delegation was Justice Minister Ernest Lapointe, and one of the other delegates was the redoubtable Nellie McClung, a prominent figure in the Canadian women's movement. How could any young MP, especially the MP for Essex East, say no? Of course, he could not. The problem was that the baby was due to be born at about the time that Martin was to leave. However, as Martin later recorded in his memoirs, the problem was solved by a certain Dr. Trottier: "Towards the end of the month, he decided to encourage the birth, and Paul Edgar Philippe Martin was born in Windsor's Hotel Dieu Hospital on 28 August."

The happy father managed to see his wife and newborn son briefly and then left immediately to catch a train to Montreal, where he and the other members of the Canadian delegation set sail for Britain on September 2 aboard the *Empress of Australia*. "It was not easy to leave them; but after a wrenching goodbye, I went on a mission of which my wife fully approved." It was not the first time and it would certainly not be the last that Martin family life would be dictated by the imperatives of politics.

For members of Parliament, there has always been an endless irresolvable conflict between Ottawa and home, between parliamentary obligations and family life. If the family moves to Ottawa, does the MP get back to the constituency often enough? However, if the family stays at home, it's a lonely life for both MP and family. Windsor is a long way from Ottawa, but there are a lot of other places that are much farther. In the early years, while Martin was still a backbencher, Nell and Paul Jr., and then Mary Anne, who was six years younger, lived in Windsor. After Martin became a minister, Nell would pack up the family in September to move to the nation's capital, and then pack up everyone again at the end of May to spend the summer at the family cottage in Colchester on Lake Erie.

Inevitably there were family crises made worse by distance. It was in the summer of 1946 that Martin was called from a cabinet meeting to be told that young Paul had been rushed to hospital with polio. In those days polio was terrible news. Many died and thousands were crippled in the epidemic that summer, so C.D. Howe, the powerful Industry minister, arranged for Martin to fly to Windsor on a government plane, in those days "a scarce and carefully husbanded resource." In the end the illness was not as serious as it might have been: "There he was, our handsome eight-year-old son, paralyzed in the throat and unable to speak. Despite our great consternation, Paul appeared to take it all as something of a joke; he was smiling and wriggling around in the bed. Mercifully the crisis passed fairly quickly and Paul began to mend, even though it took almost a year before he recovered fully."

If the sudden illness was searing for his parents, Paul Jr. in later life remembered very little. His last memory was of playing on a neighbour's swing; then, suddenly, he woke up in a hospital ward. "The odds were that I would have either died or been in an iron lung—that's what happened, apparently, to most people who got polio at that stage, with the kind I had. The odds that I would have had a full recovery were slight at best. And I ended up with a full recovery." He missed four or five months of school, but what seems to stand out in his memory of that period is that he was under strict orders not to play football while he was recuperating; however, inevitably he did play football, and his mother was very cross.

School in Ottawa was difficult at first. The family had always spoken English at home because Nell spoke no French, but when they moved to Ottawa they decided young Paul should go to French school. He was enrolled in Grade 3 at Ecole Garneau on Cumberland Street and he was, of course, completely baffled. And with the bafflement came the harsh trials of the schoolyard. "New kid at school, what do you do? You fight. I mean, it's nothing traumatic, it's a perfectly natural thing." And to complicate his life even further, he had to walk home past St. Joseph School, which was Irish Catholic. So at Garneau he got into fights because he was English; going home, he got into fights with the Irish kids because he was going to the French school. In time his bafflement diminished; after Garneau he went to the Ottawa University high school, which was bilingual before bilingualism became fashionable.

Whatever the strains of having a father who always seemed to be going to Windsor or to somewhere more exotic—or just coming back— Paul Jr. professes to have grown up in a fairly conventional life. Politics is not easy on family life because, as he said, "my father was away a lot, and even when he was here, he wasn't always here." But his mother, whom he adored and resembled, made sure that he and Mary Anne had a normal life: "My mother was the be-all, the end-all, the glue, the everything. But I think that's not untypical....I was incredibly close to my parents and my sister. I certainly give credit on this to my mother. I had a very happy childhood. We didn't have any money. But I had a very, very happy childhood and I never felt that I wanted for anything."

His earliest introduction to politics was travelling around the riding on weekends while his father met people, shook hands, chatted, inquired of their nearest and dearest. If they were out on Sunday, they went to a different church every week and Paul Sr. chatted on the church steps after mass. Later in life Paul Jr. would recall those political travels with some warmth, although at the time they were perhaps not terribly exciting. Sunny Conacher, the widow of the great hockey player Charlie Conacher, recalls that several times a year Paul Sr. would arrive at their home in the northern outskirts of Toronto. Martin liked those visits because the gregarious Conacher seemed to know everybody and to talk to everybody and was a shrewd barometer of the political climate of the country. On a number of occasions Martin had arrived with his teenage son, and Mrs. Conacher's recollection is that the youngster was very bored.

In his memoirs the father offered just a glimpse of a certain unruly streak in his son. "Nell handled the first stages of his adolescence well, but Paul sometimes had his mother and father in a daze. Like most high-spirited children, he was never at a loss for a means of expressing himself, whether it was pitching stones at the Soviet embassy or proposing a motion at his high school that 'Windsor is superior to Ottawa'."

A high school debate about your favourite city should not be a matter of great concern but in the course of his speech the young Martin referred to Charlotte Whitton, the veteran and venerable mayor of Ottawa, as "an interfering busybody." A busybody she undoubtedly was, but she was infuriated that anyone would have said so, and what probably made it worse was that it was said by the son of a Liberal cabinet minister. The mayor would not have hesitated to make clear her views on young Martin to his father in graphic and specific detail.

As for pitching stones at the Soviet embassy, Martin admits to throwing rocks at the embassy one day on his way home from school. It was the height of the Cold War, a reaction to the political times, he says. He was not arrested or charged, but the incident did get him a severe scolding from the police and his embarrassed father.

His own recollections of his school days in Ottawa suggest a fairly typical teenage boy: "I wasn't very studious at all. I was probably pretty typical. The only thing that counted were sports, and I guess I played every sport there was. If you grew up in Windsor, you weren't a very good skater and you played a lot of basketball and you didn't play much hockey. I really love hockey, but I was a lousy skater. I was not a bad basketball player. I had great ambitions to play professional basketball. The problem was that I couldn't jump and I was too short."

Son and daughter were both devoted to their father, but the senior Martin's memoirs suggest that there were long spells when he saw little of his children. Although Health and Welfare was his portfolio, he was one of the ministers on whom King and then St. Laurent could rely to represent Canada at the United Nations. He would spend weeks in New York, broken only by flying visits to Ottawa for cabinet meetings or to Windsor for weekend politicking. Occasionally Nell would spend time with him in New York, but that proved not really satisfactory because he was working most of the time. His schedule was occasionally bewildering. Once he recorded a flight to Ottawa for an early morning meeting, back to New York for the General Assembly that same morning, to Windsor that afternoon for the constituency dance, and back to New York for a delegation meeting the following morning. It did not leave much time for children.

Occasionally there were longer trips, farther away, as over Christmas and New Year 1956–57 when Martin and Nell spent two months in Asia. When their parents were away, young Paul and Mary Anne were cared for by their father's sister Anita, who lived in their rented house on Daly Avenue. Mary Anne was faithful in writing letters, her father reported, but her brother was less so. "Paul, who early in life had developed almost illegible handwriting, would promise to write but usually appended a few brief lines to his sister's more substantial letters. That fall, I could not be there when Paul's high school team won the football championship. I do not think the two of them ever knew how much I regretted missing many of those events that are so important to children. It cut me up when I would get a letter that ended 'When are you coming home?'"

In September of 1957, just after his 19th birthday, Paul Jr. enrolled in St. Michael's College at the University of Toronto, just as Paul Sr. had done, to study philosophy, just as Paul Sr. had done. Mary Anne says that her brother had wanted to study political science and economics but that their father had insisted on philosophy. Paul Jr. maintains he took philosophy because he figured he would read the world's great books on his own but he would never read philosophy on his own, so he enrolled in philosophy. His account of his years at St. Mike's is discreet and modest: "I was smart enough to get through without a hell of a lot of work, but not smart enough to get great marks. Wouldn't that be a description of most people?"

Mary Anne provides a more revealing sketch of her adored older brother's undergraduate life: "Paul was a very good-looking guy and he liked girls. He was probably in the top third of his class but that's only because he was smart. He didn't work hard at all; my father worked hard. He loved sports, and that's what he did in college, and he loved girls. He was a big party guy."

Bob Fung, who later became an investment banker and a driving force behind plans for the redevelopment of the Toronto waterfront, remembers Martin as probably the first Canadian he got to know. Fung had just arrived at St. Mike's from Trinidad and found he was living in the same university residence as Martin; they later shared an apartment in the university area. He agreed with Mary Anne's description of a life of sports and girls and not too much studying. "He was just like anybody else. Paul was just like the rest of us."

In one respect at least he was not like everybody else. Other fathers were seldom seen but Paul Sr. was a frequent visitor to the residence, always formally dressed in a dark suit, always delighted to see his son, but always visibly dismayed by the chaotic mess of the residence: "Paul was not the tidiest guy at school." Even then Fung was struck by the closeness of the relationship between father and son. In those days Paul Sr. led the relatively more relaxed life of an opposition MP. The Liberals had been dethroned from power by John Diefenbaker in 1957 and did not return to power, albeit as a minority government, until 1963. Fung, who spent his holidays at the Martin house in Windsor, got a first-hand introduction to Canadian politics through Paul Sr. In the 1962 and 1963 federal elections, he was an eager chauffeur for the Liberals of Essex East, driving Paul Sr. around the riding and ferrying elderly Liberal ladies to the polls on election day.

For Paul Jr. the introduction to politics was earlier and harsher. As he described it much later, when the university Liberal club heard that Paul

Martin's son was a student they asked him to join the club on the grounds that he was his father's son and simply had to be involved. Almost in spite of himself, he did become involved and made a lot of good friends, but he made up his mind that he would not devote his life to politics.

Indeed, if there was ever a time when he might have been turned off politics permanently, it was 1958. In January he watched as his father lost the leadership of the Liberal Party to Lester Pearson by an embarrassingly wide margin. Paul Sr.'s memoirs reported that his son and daughter bore the loss the hardest: "Paul had to contend with his classmates at the University of Toronto, so many of whom had campaigned for Pearson. Mary Anne wept because her father had been rejected." John Diefenbaker called an election two weeks later and young Martin found himself more involved than he had expected. He and a group of friends had gone to Massey Hall in downtown Toronto as a loyal claque at a Liberal rally. As he tells it, there was a crowd of perhaps 300 on the street outside Massey Hall when the police told them to move on; at that moment he became the leader of the group and told the police that, in the name of civil rights and freedom of speech, he would not move on. Everyone else had accepted the police suggestion that they move on, and the police solution to the one guy who was giving them lip was to throw him into the paddy wagon. He spent the night in jail and appeared early next morning in front of a magistrate who told him to go home. His father heard the news of the arrest on the radio; he was not happy with his son. And the sheepish son admits, "It was totally me and my mouth." The final straw came two weeks later when the Liberals suffered the most devastating defeat in Canadian political history.

Although Martin later insisted that politics did not figure in the grand design of his life, those around him always assumed it did. Mary Anne, for one, says she always knew he would end up in politics: "It was one of the things that was taken for granted, that Paul was going to go into politics." Similarly, Bob Fung: "I can't recall him sitting down and talking politics, but you always knew it was there. There was an interest that none of us ever had, but it was an interest he had. I don't think any of us in those days ever really knew what we were all going to do. But I think we all knew that he was going to end up in politics in some way, shape or form, whatever that meant."

For Fung, at least, some of that judgment may have come from his own perception of Martin as a social leader. He was someone who always seemed to be surrounded by friends: "He was just an ordinary guy, a really nice ordinary guy. There was a degree of loyalty to Paul, even in those days. Paul had something that was unique. You have a group of people—again, kids—but there was always someone who was the leader and Paul had that unique ability. It had nothing to do with politics. It was just Paul. He had a leadership ability; he had a magnetic ability. Paul was always—I wouldn't say the centre of everything but the kind of person people would congregate around. People liked him."

A variety of summer jobs gave him a glimpse of the world beyond academe and politics. His first job was a lesson from his father. When Paul Jr. was about 13, they were driving through the countryside and as they passed a field of people picking tobacco, he said, thank God he didn't ever have to do that kind of work. "My father said, 'You may think that's the way it's going to be, young man, but you have something to learn.' And the next thing I knew I was taken out to one of the farmers—I had two uncles who were farmers—and found myself in a field picking tobacco. I did that for about three weeks, and it was just as tough a job as I've ever had. Well, I was 13. And that's why I went and got a job on a fishing boat. I finally said, 'To hell with this,' and I got a job on a fishing boat for the rest of the summer." Later, he was a deckhand on a tug that operated up and down the Mackenzie River and on a ship carrying bauxite from Jamaica to Norway. One of his earliest jobs was at the Coca-Cola bottling plant in Windsor. His immediate boss was Ed Lumley, who was later a minister in Pierre Trudeau's cabinet. That summer Lumley was in charge of assigning helpers to various regular Coca-Cola drivers. He figured the Martin kid, the politician's son, was a bit of a mucky-muck so he stuck him with the toughest driver on the toughest route. The Martin kid would finish the day with his hands bleeding from the Coke cases but he did not complain.

The job that was ultimately the most successful started off as a disaster. He was reading gauges in the Alberta oil fields and decided his time would be better spent one evening at the Calgary Stampede. Taking the truck without authorization was a bad move; crashing it into a ditch on the way home was even worse. He was fired.

By that time Martin had finished his undergraduate studies and had moved on to more practical concerns: "I like philosophy but it became pretty clear to me by the time I got into the fourth year that, much as I enjoyed it, the opportunity for me to make a living as a street-corner philosopher was probably not extensive. So I went to law school." He decided fairly early on that he did not want to become a lawyer and set his sights on the Third World. He was, as he said, "very much part of that Sixties generation, wanting to solve the problems of the world."

It occurred to him that someone who might help him on that mission was Maurice Strong, the man who had fired him for crashing the purloined truck. Strong was something of a Renaissance man; he had an international reputation as an environmentalist, a businessman, and an adviser on Third World development. At that stage he was head of the giant conglomerate Power Corp. Strong's advice was not what he was seeking; Strong told him that the last thing that some African village needed was a recently minted Ontario lawyer. Instead, he should go into business and find out something about the real world. In fact, why wouldn't Martin go to Montreal and become Strong's personal assistant at Power Corp.? There did not seem to be a good reason to say no.

If Martin surprised himself with the decision, he astonished friends like Bob Fung: "I don't think Paul ever had a big grand plan. None of us did. I remember we used to laugh—it was a big joke—when Paul was going off to Power Corp., because none of us were business people. We were kids at college. And I remember when he went off to Power he would call us with different things to make sure he understood them, whether it was engineering, or whatever. There was a group of us just shaking our heads thinking of Paul the businessman at Power Corp. It was so far away from anything that any of us ever thought about."

CHAPTER 3

The Businessman

EVEN IF HE HAD NEVER GONE INTO POLITICS, Paul Martin Jr. has achieved a level of success that would make most people envious. After 22 years in business, he was a rich man, a very rich man. At the age of 50 he was the sole owner of a fleet of 33 ships that carried bulk cargo through the St. Lawrence Seaway and the Great Lakes, along the East Coast of the United States, and across the Atlantic to Europe. The list of his other business interests, filed in a 58-page report to the clerk of the House of Commons when he became a Member of Parliament, included three movie theatres, 22 multiple-unit apartments, a bus line, two office buildings, 66 beef cattle on a 400-acre farm in Quebec's Eastern Townships, five cars, 60 works of art, a 50 per cent share of several shipyards in Ontario, an Alberta oil and gas development, and four unsuccessful movies. Among his various holdings were 35 subsidiaries of Canada Steamship Lines. Whatever had driven him into politics, it was not money.

NOTHING IN HIS EARLY YEARS foreshadowed Martin's entrance in 1966 into the august office building in downtown Montreal from which Canada Steamship Lines ran its business, except perhaps the summers he worked as a deckhand on ocean freighters while he was at university. He has been fascinated by ships since he was a boy, since the days when he would watch the armada of freighters that funnelled past Windsor on the Detroit River on their way up or down the Great Lakes. But he had been in business for seven years before he got close to a ship, and that was running the unhappy Davie Shipbuilding in

Lauzon, across the St. Lawrence from Quebec City. The best that can be said about the Davie experience was that Martin survived when it appeared that he and the shipyard were destined for disaster. The shipyard, a division of CSL, was suffering horrendous losses, poor labour relations, and bad management. It must have seemed like something close to divine intervention in late 1973 when Paul Desmarais asked whether he would like to forsake Davie to become president of CSL.

It was not just CSL that seemed to be improbable serendipity. His background offered no reason to believe he was ideally suited to any one of Power Corp.'s various endeavours—except, of course, that he made a good impression on Maurice Strong. Martin had first met Strong because his father and Strong had crossed paths; then he and Strong had crossed paths when Martin managed to crash the company truck after his little romp to Calgary when he was a headstrong 19-year-old. It was shortly after that episode that Strong went to Power Corp., as executive vice president in 1961 and then became president two years later. Not long after that, Strong met up with Martin again and suggested he postpone his fantasy of going off to the Third World; instead he should get a little practical experience of life, and that was what led Martin to Power Corp. as Strong's special assistant.

Maurice Strong, still in his mid-30s, was already a figure of dazzling reputation. Even in the official history of CSL there is something breathless about the spectacle of the 14-year-old from rural Manitoba who arrived in Fort William and for the first time saw a big ship. The ship was the *Noronic*, later to be destroyed in a terrible fire; young Strong asked whether he could get a job aboard the vessel. He was told to see the second steward: "The second steward told him it was too late since the ship was about to leave, but to come back in a week when the ship was due back in port. When the bell rang, indicating that the ship was ready to leave, young Maurice hid in a closet. After the ship left the port he sheepishly went back to the second steward, told him he hadn't disembarked in time and could he work on the ship. He was given the job of kitchen assistant: peeling potatoes, washing dishes and generally helping the cook, whom he recalls as being an elderly Chinese man of kindly nature."

The brashness of the 14-year-old was impressive, and it gave a hint of the corporate career that was to follow. He worked as an accountant for a mining firm in Toronto; he went to work for the secretariat of the fledgling United Nations in New York; he made his way back to Manitoba, where he began working for James Richardson and Sons in Winnipeg as an oil and gas analyst; from there to Alberta where he worked for Dome Petroleum, ran his own firm, M.F. Strong Management Ltd., and various other energy companies that helped to shape the west, including, much later, Petro-Canada. For three years in the 1990s he ran Ontario Hydro, North America's largest utility. Martin has long cited Strong—"one of Canada's truly extraordinary people"—as one of the formative influences on his life. Strong was interested in Third World development before that became fashionable, he says, and he was an environmentalist before anyone knew what the word meant. The demands on him as an international bureaucrat were endless: he was secretary general of the 1972 United Nations conference on the human environment in Stockholm and the 1992 Earth Summit in Rio, and, as late as the winter of 2003, when he was 73, he travelled to Beijing and Pyongyang as the emissary of the United Nations to negotiate the perilous problem of North Korean nuclear weapons. (Not everyone is so admiring. In 1997 the right-wing *National Review* saw Strong as apparently hell-bent on taking over the world: "Militia members are famously worried that black helicopters are practicing manoeuvres with blue-helmeted UN troops in a plot to take over America. But the actual peril is more subtle. A small cadre of obscure international bureaucrats are hard at work devising a system of 'global governance' that is slowly gaining control over ordinary Americans' lives. Maurice Strong, a 68-year-old Canadian, is the 'indispensable man' at the center of this creeping UN power grab.")

It was Strong's knowledge of the energy industry that made him attractive to Power Corp., a modest conglomerate of electric utilities that had grown into a very rich conglomerate by the early 1960s, when the Quebec government nationalized the hydroelectric power companies in the province and left Power Corp. in command of a lot of cash and an appetite to buy. At about the same time that Power Corp. was coming into its windfall of cash, Algoma Steel Company needed some cash to finance an expansion program. It happened that Maurice Strong was already wondering about CSL as an investment opportunity; conveniently, Algoma held 50 per cent of the shares of CSL. So a deal seemed reasonable, and Algoma sold half of its interest in CSL to Power, which gave Power a minority share—a matter of no particular surprise until Power suddenly demanded four seats on the board of directors of CSL and a place on the CSL executive, which went to Strong.

But Strong's career at Power Corp. was to be short-lived. Martin had arrived in Montreal in the spring of 1966 as Strong's assistant, only to discover a few months later that his mentor was leaving for Ottawa where he would become head of the new Canadian International Development Agency. For Martin it was a rough introduction to the world of business: "I thought I was going to lose my job for sure; here I had been there not very long, a matter of months, and all of a sudden he's hired and he goes off to the government. But anyway, the new president, Bill Turner, made me his executive assistant and I stayed on. It turned out that I just had a natural aptitude to do deals. I was young, I didn't know very much about business, so they would give me more or less hopeless cases, and I was quite lucky and pulled them off."

Martin was certainly not lacking confidence. In December 1967, when Lester Pearson announced that he would be stepping down as prime minister and leader of the Liberal party, Martin had been working for Power Corp. for barely 18 months and for his new boss, Bill Turner, for scarcely a year. But he went to Turner and calmly asked for a leave of absence so that he could help run his father's leadership campaign. At the start of his leave of absence, he and his father and a lot of other people thought that Paul Martin Sr. would be the next prime minister of Canada. Then, quite suddenly, Pierre Trudeau became a player on the national political scene, an apparently reluctant candidate, and Paul Martin began the long slide down. His son learned only too soon how fast that slide had become because his particular responsibility was his father's campaign in Quebec. As a francophone, albeit a Franco-Ontarian, the father thought that the strength of his support in Quebec would carry him to victory. When Trudeau entered the race, whatever support Martin may have had melted away to Quebec's new and dazzling native son. So it was a bruised and sorrowful Paul Martin Jr. who finally returned to his job at Power Corp.

When he walked into the Power Corp. offices again, Martin discovered there was a new man in control, a man whose nerve and wizardry in money matters impressed even those Power Corp. veterans who had seen Maurice Strong at work. Paul Desmarais, who became another of those people who had a profound influence on Martin's life, had started his business life in his hometown of Sudbury, Ontario. His father had handed him the small family-owned bus company that was teetering on the verge of bankruptcy with 16 buses and a massive debt at the bank. Desmarais and his brother Louis and their partner, Jean Parisien, slowly and carefully pulled the Sudbury-Copper Cliff Suburban Electric Railway company out of debt, then turned their acquisitive attention to other bus companies, Provincial Transport in Quebec and Colonial Coach Lines in Ontario. After two decades they had created a conglomerate of their own, the Trans-Canada Corporation Fund, parlaying a backwater bus company into an empire that included all but one of Quebec's major French-language newspapers, insurance companies, furniture manufacturers, and racetracks. To Power Corp., Trans-Canada seemed like an attractive partner in a merger, but it was a merger only briefly. It was agreed that Desmarais would run the merged company while Peter Thompson, the son of the co-founder of Power Corp., would be chair. Within months Desmarais had used one of the reverse takeover bids that had become his trademark to acquire majority control of Power Corp. So when Paul Martin arrived back for work, Paul Desmarais was the new man in charge.

Martin recalls the conversation vividly: "All of a sudden I walk in to reclaim my job that I had taken this leave of absence for, and he knows me from Adam, and he sort of said, well, what do you do here? And I told him, I said, well, I had done the odd deal and everything else, and he said what do you want to do? At that point I had been at Power Corp. for a year and a half and I said I had enough of business and I'm going to quit. I had always had this desire to go off. It would have been a very interesting thing to know—if I had said I'm going to stay, I want a job, he might have said, well, we don't need you, go away. But when I told him I wanted to quit, he said, well, no, don't quit; let's see what you can do here. Well, I was married and had one child and everything else, so I said, well, maybe. And at that point I really became a firefighter."

It was a job made for a young and eager troubleshooter. Power Corp. had a lot of money but it also had a lot of troubles that needed fixing. In the next five years Martin trimmed, hacked, fired, sold, or shut down a succession of branches and divisions and companies in Canada and the United States, ranging from Inspiration Construction and Dominion Glass to Consolidated-Bathurst and Davie Shipbuilding. It was a wide-open field: "If you were an established person in the business world you were not going to take on some god-awful mess and totally damage your reputation. Well, I had no reputation, so I became the person that they would send in to fix up the company and sell it, or figure out what the hell the problem with it was." It was late in 1973 that Paul Desmarais asked him whether he would like to be president of Canada Steamship Lines.

Although Canada Steamship Lines was created as a company in 1913, some 60 years before Paul Martin became the president, its roots can be traced much farther back in the mercantile history of the Great Lakes and the St. Lawrence River. It began in 1845 with a small paddlewheel steamboat and a barge, built by Jacques-Félix Sincennes, a merchant from Sorel, which is about 40 miles down the St. Lawrence from Montreal, at the mouth of the Richelieu River. The enterprising Sincennes, who had some experience as a pilot on the St. Lawrence, knew that the farmers of the Richelieu valley had difficulty getting their crops upriver to market. The steamboat *Richelieu* and the barge

Sincennes would be the answer to their needs. As boat and barge made their way down the Richelieu, the farmers wheeled their carts onto the barge and wheeled them off at the Bonsecours Market in what is now Old Montreal; when the market day was over they would return down the St. Lawrence and up the Richelieu. Competitors appeared and quickly merged with Sincennes to create La Compagnie du Richelieu. When railways ate into the traffic from the valley, La Compagnie abandoned the Richelieu and concentrated its efforts on the St. Lawrence.

Those were the golden days of steam on the St. Lawrence and they had their own madness. Speed was the measure of success for passengers, for spectators, and for the owners. Steamboats would race between Montreal and Quebec to see which would be first to arrive and lower its gangplank. Because the shipping channel was frequently quite narrow, there was no thought of keeping a safe distance from a competitor, so the vessels were constantly courting danger, cheered on by the heedless passengers on their decks. To increase the heat in the furnaces, stokers would throw in barrels of resin or grease. Inevitably, disaster happened. On June 26, 1857, La Compagnie's *Napoléon* was racing the steamboat *Montréal* upriver from Quebec when flames suddenly burst through the deck above the *Montréal*'s overheated boilers. The captain turned the vessel towards shore but it ran aground in six and a half feet of water, 800 feet from shore, with the tide running downstream. In 15 minutes it was all over; of the 300 passengers aboard, 253 were burned alive or drowned.

That was the end of racing on the St. Lawrence but commercial competition continued and flourished. In 1874 La Compagnie merged with the Canadian Steam Navigation Company, an operation based largely in the Great Lakes, to form the Richelieu and Ontario Navigation Company. The success and prosperity of the R&O was eventually its doom as an independent company; it was an obvious target for the variety of British interests that were eager to consolidate eastern Canada's inland shipping. After a prolonged and bitter takeover battle led by a financier named Grant Morden and bankrolled by the Furness Withy shipping interests and Vickers shipbuilding, R&O finally succumbed in 1913 to a merger with Inland Navigation, Northern Navigation, and a number of smaller companies. Thus was born Canada Steamship Lines. Within a year Canada was at war and CSL was fully committed to the war effort; by war's end CSL had lost 16 ships.

The war and the financial problems that lingered in its wake nearly bankrupted CSL. It took the intervention of New York financiers and a shakeup of CSL management to get the company back on its feet, but that opened the way to a period of impressive prosperity. The Great Lakes and the river were the way to send cargo and the way to travel for pleasure. The Great White Fleet carried passengers from the Great Lakes down the St. Lawrence and up the Saguenay River; the CSL resort hotels on the St. Lawrence were the envy of their competitors; five shipyards stretching from Lauzon to the Lakehead built ships for CSL and its competitors and built ocean-going vessels to ferry troops to Europe during the Second World War. The shipping company also diversified into unrelated areas, particularly the Kingsway Transport trucking company. Curiously, in the early 1920s CSL pioneered a system of emptying cargo from freighters, but the new system was little used until the self-unloading technology became CSL's passport to prosperity 60 years after it was first developed.

The opening of the St. Lawrence Seaway in 1959 changed forever the pattern of shipping on the St. Lawrence and in the Great Lakes. The economics of freight by water had long demanded increasingly larger ships, and suddenly this was possible. There had always been a strange division in the inland shipping industry of eastern Canada. Ocean-going freighters would deliver cargo to Montreal or Quebec or the lower St. Lawrence; the cargo would then be transferred to smaller freighters that could use the short and narrow canals along the St. Lawrence that were built to skirt the Lachine and Long Sault rapids; the cargo would then be transferred to the larger freighters that travelled the Great Lakes. The Lakes freighters were a curious anomaly; they were trapped forever in the world to the west of Kingston and Prescott. Usually the lakers were built on the Great Lakes but sometimes they would be built at the Davie yards, sailing up the St.

Lawrence with their mid-section on their deck as cargo, to be assembled as much longer vessels at shipyards on the Lakes, but forever hostage as lakers because they were too big to leave. The opening of the seaway fundamentally changed that whole world.

Other parts of the St. Lawrence empire were also changing. The Great White Fleet of passenger liners was a source of particular pride to Canada Steamship Lines, but the company was more devoted than were its potential passengers. Travel down the river on a passenger boat was quaint, but quaint could not compete in a changing world of cars and airplanes. Cruise vessels occasionally had to sail with as few as 50 passengers aboard. Besides, the boats were a menace because they were top-heavy; when one of the vessels went to the Saguenay and whales were sighted, the rush of passengers to one side caused a tilt so severe that plates slid off the tables in the dining room; it would be only a matter of time before one of the vessels tipped over completely. CSL had already suffered terrible fires aboard two ships in which more than 100 people died; the company could not afford another disaster. In November 1965, CSL announced that the days of the Great White Fleet were at an end.

Martin's early years at CSL were a time of easy prosperity. The basic business was hauling grain down to the lower St. Lawrence and hauling iron ore up the Lakes on the return trip. For shipping companies it is a particular luxury when there is more cargo than your ships can carry. Not long after Martin took over, CSL unloaded the Davie shipyard that had been hemorrhaging money. So the books were looking good but Martin, as he confessed much later, was becoming restless; he was president and CEO, but Paul Desmarais was ultimately still the boss. Martin kept brooding about going off on his own, running his own show, being his own boss. Then one day in the spring of 1981 he got a call from Desmarais, who announced that he wanted to sell the company out from under him. Desmarais had long nourished a dream of taking over Canadian Pacific Railway, but to do that he was going to need some cash. Anyway, the regulators in Ottawa would probably take a dim view of Desmarais controlling two huge transportation companies. So would Paul please find a buyer for CSL? On the spot Martin announced that he wanted to buy the company and a moment later had to acknowledge that he had no money. Apparently unfazed by such bravado, Desmarais laid down the terms for a deal. Desmarais would call the bank and tell them that Martin would come calling to discuss a loan with his permission. Martin said he would need a partner, and Desmarais said he could approach one prospective partner—but only one—to see whether they could work out an offer between them. But there could be only one approach, and if there was no agreement with that one partner, Martin was out of the picture as a buyer because that would mess up the market for Desmarais. Martin agreed to the conditions and walked out of his office and across the street to the offices of Laurence Pathy, a friend, who also happened to own Fednav Limited, the largest international shipping company in the country.

"I already had a pretty good financial mind," Martin says, "so I put together the deal walking across the street."

The two men talked about it for 15 minutes, came to an agreement, and shook hands on it. Armed with Pathy's agreement and Desmarais' sanction Martin went to the Royal Bank to arrange for financing. Two weeks later, when Desmarais returned from a trip to Greece, Martin laid out the terms of the agreement he and Pathy had reached. Desmarais immediately replied that the offer was too low, but that opened the way for negotiations that lasted the better part of two months and, as Martin said later, it got more expensive with every negotiation. His own calculation is that he and Pathy paid too much—$180 million—but it could have been far worse for them. On August 8, 1981, the day the deal was finally signed, interest rates rose to 22 per cent, the highest level in Canadian history. On that day one of the gurus of Wall Street predicted interest rates would go as high as 30 per cent; Martin knew that if they did go to 30, he would be finished. In fact, the guru was wrong; instead, the rates dropped fairly quickly to 14 per cent and the deal was safe. It was, he admits, a gamble, but if he had not taken the gamble and risked every penny he had, he would not have got the company—"so you can play it either way." Seven years later, not long before he went into politics, Martin bought out Pathy because by that time CSL and Fednav were starting to compete with each other and it did not make much sense. For the first five years a handshake was what bound the deal; they had never got around to putting anything on paper, although occasionally they would have to get together and reconstruct their first conversation to make sure they had actually agreed on what they thought they had agreed on. When they did finally put the agreement down on paper it was only out of a concern that one of them might die and there would be no record of the deal. In later years there were bigger deals, but at the time the $180-million purchase of CSL was the largest leveraged buyout in Canadian history.

The purchase of CSL reveals a curious dichotomy in the character of Paul Martin. He is at times the most cautious and deliberative of creatures and at other times an apparently reckless gambler who revels in the adrenaline of the game. In his eight and a half years as Finance minister he gnawed at problems to the point that his officials despaired of ever getting a decision; Martin and his senior officials spent up to 18 months on some problems, debating solutions, searching for pitfalls, endlessly rehashing. For that he makes no apology: "If you don't have to take a risk in making a decision, then I don't know why the hell you should take the gamble. If you can do it risk-free, do it risk-free." He is ready to acknowledge that an instant decision is not necessarily shrewd when you are gambling $90 million: "Now if I had two weeks to make that decision, I might have taken two weeks. I would have taken whatever time I had to make the decision because I could have done more analysis, more thinking about it and everything else." Yet the gambling side of the shipping business is obviously a large part of the appeal. He loves to talk about shipping as one of the bastions of free enterprise, a throwback to buccaneering capitalism—"the most speculative, hard-nosed business in the world." The nature of the shipping business is always a gamble because, he says, when you are building a ship, nine times out of ten you are doing it against a market you hope will be there. But you can't build just a tenth of a ship, the ships are big and terribly expensive, and shipping is one of the last totally unregulated businesses—just market forces and entrepreneurship, with no government protection. With that Martin gives the confident shrug of a gambler who gambled and won: "It is one of the riskiest businesses around—which is why there are great fortunes made and great fortunes lost. Careful stewardship is not the way I would describe any shipping company that's been successful."

At the very moment Martin and Pathy had signed their deal with Desmarais, shipping on the Great Lakes and the St. Lawrence was headed for trouble. Iron ore shipments up the Lakes declined dramatically, partly due to the recession, partly due to structural changes in the steel industry. Steel production in the United States was down by half, in Canada by a third. Grain shipments were also down because rail subsidies made it cheaper to transport grain to Vancouver by rail than through Thunder Bay by ship. A third of the ships in the Great Lakes fleet were laid up because there was not enough cargo to carry. CSL managed to increase its share of the market, but the size of that market was shrinking.

As Canadians would discover later when he was a Finance minister determined to balance his budget, Martin was not a man to shrink from harsh measures. Sentimentality did not intrude. With little prospect of future markets, he closed down the Collingwood shipbuilding operations; 600 jobs were lost and with them went the last of the shipbuilding tradition on the Great Lakes. More painful for Martin personally—his hardest decision at CSL, he says—was the sale of Kingsway Transport. The big trucking company needed a lot of investment to consolidate its position in the trucking industry. For Martin it was a difficult choice; he had concluded that you had to be international to succeed, whether it be in shipping or trucking, because you needed a big market. He figured CSL did not have the money to go international in both industries, so it was Kingsway that was sacrificed.

For Martin, it is a harsh and inelegant jungle: "If we aren't prepared to compete anywhere in the world, people will come in our backyard and beat our brains in."

CSL's exploration of ocean travel began as a result of rising ship-building costs in the 1970s. One of the curses of the laker business was that ships were laid up for three months of the year because of ice in the Great Lakes; to get that three months' revenue out of the vessel, the solution would be to strengthen it to a standard that would permit ocean travel in those three months when it would otherwise be laid up in an ice-bound port. Thus were born "salty-lakers." The bonus for CSL was that when the recession of the early 1980s crippled shipping on the Great Lakes, the salty-lakers were used 12 months a year on ocean service.

Whatever satisfaction came from the adaptability of the salty-lakers, far more important for CSL was the self-unloading technology that the company had virtually ignored for more than half a century. The principle was easy enough: each vessel is equipped with a series of conveyor belts that carry cargo—whether it be iron ore, grain, or some other bulk commodity—from the depths of the hold to the level of the deck. From the deck level the cargo is carried on a conveyor belt to its destination on a long boom that can extend up to 250 feet. The self-unloading technology was designed specifically for the economics of the Great Lakes and the St. Lawrence. For ocean-going vessels it was reasonable after a long trip to spend four days in port while cargo was unloaded by old-fashioned cranes; but on the Lakes, where trips could be a matter of hours, shippers cannot afford to spend four days in port. Rather than four days, the conveyor-belt technology can unload a ship in eight hours.

The self-unloaders were not widely used at first because most ports had already made a major investment in conventional cranes. But in time the new steel mills on the Lakes found the self-unloaders were perfect for their needs. Cargo can be dropped quickly—up to 6,000 tons an hour—and neatly into an intended destination with far less dust and other environmental disruption. The 250-foot boom meant that vessels did not have to go right into shallow or crowded ports; the booms also meant that cargoes could be transferred from smaller freighters into, for example, gigantic coal carriers without either vessel going into port. The self-unloaders solved a different kind of problem in CSL's first major contract in Europe—a coal-fired power plant in southern Portugal that was 100 miles from the nearest suitable port. Instead of worrying about a port, CSL's *Atlantic Superior* poured coal across an oil terminal, through a hopper and conveyor system, and from there to trucks that carried the coal to the plant three miles away. Without the self-unloader and the contract to deliver three-quarters of a million tons of coal a year, the plant could not have operated.

When Martin headed off into the world of politics in 1988, his business interests were thriving. CSL was established as an international company, and its self-unloading fleet was the largest in the world; he could step back from the business in the knowledge that it was in the hands of his own hand-picked executives, and within a decade CSL would be debt-free. Then, to his surprise and embarrassment, the shipping company suddenly came to be seen as the fatal flaw on his progress towards 24 Sussex Drive.

CHAPTER 4

The Martin Women

GIVEN THEIR FIRST CHOICE, Nell Martin and her daughter-in-law, Sheila, would never have chosen husbands who were determined to make their life in politics. Sometimes, however, the choices in life are never entirely straightforward nor the outcomes entirely predictable. On the other hand, Mary Anne Bellamy, daughter of Nell, friend and sister-in-law of Sheila, made up her mind about politics when she was a flower child in the 1960s. For all of her life, she had been a privileged spectator of politics. She had watched her father suffer two terrible defeats in politics, the first when she was just 14, the second 10 years later. Immediately after the second defeat, she fled to India and fell in love with a volunteer in the U.S. Peace Corps. Twenty-five years later, from her home in St. Paul, Minnesota, she still insists that she could never see any justice in Pierre Trudeau's victory in the 1968 Liberal leadership race. And 25 years after her father lost, she agonized from a distance, from her home in the United States, at the thought of her brother running for the leadership of that same Liberal Party, running the risk of the same loss and humiliation. Unlike Mary Anne Bellamy, Nell Martin and Sheila Martin came to terms with politics and the burden it imposed on their lives. Reluctantly, perhaps, but that is the nature of life and politics.

FOR PAUL MARTIN SR., THE NEW LIBERAL MEMBER of Parliament for Essex East, the complications of domestic bliss began on an early winter evening in 1936, about a year after he was first elected. In his bachelorhood he had become accustomed to smoking a cigar as he read a book after dinner. On that particular evening he discovered that he had no more cigars, so he drove to the drugstore at the corner of Tecumseh and Windermere to buy a 10-cent Punch panatela. "As I walked in, a young woman behind the counter glanced my way while saying to another customer, 'Well, you know, I'll never get married.' For some extraordinary reason, I found myself saying, 'Oh yes you will, for some day you will marry me.' We laughed merrily. When she gave me my cigar, I had a full view of a beautiful Irish face and rich blue eyes."

The abiding image of Paul Martin is of the elder statesman, the veteran politician who was cordial, correct, and formal, a man who could not say hello in less than five minutes. In later life he did not seem like the sort of man who, even lightheartedly, would have announced to a complete stranger that he would marry her. Nor did it seem likely that he would have returned home that evening, phoned a pharmacist whom he knew to find out the name of the young woman who had sold him a cigar, and then phoned her, announcing that he was the MP for Essex East, to ask her out. Quite properly Nellie Adams told him she knew nothing about politics and could not go out with him that night, even if he *was* leaving for Geneva in the morning.

The eager MP sent a succession of postcards from Geneva to the young Miss Adams and began to court her as soon as he returned to Windsor. For a time, as he wrote later, she was hesitant. "The tempo of my life disturbed Nell. Was there no time for pursuits other than those connected with politics? she asked. From what she could see, my life was all work—engagements every day of the week; even on Sundays there were church dinners and functions. Nell, ten years younger than me, was overawed by the responsibilities of the life I led and was now urging upon her." However, she apparently overcame those hesitations for she arrived at her suitor's law office one day with a straightforward question: "Are we going to get married or not? I'm too young to spend my life waiting for you to make up your mind." They married a few months later.

When did Nell Adams come to terms with this life in politics that had seemed at first so alien? The answer is unknowable but the best guess may lie in a story told by Paul Jr. in the moving eulogy he delivered at his mother's funeral in December 1993. As he described it, when things were not going well for his father, she was there to help him up; when things were going well and he was perhaps flying a little too high, she would bring him down to earth. He told of an incident when she was still a young bride, "and Dad was walking down, very much the important MP, walking down Ouellette Street, the buttons bursting from his vest, huge cigar, very much the master of all he surveyed. And my mother realized she wasn't going to be able to put up with this for 50 years. And so on the corner of Ouellette and Wyandotte, my father was walking down, dispensing everybody with great glances of superiority, my mother sat down on the curb. And refused to move. And a crowd gathered around and my mother said I am not going to move from here, Paul, until you stop being so pompous. And she just wouldn't let him go. And so consequently he promised that he would never be pompous. The 30 people applauded." With a timing his father would have admired, Paul Jr. paused and added: "I've now met 5,000 people who watched this happen."

From then on Nell Martin seems to have adopted a dual line of attack on the matter of politics. She held herself at arm's length from politics and public life until she decided to overwhelm it. Confronted by her first election campaign in 1940, she refused to sit on the platform, as politicians' wives were expected to do in those days, but she would wave from the audience when introduced. She did her best to avoid teas and soirees, but when she went her husband boasted that she was the liveliest person in the room. If she went to a meeting, he said, "she was as likely to take a high step over her chair as to sit on it." On one occasion the MP for Essex East checked in on his election campaign committee room to find there was not a soul there; he discovered the entire campaign staff across the street in a pub, having a party with Nell. On another occasion Nell and some campaign workers were taking down Conservative election posters when they were spotted, setting off a midnight chase through the county; to the relief of Martin Sr. his wife and his campaign workers were faster than the Conservatives.

She brought the same cheerful irreverence to official Ottawa. Early in their marriage both Martins had become close friends of M.J. Coldwell, then the newly elected leader of the Co-operative Commonwealth Federation, which was later to become the New Democratic Party. So when Martin was at the United Nations and discovered he had forgotten his pyjamas at home, it seemed natural enough to borrow a pair from another member of the Canadian delegation, Coldwell, who had an extra pair. Back in Ottawa some time later, the Martins were having lunch in the parliamentary restaurant, an institution that has always had large ears. Nell waited until Coldwell walked by when she said in a rather loud voice, "M.J., I must remember to return your pyjamas."

Mackenzie King was particularly fond of Nell, and the doting husband acknowledged that "my way with the prime minister was eased by his liking for Nell," but there must have been moments of uncertainty for both prime minister and husband: "At parties Nell could always be counted on to liven things up. One night after dinner at the French embassy, we were saying farewell to the ambassador and his wife at the top of a long marble staircase that sweeps down to the main entrance. All of a sudden Nell jumped on to the banister and, with gleeful abandon, slid on down."

Time did not persuade her to revere official Ottawa's reverence for itself. During the 1970 Quebec crisis, the home of every cabinet minister was assigned armed military guards as protection against a possible terrorist attack. The Martins also had their guards but when Nell decided that the worst of the crisis was over she invited the soldiers into the living room to play gin rummy.

Only rarely did Martin recognize that his wife may have harboured a different view of his political destiny. Throughout the 1958 leadership campaign against Lester Pearson, the loyal Nell had been "a shock absorber" for him, but much later when he came to reflect on his defeat he stepped back from his own grief: "Nell faced it like a trooper and took the greatest care of us all. While she was sorry for me, I think deep down she did not bemoan the result. The life of a party leader's spouse is a tough one. She would have seen even less of me than before and would have had to bear more burdensome family and social responsibilities." Ten years later his two children staunchly opposed his departure from the House of Commons but his wife, he reported, was less opposed. Indeed, she rejoiced that she had poured her last cup of tea and gone to her last campaign supper. Ahead of her lay the demands that come of being the wife of a senator and then of a High Commissioner to London, but after more than 30 years she was finished with daily politics.

AS FOR THE NEXT GENERATION, when Sheila Cowan first made the acquaintance of young Paul Martin in the early 1960s, politics, as she said later, was not part of the scene. His father was a politician; that much she knew. But the son was headed in other directions—business or law or something, but not politics. Several years before, the Martins had moved into a house on Devonshire Road, two houses away from her own family in Walkerville, one of the most prosperous neighbourhoods of Windsor. Inevitably the paths of the two families crossed because William Cowan and Paul Martin Sr. were partners in the same law firm. Sheila had soon got to know Nell Martin and Mary Anne, who was her age and in the same class, but it was some time before she met young Paul, because he was off at university or working at summer jobs, very much the absent older brother.

Her first real meeting with the older brother had all the hallmarks of a social disaster, and as she talked about it 40 years later she looked uncomfortable all over again. She had been invited to the family cottage at Colchester, about a 45-minute drive away, and Mary Anne had suggested that Sheila could get a ride with her brother. That seemed reasonable, except the ride involved going first to Stratford with another couple, seeing a Shakespeare play at the Festival Theatre, and then going all the way back and south of Windsor to the cottage. It was not a happy experience. She was 17, five or six years younger than everyone else: "Here I was with all these older people; I just didn't know what to talk about." Besides, the other couple spent the entire trip necking in the back seat of the car, and not surprisingly Sheila wondered what she was doing there and what was going to happen. In fact, nothing happened and she got to the cottage without misadventure, except that she discovered that Paul was "such an awful driver." That has not changed over the years: "He gets in a car and his mind clicks on to something else. It's not that he's a bad driver. He just doesn't know what he's doing or where he's going, and his mind is not on it. But he's never had an accident."

What is bizarre in retrospect is that Paul always describes the Stratford trip as their first date: "He remembers what I was wearing. So does my mother. But I don't."

They did not see each other for another three years, until Sheila was in her third year in University College at the University of Toronto, studying English Language and Literature. She had a friend who was going to Detroit for Thanksgiving weekend and she phoned Paul, then in law school, to see whether he was driving to Windsor and might give the friend a lift. A week later he phoned Sheila and invited her to go bowling—"and that was it." She had been going out with someone else but gave that up. They were married two years later, in September 1965.

As she describes their courtship, it sounds like a classic romance. He was handsome, funny, kind, and lots of fun. Everything he did came easily, first law school, then articling with a big Toronto firm. She never had any doubts that he would do well in life because, as she says, everything came so easily. Except that there were flashes of devastating awkwardness. At the first Christmas after they started going out together, but before they had told their parents of their romance, Paul had insisted that they exchange presents privately in the alley beside one of their houses: "I remember that my grandparents were there and he just didn't want anybody to know. So I had to pretend." The strangeness of the venue for exchanging presents was not improved by Paul's choice of a present for his new girlfriend: "He had actually bought me this ghastly blouse that he thought was wonderful. We've never had the same taste. From the very beginning!"

Was she smitten from the first? Across her face there is a flicker that is hard to read: "I was probably less smitten than he was, because I was still going out with somebody else—who I bring up in my worst moments—who I'm sure I could have stuck with if I had known about politics."

Although it would be a couple of decades before politics transformed their lives, the political beast reared its head as soon as the Martins got to Montreal in the spring of 1966. Paul had barely started working at Power Corp. when an old friend called to suggest he should do some canvassing for a young Liberal who was regarded by senior people in the provincial party as a man with a future. His name was Robert Bourassa, an economist who was running in the Montreal riding of Mercier. Afterwards they dropped in on another Liberal campaign headquarters and Paul, curious about the political culture of his new city, left his friend and wandered up the street to the offices of the independent candidate in the riding; he found nobody there so he helped himself to a couple of election pamphlets and sauntered back to rejoin his friend. Moments later, as he tells the story, two organizers from the independent candidate arrived; the independent candidate was the brother of a professional wrestler, and the two organizers were cut from the same mould. There were accusations and shouting and bad temper all around; Paul suddenly realized he had been the cause of the uproar and went to explain things. But rather than apologizing and explaining, he pushed them away from the door with a hand on the chest of each of them, saying they were going to settle things—"*on va le regler.*" The next thing he knew, "I'm flat on my butt with a broken nose."

That evening Sheila was entertaining friends, still expecting her new husband home for dinner, when the doorbell rang at about 11:30. She opened the door to discover Paul leaning against the doorway, covered with blood, his nose plastered to the side of his face. Her thought was "Oh, my God, this is Quebec politics!"

Their next brush with politics brought a different kind of pain. Paul took six months off his job at Power Corp. to help manage his father's 1968 leadership campaign and the entire family bore the burden of that loss. For Sheila, that was the first experience of the hard knocks of politics. She was surprised by how well her father-in-law took his defeat; he got up the next morning and got on with his life, as did Paul when he was defeated by Jean Chrétien in 1990. Contrary to the stories afterwards, she insists, the loss certainly did not inspire him to set out a long-term plan to avenge his father's humiliation: "I think he took the loss hard but I think he could also see it coming. I think that anything to do with himself he can handle, but he just felt very badly for his father." Still, it was not an encouragement to enter politics any time soon.

In Quebec of the 1960s and 1970s, however, there was no escape from politics. While Pierre Trudeau was putting a Quebec face on federal politics, Quebec nationalism was blossoming into separatism. The heady times of Quebec's Quiet Revolution suddenly became the anxious times of the 1970 October crisis. For the Martins the crisis was more acute than for most others because Power Corp. and Paul Desmarais had been singled out in the manifesto distributed by the Front de Libération du Québec. Until then the succession of bomb attacks by the FLQ had been remote from the lives of most Montrealers. Suddenly the country was under the War Measures Act and the city was not quite so much fun for people like the Martins. Paul Desmarais himself left the country for six months. During the day, Paul was at the office and Sheila was in a home that felt as though it were under siege, with two boys: Paul W., who was still only a toddler, and Jamie, who was an infant. Police told them to put an alarm on their house, to park their car in a garage, never to take a cab directly to the house, and never to call a cab to the house because the cab companies were infiltrated by FLQ collaborators. "I always tend to internalize everything; I remember it was just like having a big lump in your stomach all the time when you walked your kids to school. I remember that Halloween: they couldn't go out. In retrospect you can be cool but I still can feel the tension." As she talks of those "horrendous few months," she recalls particularly the Saturday night that police discovered the body of Pierre Laporte, the Quebec cabinet minister who had been murdered by the FLQ gang that had kidnapped him. Three decades later the horror remains. "That was a very, very scary time. You know, you were young and you just didn't know."

Crisis became a condition of life in Quebec in those days. Six years after the FLQ crisis, the separatist Parti Québécois was elected as the Quebec government; the PQ victory was the signal for thousands of anglophones to leave Quebec. But as many of their friends fled to the high ground to the west, the Martins promptly went out and bought a 400-acre farm in the heart of the Eastern Townships, south of Montreal. A great farm it was not; Martin describes it as mostly rock, swamp, trees, and perhaps 100 acres of pasture, but it was their proclamation that they were not leaving. "Boy, I'll tell you, if there was anything that was going to make me stay in Quebec it was the fact that the sovereigntists had won."

Although politics pervaded everything in Quebec in those days, it was incidental to their life. Paul had gone from being a firefighter at Power Corp., dispatched to whatever corporate problem seemed most acute at any particular moment, to the presidency of Canada Steamship Lines, a subsidiary of Power Corp. As Sheila described it much later, Power Corp. was an exciting place, small and personal, which allowed them to meet all kinds of interesting people, and then CSL became part of the family. Montreal returned to being an appealing city, with English and French rubbing shoulders and only occasionally bumping, when, as Sheila says, "you put up with some rudeness." They had a third son, David; all three kids were thriving; she and Paul were happy and enjoying life.

If life was happy for her, it was certainly different from the ordered life she had known when she was growing up in Windsor, when there was a family dinner every night. If her father had to work in the evening, he came home for dinner and later returned to the office. There was a different pace to their life in Montreal. Paul was not a nine-to-five businessman. Family dinners, if they took place, were on the weekend when the family, including the kids and their friends, headed to the farm on Friday evening. During the week she never expected Paul home for dinner. He got home when he got home. Sheila suggests that if microwaves had been invented then they would have saved a lot of grief, but that is debatable. Domesticity is apparently neither to his taste nor his talent. Sheila did not expect him home to bath the boys when they were small. She cannot remember him ever taking care of the kids on his own because, she says, he was so nervous. He has never carried a key for their house in Montreal or their farm, and relies on Sheila to be there; his secretary is forever getting keys cut for his Ottawa flat because he has to carry that key and he always keeps losing it. His favourite food is Kraft Dinner, and Sheila's one complaint about her husband is that after almost 40 years of marriage he never learned how to make it: "I mean, if only he could just make it my life would be easier."

In fact, neither of them is particularly concerned about food. His mother did not like to cook, and Sheila says that her own mother was such a good cook that she never bothered to learn. So there were the command turkey dinners at Christmas and Thanksgiving, but after that it was chili and meat loaf and tuna casserole: "So I had very easy-to-please children. In fact my kids are the only ones who go to university and like residence food. So they tell me. Which isn't a slur, they say—but. So I'm thinking, gee, what was I like all those years? Maybe I didn't feed them properly. But they're all healthy and fine. And I've been very lucky that Paul isn't a connoisseur either. We just decide to order in or we go out. I can make things actually. I mean, I can cook. But I don't much."

Sheila Martin got her reading of politics and its effect on family life from watching the life of the family two doors away on Devonshire Road in Walkerville. Paul Sr. was away from home on state or political affairs far more than Paul Jr. was on business. Over the years it had been Nell who raised young Paul and Mary Anne; she was the one who gave them their grounding in life, and doing it alone was hard. Sheila concluded that her mother-in-law had been wonderfully adaptable, had a delightful sense of humour, and put on a great public face, but she did not relish the role that politics had given her. Her respect and affection for her mother-in-law is boundless—"she called a spade a spade and didn't put on any airs. She was great fun. She was wonderful." But she came to understand the impact of politics on Nell's life when it appeared that Paul Jr. might himself go into politics. Nell was upset; she hated the idea.

It was a gradual assault that politics made on Sheila Martin and her comfortable life. The beginning was probably first noticeable in the late 1970s and early 1980s when people started to invite Paul to meetings of various reform groups on the discontented fringes of the Liberal Party. And then there were invitations to address or moderate conventions or party functions. Indeed, some of those on the fringes and in the core of the party wondered whether Paul should not contest the leadership as a dark horse candidate when Pierre Trudeau stepped down in 1984; he too considered the possibilities. Four years later, although the leadership had passed him by, he decided to run for Parliament, and by then Sheila was into the political glue and there was no getting out. So Paul was a member of Parliament and soon there was another leadership race, and that time he was running.

She says she enjoyed the 1990 leadership race. She liked travelling across the country and meeting people, and all three boys went out to Calgary for the convention. She says she did not mind that he lost because that's what he had expected: "I think we knew we were never going to win it, so that was a little easier. I think it would have been very hard to lose a tight race. But we knew we weren't going to win. Nobody was heartbroken." A true political junkie would add, "And there's always next time." On that Sheila Martin is silent, but she talks now like someone who is almost reconciled to the life of politics: "I didn't come from a political family the way he did, where you grow up knowing what elections do to you. I think I'm glad that we didn't do it when the kids were young, but I have to say it's not all bad. You just sort of adapt to it. And we've had a lot of great times. I guess it didn't disrupt our life as much because the kids were older, and the kids were all very self-contained or independent."

Even as the wife of an MP she has been able to keep politics at a distance. The Martins do not live in his riding, LaSalle-Emard, which means that she is not on show 24 hours a day as the wife of the MP (she shakes her head sympathetically about the wife of an Ottawa cabinet minister who feels she has to get dressed up to go shopping, lest the constituents decide that their MP's wife is slothful). She goes occasionally to functions in the riding; they throw a Christmas party for the volunteers every December and they invite the volunteers out to a party at the farm during the summer. After a decade and a half, LaSalle-Emard is almost family.

For a time they flirted with the idea of moving to the riding. Paul was preparing to run for Parliament; he and other eager Liberals thought it would look better if he lived in the riding, or at least he could claim that he owned a house in the riding. Sheila was not amused by the house-buying adventure: "That was one of our little mistakes where he jumps in too fast and doesn't think things through. There was no need for us to buy a house there or talk about moving there, so we got rid of it. It was just another house to look after. In fact we moved twice. We started out with a semidetached on a street until we got people complaining that the lawn wasn't cut, and I said, Paul, now this is really stupid. That was a corporate decision made by the people running the campaign and it was just totally wrong. It was something we didn't need to have done...." So they bought a condo where they did not have any responsibility for cutting the grass, they rented it out for a while, then finally they sold it and stopped worrying about the fact that they lived in a very large house in Westmount. Later they moved to a smaller and elegant Edwardian townhouse on Summerhill Avenue, just above Sherbrooke Street.

Sheila divides her life between Montreal, Ottawa, and the farm and complains that she does not have enough time to indulge her passion for gardening. Keeping track of her family is not always easy. When Paul was Finance minister, he was travelling all the time, across the country and around the world. Paul W. is working in Singapore for Canada Steamship Lines and travels home twice a year to see his family. Jamie lives in Toronto and works as a screenwriter, and David is working as an investment banker in Montreal. Sheila is anxious whenever they travel; whether it is Paul or the boys, flying or driving, she insists that they phone when they have reached their destination. "I thought I'd outgrow it. It's not just him. It's the kids too," she says. "They all phone. They're very good about it."

Sheila has always taken Ottawa in small doses, usually two or three days a week, and not all of it is political Ottawa. She and Paul occasionally go to embassy receptions but they don't attend many dinner parties because they are not in Ottawa on the weekends. Her happiest time in the capital is working for Politics and the Pen, a committee of the Writers' Trust, which awards literary prizes and helps to finance indigent writers. The committee work reflects her own literary tastes, and, best of all, nobody is involved in politics. Unlike her husband, whose reading in recent years has always been an offshoot of work, she reads as much contemporary fiction as she can; at a minimum she tries to read the most prominent recent Canadian fiction, all the novels nominated for the Giller Prize and the Governor General's award. When she wants to play hookey from serious reading, she devours Ruth Rendell and P.D. James.

There are other Canadian men and women who would make almost any sacrifice to move into 24 Sussex Drive, the elegant home of the prime minister, there to read fine novels or settle the affairs of state, or to prompt a spouse to do so. Those afflicted with such a passion could dwell on the possibility for years. But Sheila Martin has nourished no fantasy about wearing the cloak of politics all day every day. That said, she decided long ago that if she became the wife of the prime minister, obviously they would be living at 24 Sussex Drive. But she tries not to think about it, and, magically, the best address in the country is gone from her mind.

"Oh, God, I don't want to do this at all, so I just don't think about it. Months will go by and months will go by, and we'll handle what comes.... I just have no idea and I don't think that far ahead."

Small wonder that she remembers fondly the days when Paul Martin was just an average obsessive, driven, workaholic, ambitious shipping magnate. She smiles ruefully at the recollection: "Business I look back on as being Utopian."

CHAPTER 5

On the Fringes of Politics

Pierre Trudeau was still prime minister, still a figure of reverence and awe among most party loyalists, when Paul Martin Jr. began to be noticed around the fringes of the Liberal Party. It was a time when a number of young Liberals were wondering how the next generation of Liberalism should unfold, and that was when the agreeable businessman from Montreal just seemed to appear out of nowhere. Quite suddenly, Paul Martin Jr. became a fixture at gatherings of Liberals, especially young Liberals who thought of themselves as reformers. Then, in the space of a couple of years, his became a name to conjure with. Paul Martin Jr., they said, was a guy to watch. It was a name, after all, with a certain lustre in the party's history. For four decades his father had been the tireless champion of small-l liberalism within the party, so anyone bearing the Martin name was going to be noticed, and inevitably people would begin speculating about his political future.

For the Liberals, they were curious times. By the end of the 1970s it was clear that the Canadian romance with Pierre Trudeau had dimmed. He was impatient with his electors and his electors were impatient with him. When Joe Clark and his Conservatives won the 1979 election by a narrow minority, it was almost a relief for some Liberals. Now they could get on with the next stage of their lives. They had been in power since 1963, first under Lester Pearson and then under Trudeau, and after 16 years they had long since used up the last of their fresh ideas. Hugh Faulkner, who had been a minister for seven of those years, summed it up neatly when he said that by the time of that losing election in the spring of 1979, "there was not much energy left, and it showed."

For many Canadians, including those who had once voted for him, a broad malaise found a focus on Pierre Trudeau. In Faulkner's judgment, more than anything else the loss probably reflected growing antagonism towards Trudeau: "What I remember through those last years before the defeat of 1979 was that Trudeau became edgy and caustic in word and sometimes in gesture with some of the public. The economy was not performing brilliantly, many of the public were upset/angry/critical and he seemed less than sympathetic and often rude. But we all knew that when confronted, his instincts were to hit back. Typically those moments got lots of press and pissed off lots of people."

Faulkner and others thought that the defeat in 1979 would mean that the Liberals could settle down to the task of renewal. However, that was not to be, not right away, anyway. Within a year the Conservative minority government had stumbled into disaster, and Trudeau, after first deciding he was through with politics, returned to claim the vacant leadership and lead the Liberals back to power with a majority in the House of Commons. The new government could not reinvent itself, but there was some effort at a fresh face. When the new Trudeau cabinet was announced in March of 1980 there were a dozen new ministers around the table. But the power still lay with the man at the head of the table who had become prime minister 12 years before, and he was not particularly in a mood for rejuvenation.

The event that came to symbolize that reluctance to rejuvenate occurred a year later, in the summer of 1981, when Peter Stollery, who had served without distinction on the Liberal backbenches for nine years, suddenly found himself vaulted from the Commons into the velvet cushions of the Senate. All this so that one James Coutts, principal secretary to Trudeau and the political smarts of the prime minister's office, could run in a by-election in the downtown Toronto riding of Spadina, a safe Liberal seat that would win his passage to the House of Commons. Nobody ever disputed Coutts's smarts, and even his critics were willing to admit that he might make a good cabinet minister. But why should Stollery get that extravagant buy-off? Why should Coutts get a guaranteed Liberal seat while others had to scramble? And, besides, why the hell should there be any kind of reward for the man who more than anything else had come to represent the remoteness and arrogance of the prime minister's office and Pierre Trudeau's style of government? For Trudeau, the answer was easy enough: Coutts and Keith Davey had guided him back to victory in 1974 after minority government and again to victory in 1980 after the Clark government, so if Coutts wanted a seat in the Commons, well, perhaps he deserved it. Certainly there was no political risk in Spadina; except for the extraordinary Diefenbaker elections of 1957 and 1958, the riding had always been solidly Liberal. However, even Liberals chuckled bitterly a few weeks later when an unknown New Democrat, Dan Heap, won the by-election in Spadina by 214 votes over Jim Coutts.

In the months afterwards there were three words that would fan the flames of discontent in almost any group of Liberals, and the words, of course, were Coutts, Stollery, and Spadina. But uneasiness within the party did not begin with the Spadina by-election. Since the mid-1970s about three dozen young Liberals had gathered, usually on the first weekend after Labour Day, on Grindstone Island in Big Rideau Lake, 50 miles southwest of Ottawa, to drink Scotch and talk reform. A number of Grindstoners were also invited to sit in with another group of reformers who met about once a month to talk politics across the river from Ottawa at the Country Club in Hull. After he went down to personal defeat in the 1979 election, Hugh Faulkner invited a variety of friends and acquaintances—liberal in thinking but not necessarily Liberal, he said—to get together periodically to discuss public policy and to get good people committed to running for Parliament. He had started calling it the No Name Committee but others soon decided it would be easier to call it the Faulkner group.

The Faulkner group was smaller and its members older than the other groups, which were made up of young Liberals, most of whom had their introduction to politics and government as ministerial assistants on Parliament Hill. Only rarely did members of the Liberal establishment attend these gatherings because they were not invited and would not have been welcomed among those who believed the establishment was suffocating the party. Although the various groups existed quite independently, there was at least one particularly interesting thread that tied them together. A regular participant in the gatherings of each of the groups was a Montreal businessman by the name of Paul Martin Jr.

It was a reflection of the times that Paul Martin was as attractive as he was to a new generation of Liberals. Those who remember him from the late 1970s and early 1980s all say the same things about him: he was endlessly curious, he was bright and energetic, and he had an insatiable appetite for ideas and debate about public policy. The Liberal Party has always been a magnet for bright young people; that is the appeal of power, and the Liberal Party has had more of that appeal because it has been in power longer. So Martin certainly wasn't a novelty. But what the Liberals were significantly lacking in that period was a stable of potential leaders. John Turner and Donald Macdonald had both left politics, each in his own way impatient with Trudeau and the narrowness of his political agenda. Occasionally Trudeau himself would complain in private about how English Canada was failing to produce political leaders. He did not say, "Look at the Liberal benches and you will see what I mean," but he might just as well have done so. What Trudeau did not acknowledge, if it occurred to him, is that there is only so much oxygen available in any group; when someone is as strong and dominant as Pierre Trudeau, there is not much breathing space for other strong egos. Politicians, especially those with the talent and ambition to be leaders, are not by nature timid and unassuming. So Turner left and Macdonald left, and when someone like Paul Martin appeared on the scene, people noticed.

Among those who noticed were Terrie O'Leary, Peter Donolo, and Alfred Apps, all of them as eager as eager young Liberals could be. In the autumn of 1981, not long after the Spadina by-election, the three friends decided it might be interesting to invite Martin to speak to the young Liberals at a Liberal policy conference that would be held in Ottawa the following year. They called him at Canada Steamship Lines and said they would like to go to Montreal to talk to him, and he staggered them by saying, fine, come on down. As O'Leary recalled, "It didn't take 15 phone calls or anything like that. He was as intrigued with us as we were with him. It was a neat thing that at his level he had that kind of curiosity." Not quite so neat was that after they walked into his Montreal office and began talking about their unhappiness with the Liberal establishment, symbolized by Jim Coutts and the Spadina by-election, Martin immediately pronounced that Coutts was one of his best friends. Everyone swallowed hard and changed the subject. They had expected to spend perhaps 20 minutes with Martin; they stayed for a couple of hours. Apps recalls Martin as open, engaging, and receptive, happy to talk about the state of the nation or the state of the Liberal Party: "I remember walking away from that meeting and thinking that he was exactly what I hoped he would be. I remember being so delighted with ourselves—in a kind of pretentious way—that we had the chutzpah to do this, and so delighted that what we had found was more or less what we expected to find."

For people like Apps the problem with the Liberal Party was that in spite of the brilliance of Pierre Trudeau's vision of a pluralistic, multicultural Canada that could be a moral force for the world, the economics at home had gone badly wrong: "There were a lot of us who felt we needed a chief financial officer in the Liberal Party. We needed to bring back some people into the party who could bring some good basic private-sector business judgment to government accounts. We saw in Paul Martin someone who had a good, rich, soft-l liberal tradition, through his father, but who had been part of the Power Corporation empire and Canada Steamship Lines. He had a name that was synonymous with Liberal historical mythology. We saw him as a potential vessel for our hopes back then. We were sitting around trying to think of who we could have who would send a signal to the party that the Liberal tent could be redefined again to reflect some credibility in the economic management issues facing the country."

Apps is insistent that their push for reform was not particularly ideological. They at least were not those Liberals from the right wing of the party who were unhappy with all state intervention and who had objected from the start to the very idea, for example, of creating Petro-Canada so that Canada could have a direct stake in the petroleum industry. Instead it was "a lack of that other side of economic policy, the balancing of the books, the keeping of competitive tax rates, all that stuff. We were not worrying about what they were doing but what they weren't doing." They were not alone. Whatever Trudeau's genius may have been, it was not economics. The country had suffered skyrocketing inflation, relentless unemployment, wage and price controls, and the memorable occasion when the prime minister arbitrarily announced massive spending cuts without even advising his Finance minister, Jean Chrétien.

"There was a sense that Nero was fiddling while Rome was burning," Apps said later. "It wasn't what they were doing, it was what we felt they weren't doing to create a stable economic framework for private-sector decision-making. It wasn't much more sophisticated than that. I mean, we were kids. I was a law student at the time. I was a kid."

A kid perhaps, but Apps already had an instinct for rattling cages. Indeed, when the Liberal conference finally opened in the Chateau Laurier hotel, Apps almost single-handedly eclipsed Martin's speech. With Donolo looking over his shoulder, Apps drafted a long and impatient diatribe that was officially registered in the conference records as Resolution 40. It was a demand for openness and transparency, a transfer of control of the Liberal Party apparatus from the prime minister's office, and in general the kind of democracy that Pierre Trudeau used to talk about when he first launched himself into party politics. By the time he had finished reading the handwritten resolution, the rebellious young Liberals were on their feet and cheering, an experience that a bemused Apps would describe 20 years later as bizarre and electric. The Liberal Party did not get to be Canada's government party by caving in to bizarre and electric. The party establishment was at first upset by the signs of rebellion from the young Liberals, but when Resolution 40 got to the floor of the full convention the party establishment was in complete suffocation mode. The leaders of the party were determined there would be no floor fight to attract the attention of reporters covering the conference, so suddenly everyone was all in favour of openness and transparency and party democracy. Resolution 40 was approved overwhelmingly. "It was a big yawn," Apps said grimly. "It's a terrible thing when your revolution is co-opted."

As for Paul Martin and his star role at the conference, nobody remembers much except that Peter Donolo describes it as "quite a lousy speech"—perhaps not surprising because that was an era when all of Martin's speeches tended to be more worthy than exciting. Still, he made an impact by just being there. Richard Mahoney, who was then still in university and had just joined the party, was at first shocked by the attitude of the other young rebels. He had not expected a lot of criticism of the prime minister and his office and his colleagues and the Liberal MPs. But it was at that conference that he introduced himself to Martin, the businessman from Montreal whom everyone was eager to talk about and eager to meet.

The association between Martin and Mahoney was not untypical. Afterwards Mahoney became a power in the Young Liberal organization and frequently turned to Martin as the voice of a new Liberalism. A few years later when Martin ran for the party leadership, Mahoney was his executive assistant and then continued as a major figure in the large but ill-defined Martin organization. David Herle was a Young Liberal in Saskatchewan when he met Martin, and he too kept in touch as he rose in the ranks of the Young Liberals; Herle went to work for Martin at CSL, and then from the time the Liberals returned to power in 1993, Herle was Martin's senior adviser. Mike Robinson met Martin at Grindstone Island, ran his 1990 leadership campaign, and remained one of his senior advisers. The trio of Apps, Donolo, and O'Leary followed different paths, never far from Liberal politics. Apps became a partner in a major Toronto law firm but continued as a gadfly within the Liberal Party, signing on briefly to work for John Manley in the eventual leadership race; Donolo became Chrétien's director of communications, one of the shrewdest and most engaging people around Chrétien after he became leader of the party and then prime minister; O'Leary went to work for Martin as his executive assistant in 1989, an explosive adviser on politics and policy whose toughness and shrewdness astonished bureaucrats and politicians alike and whose boss rated her "probably the best political judge, or certainly one of the best political judges and analysts in the country."

It is a significant footnote to that meeting in Montreal in the autumn of 1981 that O'Leary and Donolo came to be critically important in preserving the relationship—albeit occasionally stormy— between Chrétien and Martin when they were one of the most successful teams in Canadian political history. Both eventually took their leave of the Ottawa pressure cooker: O'Leary left Martin in 1998 to work as Canada's executive director at the World Bank; Donolo left Chrétien in 1999 to become consul general in Milan. Apps is not alone in believing that after their departure the partnership of Chrétien and Martin was doomed:

> I think they understood in an historical context their roles in retaining that unity in the party, that big tent, and I would argue that that was what they were made for, that was what they were trained for, that was the role they grew up to perform, and they understood its essential importance to the party throughout that period. I don't think people have understood the extent to which things started to fly apart when they both went their own ways. [If they had remained] it would have been much better managed, it would have been handled in a way that was much less dominated by background noise and bit players. In other words, the whole thing would have been much more professional, controlled, and elevated in its character and tone than it was ultimately. There was a vacuum that was taken over by what I would call a lot of thugs in the Liberal Party—on both sides of the equation.

There is an odd disconnect in measuring the relationship between Paul Martin and his friends and allies in the Liberal Party. The problem is a time warp between the Liberal Party and its problems and inspirations when Martin first became associated with the party, and its reality a generation later. In the years after the late 1970s and early 1980s, the Canadian political culture progressed from Pierre Trudeau to Joe Clark, back to Trudeau, and on to John Turner, Brian Mulroney, Kim Campbell, and finally to Jean Chrétien (not to mention the clutter of misfits who masqueraded as the various leaders of Her Majesty's Loyal Opposition).

From Trudeau's departure in 1984 to the date that Chrétien set for his departure from politics there was a gap of 20 years, yet it did not seem a great leap. Chrétien's view of Canada was little different from that of his former boss, although his view of government was minimalist; he began his political life in 1963 with a limited vision, and four decades later not much had changed.

In the days when Terrie O'Leary went to Montreal to see Paul Martin she had also been involved with a Liberal recruiting campaign in university and college campuses across the country. She recalls big black and white challenging posters: "You're young, you're committed, you want to shake up the Liberal party of Canada. We dare you." A generation later, O'Leary and the students to whom her poster campaign was directed were all in their early forties; Paul Martin, whose freshness and curiosity made him something of an icon for a generation of young Liberal enthusiasts, had reached an age when most people retire.

It is surprising to think back on it, but such was the state of the Liberal Party in the early 1980s that to some young and reform-minded Liberals, Paul Martin Jr. seemed a perfect candidate to succeed Pierre Trudeau whenever he decided to step down as party leader and prime minister. Improbable though it must have seemed to some, it did have a certain logic. He had evolved outside the conventional channels of political advancement and had escaped the curse that seemed to have marked many of those who had served in Trudeau's governments. Martin was a fresh face, and those with even quite short memories knew that much of the appeal of Pierre Trudeau in 1968 was that he too was virtually an outsider. When Pierre Trudeau declared himself a candidate to succeed Lester Pearson as the leader of the Liberal Party, he had been in the cabinet for just a year; indeed, he was best known as a quite savage critic of the Liberal Party, which he regarded as corrupt and brain dead, so he personally had escaped the aura of sourness that had sullied much of the politics of the 1960s. A generation later Martin had a similar appeal, at a time when the Liberal Party and the country wanted a change, as the next election would demonstrate.

Perhaps because his father had come to be seen as a man devoured by ambition, Paul Martin Jr. has always been reluctant to acknowledge publicly his own ambition. Before he ran for Parliament for the first time in 1988, he thought about it for a long time and, in fact, he said, "I darn near didn't run in 1988." But he certainly was not thinking about the leadership when he ran for Parliament. No, he just wanted to be an MP. As Martin tells it, only when John Turner announced he was giving up the leadership did the thought occur to him. "I said, what the hell, let's go." By itself that seems surprising, especially since most Liberals had devoted all their waking hours to predictions of Turner's political demise since he had been swamped by Brian Mulroney in the 1984 election.

It must be doubly surprising for a variety of political friends who had urged Martin to contest the Liberal leadership not in 1990 but in the early 1980s, in anticipation of the eventual departure of Pierre Trudeau. It may have seemed utterly fanciful—after all, he had no political experience and the Liberals were in increasingly bad odour across the country—but Martin's friends urged, and he at least considered. A number of those friends recall such conversations with Martin. Still, they are reluctant to contradict publicly a friend who had finally become a declared candidate to be prime minister. As one veteran of those early days recalls:

I know he did give some consideration at least to the idea of running for the leadership in 1984. I encouraged him strongly to run for the leadership in '84, and I was by no means alone. I think he made it clear to many of us that it did not fit his personal situation at that point—his family life, his business life. He had just taken over ownership of CSL and, you know, a debt to go along with the ownership. He was fairly clear about what an awkward and improbable circumstance that was in terms of considering it, but it was a major topic of discussion amongst many of his friends and admirers during that whole period.

He was quite political. It was not very hard to get into a very intense, partisan, political discussion with Paul Martin. People talked about him that way 20 years ago; he knew that they talked about him that way. They talked to him that way. He demurred but he did not lock the door. His putting off of that discussion was a timing putting off—"not the right time for me."

Nobody disputed the virtual impossibility of Martin seeking the leadership in 1984. The Martins had three boys, two of them teenagers, the other just short of his teens, still living at home. He had become half-owner of Canada Steamship Lines less than three years before and he was in hock to the banks to the tune of about $90 million. The odd thing was that he was sufficiently interested to talk about it and sufficiently interested to say that he could not win and he would not run if he could not win.

If there was any doubt about the intensity and urgency of his son's interest in politics, it is resolved by Paul Martin Sr. During his time as Canada's High Commissioner in London, from 1975 to 1979, he maintained a meticulous diary of his own observations on the affairs of Britain and the world and also on the interests and activities and dreams of his son. In particular he records the eagerness of Paul Jr. to enter politics. In the late 1970s, as he wandered the fringes of Liberal Party politics in Ottawa and across the country, the Montreal businessman, full of curiosity and hungry for ideas, was also apparently seething with a desire to throw himself into electoral politics. The son is always at pains to mask his ambition, but the father's diary suggests that such ambition is beyond debate: "A letter received today [March 9, 1976] from Paul revives his desire to get into public life and politics."

Three years later, after the defeat of the Trudeau government by Joe Clark in the 1979 election, his ambition was not just to get his feet wet in Parliament but to get ready for the prime ministership.

> Off and on, Paul talks about getting into public life. This I have dis-
> couraged.... It always seemed to me wrong for him to interfere with his
> business career at this stage. Prompted as I was by my own experience as
> an early participant in pubic life, I sought to advise him that he should
> not go into politics until perhaps around the age of forty-five. Last
> night he said, "Dad, I want to have a talk with you soon. Now is the
> time for me to get my feet wet." He even went further and said, "Now
> is the time for me to begin to become a candidate for the prime minis-
> tership." Shades of the father!...

Later in the summer of 1979 during one of his father's visits to Canada they returned to the problem of politics. By that time he was not only giving active consideration to running for Parliament, but his father revealed that he rather fancied Pierre Trudeau's seat in the riding of Mount Royal if the Liberal leader decided not to run again.

> We have known for some time that he had the political bug.
> Fortunately, he had other interests. He is certainly one of the ablest
> of Canada's younger businessmen.... I have discouraged him from
> entering Parliament whenever he raised the issue, and primarily for
> economic reasons. I would say to him, wait until you have made your
> mark in business.... Then, they will hand you the top assignment....
> Paul took my advice. Last night he wondered if he had been wise.
> Now he thinks he should have run in the last election. In any event,
> it would be fun to be in the opposition. Sometimes a reputation is
> made on its benches.
>
> It is not impossible that Paul might seek a seat in the next election.
> If Trudeau decided not to run again in Mount Royal, Paul would like
> that seat....
>
> All this speculation shows how Paul's thinking runs these days.

More than 20 years after his father recorded those thoughts in his diary Martin professed to be puzzled by it all: "This is a difference of opinion between father and son. I don't remember. It is conceivable that I talked to him about it. I probably did talk to him about it. But to the best of my recollection I had no intention of running."

Martin's declared recollection of his early days on the fringes of the political party is that it was not politics but public policy that caught his attention: "I really was not interested in politics in any way." His political friends were people like Hugh Faulkner who, like him, were interested primarily in public policy. One of the members of the Faulkner group was Hugh Wynne-Edwards, then vice president and chief scientific adviser of Alcan International. To the discomfort of Martin, Wynne-Edwards recalls an evening walk after a meeting of the Faulkner group in the early 1980s when he asked Martin whether he would run for Parliament; Martin said yes.

Confronted by this recollection, Martin has the look of a man who, no matter what he does or says, cannot get rid of the gum that is stuck to his shoe: "I have a problem. My own view is that I never thought much about running, never really thought I would run....But I am constantly being faced by my father's words in his book to the contrary, and now you're quoting Hugh Wynne-Edwards where I said it. So I'm getting this overwhelming evidence the other way. I don't know what the hell I can tell you. You can say that 'he denies it vigorously but his case keeps getting weakened'."

As he says it, Martin does not look as though he believes he is ever going to get rid of that gum on his shoe.

CHAPTER 6

The Rivals

A S THE DAY OF HIS INEVITABLE departure from the prime minister's office approached, his remaining tenure to be measured in months or weeks, Pierre Trudeau delivered a blunt message to whichever members of his cabinet might fancy a head start on the race for his job. Trudeau glared around the cabinet table with a cold menace that was peculiarly his. He probably could not choose his own successor, he said slowly, but if anyone began campaigning for his job before he was ready to leave, he would do his best to defeat whoever was so rash.

To anyone who knew Trudeau or knew his legend of rock-hard, confident superiority, it is a surprising story, revealing an unsuspected vulnerability. But it was not the first time that Trudeau had given such a glimpse into his inner self. In the late summer of 1975 John Turner, the minister of finance, abruptly resigned from the government. The resignation shook Ottawa to its core because Turner's record in government had been exemplary; he more than anyone other than Trudeau had guided the Liberals back to a majority in the election 15 months before; and he was the Liberal's eager dauphin. In the first meeting of the Liberal caucus after Turner's resignation, Trudeau faced the assembled MPs and senators and delivered a blunt message: "There is no longer a number two in this room." Everybody knew that, but nobody knew that it was a matter of much concern to the unchallenged prime minister. To those gathered in the caucus room that day it must have been almost a shock to realize that Pierre Trudeau ever bothered looking over his shoulder. He had always given the impression that he was no more impressed by number two than number twenty-three.

If Pierre Trudeau was wary, was it any wonder that Jean Chrétien would nourish a certain continuing uneasiness about Paul Martin?

Chrétien and Martin had met long before they were partners in government. Their paths were destined to cross because they had become members of that exclusive Ottawa-Montreal nexus of power and influence and success. Chrétien was named a junior minister in the government of Lester Pearson in Ottawa just after Martin moved to Montreal and joined Power Corp. Two years later Paul Desmarais took over as head of the giant Power Corp. and began the process of drawing the country's leaders and future leaders, financial and political, into the orbit of his acquaintance. In time Chrétien and Martin were among those who went with Desmarais and friends on hunting and fishing weekends. For Chrétien the Desmarais connection was sealed later when his daughter France married young André Desmarais; for Martin, Desmarais was first his boss and then his business partner. In the Trudeau government, Chrétien moved from portfolio to portfolio as he became an increasingly trusted minister; Martin, whose father remained a member of the Trudeau government for seven years, moved up the ladder of success from corporate firefighter at Power Corp. to president and then owner of his own shipping line.

Occasionally there was golf: Chrétien and Ed Lumley, later a minister but then Chrétien's parliamentary secretary, would drive down to Montreal to join Martin and John Rae, formerly Chrétien's special assistant and by then a rising star at Power Corp., for golf and dinner. The foursome at the Kahnawake golf club was an annual event that came to an abrupt end after Lumley deserted his old boss and backed John Turner for the Liberal leadership in 1984. For a time the Martin-Chrétien relationship survived. During the leadership race Martin had been chosen to be chairman of the debates among the leadership candidates, so he had to be neutral. But as an old friend he helped out the Chrétien campaign on several occasions; when they needed buses in a hurry, Martin was the man to see because the CSL empire he had bought from Paul Desmarais happened to include a bus company.

Neighbours in the club of power and influence they may have been, but Jean Chrétien and Paul Martin had their roots in quite separate and distant worlds. One came from small-town, backwater Quebec, working class and rough. The effects of his visible facial paralysis got him teased by the other kids at school; he was tough but he was not athletic, and he moved awkwardly, as though his joints did not quite fit. He had already begun to cultivate his role as the little guy from Shawinigan, inelegant in both languages, the shrewd bumpkin; he affected indifference to the fact that he was scorned by the new generation of Quebeckers who had arrived in Ottawa, the Trudeau gang and their acolytes. And, as one Ottawa veteran described it, he had already developed that initial aggression, the need to brush up heavily against you, right away, just to assert himself, as a way of saying that you shouldn't take him for granted.

Paul Martin was a different breed of cat. He came from a middle-class family in a middle-class world, where circumstance shaped you to walk and talk with a comfortable confidence. He wore old blue jeans and fine blue suits with equal, casual grace. He had grown up partly in Ottawa, partly in Windsor where it was just part of life to cross the Detroit River to watch the Lions or the Tigers play or to be part of the excitement of civil rights marches in big-city America. He was at ease in the world of politics and government, cabinet ministers and mandarins; he did his school homework in the parliamentary library; in his stocking feet he would slide along the marbled floors of the Parliament Buildings. At university he was handsome and somehow magnetic; he was always the centre of a circle of friends. He had no need to brush up against you; he was the kind of person you noticed.

Those who knew both men then and later are agreed at least that they are two quite different people. One is intuitive, visceral, impatient, decisive; the other endlessly explorative and argumentative, instinctively reluctant to accept what seems easy and obvious. Chrétien wants to hear or read the consensus, the conclusion, of other people's discussions; Martin wants to sit down with a dozen people and start a three-hour debate. One demands brief memos; the other buries himself in weighty tomes. One makes fast decisions; the other seems at times to dither. One loves politics; the other is interested only in policy. Those who have known them over the years say they were friendly, but they were not really friends; they were cordial but not warm; they got along, but they were not close.

However friendly they may have been, it would not have escaped Chrétien's notice that even back in 1984 people were talking of his sometime golf partner Paul Martin as a future star of the Liberal Party. Indeed, there were some who said Martin should contest the leadership in 1984, though he had never been more than an interested spectator of the political process. Martin did talk about the leadership that year but he ruled himself out—not because he was not interested but because as a result of the CSL deal his signature was on a bank loan for close to $100 million. Personally, it was not the right time for him. Such talk would not have amused Chrétien. He resented John Turner's candidacy and never understood why he was such an overwhelming favourite, so it was hardly surprising that he would have no patience at all with a rank outsider like Paul Martin.

In theory, Jean Chrétien had left politics early in 1986, still seething that Turner had been elected leader of the Liberal Party, mollified only slightly by the fact that Turner seemed to be making a complete botch of it. Although Chrétien had resigned his seat in the Commons, he had, of course, not stopped playing politics. Encouraged by Turner's misfortunes, he began to focus on the leadership review that would take place in November; there would be revealed the measure of the party's discontent with its leader. The review was not a happy time for the Liberals, as Keith Davey, the party's eternal insider, described it with such obvious personal unhappiness: "The soul-destroying paranoia of John Turner and some of his people was, unfortunately, perfectly counterbalanced by the destructive mischief of Jean Chrétien and some of his people. The Liberal party was the big loser in the stakes." In despair over Turner, Davey and other established Liberal heavyweights like Marc Lalonde swung their support to Chrétien, to no avail. Turner survived the review by an overwhelming 76 per cent of the votes. Despite the margin, Chrétien and his people took that as an invitation to continue the guerrilla warfare to destroy Turner's already frail leadership.

As Turner and the Liberals declined in the polls, Chrétien ostensibly devoted himself to making money, a lot of it. The little guy from Main Street was finding consolation in the comforts of Bay Street. But politics was never far from his mind, and with the prospect of an election looming in 1988 he addressed himself to the problem of Paul Martin. For some months it had been clear that Martin was preparing to run in the Montreal riding of LaSalle-Emard. Or at least he was thinking seriously about it. He had started to take an active interest in the riding and had purchased property there. He had never taken an active role in politics, but people had already begun describing him as a star candidate for the Liberals. Possibly even a leader, some day, they said. That was enough for Chrétien. He approached Martin and counselled him to run in Windsor, in southwestern Ontario, as his father had done. He did not think that Martin should seek a seat in Quebec. Martin replied that he had never really lived in Windsor and that he had been living in Montreal for more than 20 years. If he ran, it would be in Montreal. The answer did not please Chrétien.

For Martin, LaSalle-Emard meant taking a chance. For 20 years he and his family had lived in those parts of Montreal that were more prosperous and predominantly English-speaking, the Town of Mount Royal and Westmount. So in political and social terms, LaSalle-Emard was a long way away. The riding was largely working class, half francophone and the other half a mixture of Irish, Polish, Sikh, and other immigrant communities that gave it a dynamic beyond the conventional pattern of the city. If he had stayed closer to home and run in Saint Henri-Westmount, nobody would have been surprised—Power Corp., Canada Steamship Lines, John Turner, Business Liberalism. But LaSalle-Emard allowed him to escape at least those easy labels. Besides, he said, LaSalle-Emard reminded him of Windsor. On nomination night, Paul Martin's was the only name on the list. However, if the nomination was easy, LaSalle-Emard was not an obvious route to political fame and fortune. When the Conservatives swept to power in 1984, the seat had fallen to Claude Lanthier by a margin of almost 4,000 votes; in his four years in Ottawa, Lanthier, an engineer who was already well known in the community, had done a solid job as a rookie MP. Martin's election was anything but guaranteed.

For most Canadians the 1988 election represented a profoundly unsettling choice. Four years earlier, after a decade and a half of Pierre Trudeau, the country had thrown the Liberals out of office and put Brian Mulroney and his Conservatives in their place. The country was soon so little impressed by that choice that at various times in the course of the election campaign Liberals, Conservatives, and New Democrats each led the opinion polls. Mulroney was increasingly unpopular but Turner was confusing. Mulroney had won the support of most provincial premiers across the country, particularly Premier Robert Bourassa of Quebec, for the Meech Lake constitutional accord that would have recognized Quebec as a distinct society and would have secured Quebec's signature on the constitution. To the dismay of those Liberals who still clung to the ideals of Pierre Trudeau, his successor, John Turner, was supporting the Meech Lake agreement.

The split in the country over Meech Lake was as nothing compared to the split over the free trade agreement with the United States, which had been signed in late 1987. The relationship with the United States has always been fundamental to the very existence of Canada. When two countries share a border that is thousands of miles long, where the roots of history and culture and, for the most part, language are similar if not identical, the question is not whether there is going to be a relationship but what the nature of that relationship is to be. Any suggestion of a change in that relationship is apt to bring on a case of nerves, for buried deep in the psyche of most Canadians is the conviction that sooner or later, whether in ignorance or malice, the American elephant is going to roll over.

Almost unnoticed, in its final months the Trudeau government had been moving towards a substantial reappraisal of the country's relationship to the United States, although at that stage "globalization" had not entered the contemporary lexicon. Of course, Brian Mulroney had come to power firmly opposed to free trade: "This country could not survive with a policy of unfettered free trade. I'm all in favour of eliminating unfair protectionism, where it exists. This is a separate country. We'd be swamped. We have in many ways a branch-plant economy, in many ways, in certain important sectors. All that would happen with that kind of concept would be the boys cranking up their plants throughout the United States in bad times and shutting their entire branch plants in Canada. It's bad enough as it is...." So, however logical and ordered it all came to seem a decade later, the embrace of free trade was a shock. To the delight of the business community, Mulroney seemed to have turned on a dime and thrown himself into the arms of Ronald Reagan and the United States. What nobody was ready for was the emergence of John Turner as the voice of the last defiant cry of Canadian nationalism. The leaders of business who had been so unhappy with the Trudeau Liberals in their final years thought Turner would be the answer to their problems; they rejoiced when he was elected to lead the party. Then, quite suddenly, the golden boy of Business Liberalism was leading the charge against continentalism— "I'm not going to let Mr. Mulroney destroy a great, 120-year-old dream called Canada."

In the muddy trenches of politics, the foot soldiers of the contending parties carry on their local struggles without much regard for the great issues that usually sail far overhead like artillery shells. In LaSalle-Emard Paul Martin campaigned on the same side of the Meech Lake accord as his leader, which aligned him with most Quebeckers. On free trade, as a self-proclaimed economic nationalist he announced that he was all for free trade but insisted that some provisions of the free trade agreement had to be changed, which suggested that he seemed to be learning the black arts of prevarication. To the voters of LaSalle-Emard, such debates probably did not matter immensely. But those parts of Montreal had always been Liberal in the old days, and it was probably flattering when the newspapers reported that this guy Martin was apparently something of a star candidate.

Whatever the mood in the rest of the country, in Quebec Brian Mulroney still reigned as a favourite son; indeed, on election day, although the Conservatives slumped elsewhere in the country, in Quebec Mulroney and his Conservatives increased their seats from 58 to 63. Liberal candidates managed just 12 seats in the province that used to be their stronghold; they took two seats that had been held by the Conservatives, and one of those seats was LaSalle-Emard. The margin of victory was a perilous 1,415 votes, but that was enough; for the first time in 20 years there would again be a Paul Martin in the House of Commons. Jean Chrétien was still waiting on the sidelines, but he would not be there for long, and thereby was born a rivalry that absorbed the best minds of the Liberal Party for the next 15 years.

John Turner had led the Liberals to a respectable result, but he was mortally wounded and his leadership was doomed. Six months after the election Turner announced he would be stepping down. The convention would not be held for another 13 months, until June 1990, a delay that was engineered to allow new candidates to emerge sufficiently to mount a reasonable challenge to Jean Chrétien. Before long it was apparent that there were two obvious candidates—obvious for their eagerness and obvious for their talent, but it was equally apparent that neither had a chance to shake Chrétien.

Since she first entered the House of Commons in 1984 Sheila Copps had been a star. The Liberal ranks had been devastated by Brian Mulroney and his Conservatives. In the previous election, with Pierre Trudeau leading the charge into the 1980s, the Liberals had won 147 seats; with Trudeau gone and John Turner in his place the Liberals managed just 40 seats. So the way was open for anyone with brains and nerves and lungs, and thus was born the Rat Pack. Brian Tobin, Don Boudria, John Nunziata, and Sheila Copps were like crazed foxes in a chicken coop. There were days in the Commons when it seemed there was nothing between Turner and invisibility except the Rat Pack.

Elegant they were not, noisy and effective they were. As a candidate for the leadership, Copps was an even longer shot than Martin, but her entry into the race guaranteed that things would be lively. What she had, in both official languages, was a natural electric presence, and as his friends and supporters soon discovered, that was something sadly lacking in Paul Martin.

Mike Robinson had met Martin perhaps 10 years before. Robinson had been part of the Grindstone group when Martin was invited to one of the annual gatherings and proved to be what people always said about him—bright, curious, energetic. Over the years he had met Martin a handful of times and had always been impressed, so he was disposed to be sympathetic when he was invited to a meeting with Martin and several of his friends and advisers in early 1989. He had not, mind you, gone to the meeting expecting to be offered the job of managing Martin's campaign for the leadership; so that was one surprise. The next was when he found himself accepting the job.

Nobody had really spelled it out, but everybody rather assumed that the Montreal businessman was arriving with an impressive assortment of political skills. After all, he had been raised at the knee of a grand master of political performance, a man who could speak off the cuff on any occasion and make his audience believe he had been thinking about them for weeks. Literally on a moment's notice Paul Sr. once had to deliver a speech in the House of Commons on agriculture, a subject on which it was assumed he was quite ignorant. The speech had been written for Lester Pearson and Martin had never seen it before he began to talk, but Pearson wrote later that Martin "performed magnificently, as if he had spent hours writing and memorizing the speech." The son had no such natural skill. Impressive with small groups, but with a formal speech before large audiences, by the account of friends and admirers, he was a disaster.

Mike Robinson's personal introduction to the disaster has become part of Ottawa's folklore. He had invited about 50 Liberals to his house to meet this impressive man. Martin did not rise to the occasion. When it came time for him to speak he mumbled and stumbled and concentrated all his attention on a handful of fluff he had picked up from the carpet. Much, much later Robinson admitted to a certain wry amusement, but there was not much amusement that evening: "I had just announced to my wife that I was indeed embarking on this great adventure and that I would be taking a leave from gainful employment and that I would be working as a volunteer for a year on this effort—which she thought was something that maybe I should have consulted both her and the bank manager about before I decided to do that. I was, you know, sort of proud that I would be able to introduce her to the candidate so she would understand the reasons why I was so convinced this is how I should spend my time. There is no question that by the time he had finished filling his hand with lint she wasn't quite so convinced."

What Robinson and others discovered to their surprise was that Martin had none of those skills that seem instinctive with most politicians. One early adviser described a typical Martin arrival at political meetings where he was supposed to be the star attraction. He would enter unobtrusively and disappear into the dark aisle at the side of the hall; the last thing he wanted to do was draw attention to himself. What his father had done almost compulsively seemed alien to the son. He would not look people in the eye, he would not make small talk, he would not, as the political handlers love to say, do the grip and grin thing.

"Those skills—communications skills, the sense of yourself and your presence in a room—are things that really are acquired and I don't think are natural to somebody who has operated in a business environment where, you know, they haven't spent a lot of time in front of cameras," Mike Robinson said much later.

There were a lot of things that he had never had to confront in his life before, that he had to get his head around—how to deal with this different environment where every time you walk into a room people are watching you. You know, any body language that appears to be defensive or appears to be inappropriate will get commented on. You can't assume that if you're in a room just listening that people are not going to be looking at you to see how you are responding to what other people are saying. Paul does not have a huge ego. I mean, he's still surprised to find out how much he is the centre of attention, even today. In those days he just couldn't understand why anybody would be looking at him if somebody else is speaking. It just made no sense to him.

The first task was teaching him to be a public speaker. He learned, but he learned the hard way. During the week he had his job as an MP in Ottawa and he would do what he could on the long campaign for the leadership. On the weekend a handful of coaches, advisers, and spinmasters would invade the Martins' big house in Westmount, and they taught him whatever there was to learn about being a public performer. Speeches were written and then rewritten if the message was wrong and then rewritten again if the cadence was wrong. When the speeches seemed to be right, they were rehearsed and rehearsed and rehearsed, because he could not get it right or he did not believe he got it right. Tempers flared. Martin would yell at his speech writers and his coaches and they would scream right back. The process seemed endless. A single speech could take dozens of hours. But it was Martin more than the handlers who set the task. Jack Fleischmann, one of his early coaches, said later, "He understood that he had to learn how to perform publicly, and he understood better than anyone else how important it was. He couldn't stop. He was obsessed by what he had to learn. For him it was like learning a language."

When the speeches were done, there were other tricks of the trade that would not dawn on most people until it became a problem. In Martin's case the problem was a scrum, one of those unstructured encounters with reporters that are perfect for a brief elaboration or clarification; you answer a question, you get back to your main message, and then goodbye. John Duffy, then a young speech writer, recalls one occasion in which Martin got into a scrum after a speech. It had been a good speech with a good crowd, delivered quite well, and a couple of reporters asked a couple of questions and then a couple more and it went on and on until the reporters wearied of their sport and left, the message of the speech long forgotten. The problem was that there were no press aides to extricate him and Martin did not know how to do it himself. By Duffy's watch, the scrum lasted for 25 minutes. "It was awful."

For Martin, the Liberals' 1990 leadership race was a harsh lesson in the realities of politics. From the start, as columnist Carol Goar implied, his entry into the race seemed a little presumptuous. "The Montreal shipping magnate has no political record to speak of. He does not have the oratorical skills to light up a room. He does not have the media skills to play to a television camera. And his parliamentary debut has been less than inspiring." Far less charitable was the wicked judgment by Dalton Camp: "I have read some of the speeches of Martin, the younger. The experience lends truth to the rumour, circulated by Liberals emerging dazed from an evening's exposure to Martin oratory, that admission was free to audiences attending his meetings but they had to pay to get out."

By the end of the campaign, as a result of coaching and his own dogged determination, Martin was getting to be an accomplished performer, but by that stage performance was not going to win it. The Martin strategy was built on challenging Jean Chrétien in his own backyard. He would beat Chrétien in Quebec, and in doing so would prove to the rest of the country that he was a political winner. His ace in this game would be that he was supporting the Meech Lake constitutional accord and could win the votes of young and nationalist Quebec while Chrétien was stuck with his Trudeau view of the country, a voice from the past. The strategy was brilliant except that it was fatally flawed. The federal Liberal Party in Quebec remained much as it had been when Pierre Trudeau led the party. As a Martin organizer said much later, the people to whom Martin appealed were not Liberals and they would not become Liberals. The people who were Liberals were perhaps not young and hip, but they did not like Meech Lake any more than Chrétien did, and that meant that they were not going to vote for Paul Martin.

Martin had other ideas to offer in the campaign. He talked of a more sophisticated relationship between government and the private sector and pointed to Quebec as an example of what could happen. He cited Quebec's Caisse de Dépôt as the kind of regional pool of capital that could be enlisted for entrepreneurs across the country. He wanted affordable housing as a basic right for all Canadians, a national child care program as an economic necessity in the modern world, and a 10-year program to improve education throughout the country. Eventually, almost all the ideas proposed by either Martin or Sheila Copps were overwhelmed by the debate over Meech Lake, and in the end it was Meech that left the deepest wounds.

Meech was an unlovable chapter in Canadian history. Its origins lay in the rise of nationalist politics in Quebec during the Quiet Revolution of the early 1960s. By the time Mulroney became leader of the Conservatives in 1983, Quebec's nationalism and its demands on the country's constitutional framework had dominated the political agenda for a generation. Mulroney had agreed with the constitutional approach of the Trudeau government, although his party reflexively felt obliged to be critical. Yet, when in the middle of the 1983 leadership campaign Mulroney said he would be ready to write out his own constitutional proposals on an airline barf bag, he was reflecting not only his own lack of interest but a broad public lack of interest. Once he became prime minister, certain political realities became more apparent: as a result of the great final struggle between Trudeau and René Lévesque, Quebec was still outside the country's 1982 constitutional framework, and that clearly could not continue as an open wound; Mulroney's Quebec caucus was composed overwhelmingly of conservative nationalists, and if they were to be assuaged it would be by a constitutional framework that was even more decentralized, the antithesis of Trudeau's legacy. For Mulroney, there was undoubtedly a certain vanity at play—the hope that he could get a constitutional agreement that had eluded Trudeau. For the Chrétien Liberals, Meech was a betrayal; for Liberals like John Turner and Martin, Meech was an attempt at an honourable compromise with modern Quebec on terms acceptable to at least the political leadership in English Canada. For a while in the middle of the Meech debate it was possible to believe the future of the country depended on it; looking back, it is hard to remember why. For the Liberals who were trying to choose a leader, the Meech episode was ugly and painful. When a senior Martin adviser said much later that "there's nothing uglier in the Liberal party than a fight about the constitution and the nature of the country," it seemed like an understatement.

The year-long campaign had a certain nastiness to it from the start, and that did not get better. It had started badly when Chrétien went to Martin and advised him against entering the race because he, Chrétien, was going to win. The tipping point came in early June, three weeks before the convention in Calgary, long after the delegates had been chosen and the result was virtually guaranteed. At a policy forum in Montreal young Martin supporters staged a noisy demonstration against Chrétien, chanting "vendu" and "Judas." The theme of Chrétien as a traitor and a sell-out continued to Calgary, with Martin delegates wearing black armbands to mourn the death of the Meech Lake accord. As a veteran of four decades of politics, Chrétien is not a stranger to insults, but those attacks hurt him personally. When Chrétien loyalists trace the long line of hostility between their man and Paul Martin, it is the Montreal rally to which they always return; that, they say, is where the trouble began. And, like Chrétien, they blame Martin for the long alienation between Chrétien and the people of his own province. That may be a self-serving reading of history; Chrétien was never particularly popular in Quebec, sometimes astonishingly unpopular; but to be called a traitor by the members of your own political family is understandably difficult to digest. Of all the chips on Jean Chrétien's shoulder, the largest has always been the result of the scornful regard of his fellow Quebeckers; Paul Martin was not forgiven for drawing the country's attention. Then, having challenged Chrétien, Martin did not let up even when it was obvious that he was beaten and beaten badly; the challenger was pursuing a scorched earth policy without apparent regard for the fate of the destined leader or the party.

When it was all over, the 1990 Liberal leadership race was the most expensive in Canadian history. Chrétien had spent $2.44 million, Martin $2.37 million. Sheila Copps had spent a comparatively modest $800,000. Together, the three candidates spent more than the party had spent for its entire national election campaign two years previously. For their efforts and their money, Chrétien got 57 per cent of the vote, Martin 25 per cent, and Copps 11 per cent. In his autobiography Chrétien dignified the 1990 leadership race with just two paragraphs and his opponents with one sentence: "My principal opponents, Paul Martin and Sheila Copps, were superb candidates." The Liberals had elected a leader who would soon lead them back to power, but in the process there were bitter personal wounds from which there would be no recovery.

CHAPTER 7

Why Finance?

AUL MARTIN'S MOTHER, Nell, died on November 11, 1993, exactly one week after her son was sworn in as minister of finance in the new Liberal government. She was 80 and had been ill for some time, but she held on until her only son had become a minister of a Liberal government, as her husband had done almost 50 years before. Immediately after the swearing-in ceremony, Martin had left Rideau Hall and flown to Windsor to be at the bedside of his dying mother. Martin and his sister, Mary Anne, and their families were at the bedside as Nell drifted in and out of a coma. Later, at Nell's funeral, he told of one of the moments when she was quite lucid: "And then when she saw us all there she said...she said, 'Why?' And Mary Anne said, 'Well, why...why what, Mum?' And my mother said, 'Well, why are you all here?' And so I said, 'We're here, Mum, because you've been sick, and everybody has come to be with you.' And that was fine, and about five minutes later she said, 'Well, why?' And I said, 'Well, Mum, I told you it's because you've been sick.' And she said, 'No.' She said, 'Why...why do you want to be minister of finance?'"

It's a question Martin himself would have asked a few weeks earlier. He had no desire to be minister of finance. For one thing, like everyone else, he knew that solemn lesson of Canadian politics that the ministry of Finance has always been the graveyard of political dreams—if you want to be prime minister, don't first become minister of finance. Anyway, from the time he first started to think seriously about politics he knew that he wanted to be minister of industry; he wanted to be the new Clarence Decatur Howe, the strongman of the wartime and postwar Liberal governments. He wanted to be the new C.D. Howe because his father had talked admiringly of the cabinet colleague with whom he banged elbows constantly, but for whom he had enormous respect. It was a son's proud boast that "two of the greatest of the postwar political figures were my dad and C.D. Howe." After Ed Lumley was elected to the House of Commons in 1974, whenever he found himself in Windsor, his old hometown, he would call on Paul Martin Sr., who always reminded him about C.D. Howe and counselled him that if he got the chance to be a minister he should choose Industry or any other related ministry on which he could get his hands—Regional Economic Expansion, Communications, Science and Technology. Lumley did just that because, as he said, "Mr. Martin was constantly into my head." Paul Jr. was there for at least one of those stern lectures from his father to Lumley, and he must have been quite familiar with his father's point of view.

One of the surprising things about Paul Martin Jr. was that although he had arrived in Ottawa with a lot of ideas about public policy, he did not know much about how Ottawa operated—not the process of government, not the process of politics. He knew his father's Ottawa, the small-town capital in which he had grown up in the 1950s, but he did not know about government and decision-making in the 1990s. In late October 1993, with the election results showing a Liberal landslide, Paul Martin knew exactly what he wanted when Jean Chrétien called him and asked him to be his minister of finance. No, said Martin, he would like to be minister of industry. After all, who could identify the minister of finance in the days when C.D. Howe and Paul Martin Sr. changed the face of Canada? It so happened that Paul Jr. knew who were the various ministers of finance because the Liberal cabinet in those days was almost like family, but as well as knowing who they were he knew that they did not have their hands on the levers of real power. So, no, he did not want to be minister of finance.

At about the same time that Jean Chrétien was phoning Martin, David Dodge, the deputy minister of finance, was phoning Ed Lumley. Dodge knew that Lumley, who had been out of politics for a decade, was an old friend of Martin, and Dodge's message to Lumley was that he badly wanted Paul Martin as his minister of finance. At the same time a surprised Jean Chrétien was phoning David Smith, a senior adviser and an old friend. What, said Chrétien, was he going to do about Martin, who did not want the most important job in the government? What Chrétien, Dodge, Lumley, and Smith all knew—that the Liberal government would survive or fall on the performance of its finance minister—Martin apparently did not know. He had another conversation with Chrétien and again he said no to Finance; he would like Industry. After some hesitation Chrétien concluded that Roy MacLaren might have to be his choice for Finance, but his cabinet-making was not final and he had not given up hope of getting Martin.

Lumley tried several times, going hard at Martin, trying to convince him that the world had changed:

> Mr. Martin [Senior] had, from my perspective, a real good appreciation about not only acquiring power but exercising it in the best interests of Canadians. So Paul wanted to be minister of industry. And I went to Paul after the federal election and said, Paul, you don't want to be the minister of industry. It's changed since I was there; you've got such a huge deficit that you're not going to have the tools to do the job.
>
> You can't be the minister of industry today and function. What you've got to do is you've got to solve the macro problem, and the only one who's going to do that is the minister of finance. You're going to be fighting the minister of finance all the time if you're the minister of industry, so why do you want to be the minister of industry? The concept, I think, came from his dad.

Perhaps Chrétien's shrewdest choice was his call to David Smith. Now a senator as his reward for almost 40 years as a Liberal organizer and fixer, Smith was one of the core of advisers in whom Chrétien invested great faith. The short and stocky Smith, with his curly blond hair and horn-rimmed glasses, exudes politics. He is the ultimate political insider. For Smith, political discourse is an endless series of anecdotes; the walls of his office in the prestigious Toronto law firm of Fraser Milner Casgrain are a jumble of photographs of Smith with politicians and political cronies going back to the days of Lester Pearson when Smith was the head of the national Young Liberals organization and executive assistant to Walter Gordon. He served one term in the House of Commons and was a cabinet minister in the final year of Pierre Trudeau's government. Although he and Chrétien were friends, Smith supported John Turner for the Liberal leadership in 1984 because he had served as Turner's executive assistant. Chrétien did not easily forgive those who did not support him, but he forgave Smith, and in time Smith supported Chrétien for the 1990 leadership. Those are the hard choices of politics. Smith had known Paul Sr. in the days when he was secretary of state for External Affairs, and he and Paul Jr. had been friends since university days. But when Martin went to him to ask for his support in the leadership campaign, Smith had to tell his old friend that it was the turn of Chrétien, another old friend. So when Chrétien asked him what he should do about Martin, Smith was at least on familiar ground.

His advice was the same as Lumley's: he should continue his pursuit of Martin:

> Maybe he sort of remembered his father's period and the kind of muscle that C.D. Howe had back then. But, you know, that was in a postwar period when we were in a very expansionist mode, the government was very proactive and interfering in the private market place. There were megaprojects and things like that and the commitment to make them happen. But that was then and this is now. There aren't going to be any megaprojects because this deficit is so bad that we can't afford them. The biggest single problem is going to be getting this deficit under control, and Paul has the confidence of the business sector because of his track record, to a degree that nobody else has. You send the A-team in for your biggest problem, and that's your biggest problem, and he is the A-team. And that's what I told him.

A few days later, at about 10 p.m., Martin called Smith at home. He said Chrétien told him that Smith also thought he should go to Finance and Chrétien had suggested that Martin call Smith himself. So Smith once more explained his reasons—"You send the A-team in for your biggest problem." Martin said he thought they were good reasons, thanked him, and hung up. Two days later he was sworn in as Finance minister and MacLaren went to International Trade as Chrétien had originally intended.

Three years earlier, a happy relationship—indeed, any relationship—between Jean Chrétien and Paul Martin was not something that anyone would have predicted. Rivalries within a political party are far more visceral and painful than rivalries between parties because, inevitably, they are terribly personal. For a start, Martin and his loyalists were regarded by Chrétien as supporters of John Turner, from the time Turner won the Liberal leadership over Chrétien in 1984 until he stepped down six years later. More important, although the 1990 Liberal leadership race had not been close, it was bitter. Chrétien resented the fact that Martin had undertaken to challenge him for the leadership that he thought was his by right, and he resented particularly the campaign led by Martin and his supporters on Meech Lake, calling into question, as he saw it, his legitimacy as a Quebecker. It sounds simplistic but one man who has known them both for years describes conflicting attitudes that are not much different from what you would find in an average schoolyard: "Martin is not a guy who likes losing. Nor is Chrétien. Neither would probably like anyone who ran against him. So Martin was upset because of losing, and thought he should have won, probably. And I think Chrétien was happy to win but upset that people had run against him."

Equally important in the long run was that there formed around Martin a coterie of devoted admirers who remained dedicated to his political success, convinced that the leadership was his by right and that Chrétien was an unworthy and inadequate interloper. The team that led his campaign in 1990—Michael Robinson, Terrie O'Leary, David Herle, Richard Mahoney, Dennis Dawson—never left, and they formed the core of his undeclared leadership campaign for the next 13 years, as keen as or keener than the man himself. That the Chrétien-Martin relationship survived at all is a wonder, for it is almost a truism in politics that leadership races in any party eventually lead to complete alienation; those who come second and third find it hard to stick around to serve the winner.

Yet whatever feelings may have seethed beneath the surface, it took a long time before the gracious mask of civility was cast aside by Chrétien and Martin. For the final few years their relationship was always on the verge of collapse, but for the better part of nine years, in spite of their personal feelings, Jean Chrétien and Paul Martin formed one of the remarkable political relationships in the century. That relationship restored the Liberal Party to its role as, quite simply, Canada's government party, the friendly dictatorship; by good luck and sharp politics the Liberals devastated their opponents.

Improbably, the relationship began at the caucus meeting on the day after the leadership convention; two MPs who had been supporting Martin had already stormed out of the party; Martin loyalists had been wearing black arm bands to mourn the death of the Meech Lake agreement; there was concern that other MPs and perhaps Martin himself might desert the party. But Martin did appear at the caucus meeting, and Chrétien went down to greet him on the floor when he arrived and led him up to the platform. From then on he consciously made room for his beaten rival. In the days ahead Martin asked to be environment critic; he became environment critic. Later, Martin asked to be co-chair of the Liberal election policy committee; he became co-chair. In short, Chrétien made a lot of room for Martin. Despite the leadership struggles, Chrétien understood on a very basic level that he could not afford the luxury of not getting along with Martin.

The Liberals won the 1993 election, but they had won it almost in spite of their own performance in the previous decade. Their opponents made it easy. Brian Mulroney's Conservatives had simply imploded; Mulroney's successor, Kim Campbell, was swept aside and the Tories emerged from the election with just two seats and no leader.

Without Ed Broadbent as leader, the New Democrats nearly disappeared; the Bloc Québécois and Reform arrived dramatically from nowhere but could not reach beyond the boundaries of their regional appeal. Yet, though they won handily, the party whose leadership Jean Chrétien won in June of 1990 was seriously damaged goods. The Liberals had spent much of the previous decade in bitter internecine squabbling over John Turner's leadership, and they were confused about what their political values were or what their values should be in a changing world. The Liberals' state of disarray was not helped by Chrétien himself; as leader of the opposition he had been ineffectual and might well have been the victim of a putsch if an election had not come along and made him prime minister.

When John Turner was at the top of his game, he was an impressively smooth and competent politician, a star in the Liberal firmament almost as lustrous as Pierre Trudeau himself. When he shone brightest was not long before he flamed out of Ottawa. In the election campaign of 1974 Turner played a brilliant counterpoint to Trudeau. The two men pulled the Liberals from the near defeat of the 1972 election to a comfortable majority. A month and a half after the election, Ottawa was still in its summer torpor and Turner was fretting that the newly returned government was drifting aimlessly. There were no apparent plans to call Parliament, and the health of the economy was anything but certain. Turner took matters into his own hands, calling about 20 senior reporters to his office—the elegant West Block office that had been occupied by John A. Macdonald—for his own personal report to the nation on the state of the economy in Canada and the world. There were no cameras, no microphones, no podium— just Turner, standing, facing the reporters, some of whom were lucky to have found a chair, others jammed into corners, some sitting on the floor. There was one Finance official who stood at the back, silent, just watching. Turner talked for two hours, without notes, and without apparently getting a number wrong. It was a quite masterful performance. He stayed around Ottawa for a little more than a year, then quit the cabinet and quit the House of Commons not long after that.

Turner left Ottawa because no political firmament easily accommodates the competing lustre of two stars, and the sadness of Turner's career is that when he got back to Ottawa in 1984 he no longer shone as bright. He was far from the top of his game, and until he left Ottawa for the second time six years later he seemed always to be a man under threat. There was nothing he could have done to win the 1984 election because after almost 16 years of Pierre Trudeau in power, the country was fed up with the Liberals. In the 1988 election he saved the party by his quite dazzling attack on Mulroney's free trade agreement. There was something counterintuitive about that because Turner was a Business Liberal, elected by Business Liberals to bring back economic sense to the party after the nationalist dalliances and sheer economic mismanagement of the Trudeau years, and there he was attacking the free trade agreement that was the delight of the business community. Still, whatever his business friends thought, Turner had become Johnny Canuck, the new voice of Canadian nationalism, and the Liberals suddenly had some life. Turner did not complain of the incidentals of the free trade agreement, as Chrétien and Martin would later do. Turner went all out, accusing Mulroney of betraying 120 years of Canadian history, thereby reducing Canada eventually to a colony of the United States.

The Liberals managed to improve their standing from 40 seats in 1984 to 88 seats in 1988, but Turner himself was doomed. There had already been one major attack on his leadership by supporters of Jean Chrétien, and it was only a question of time until there was another. A few months after the election, he acknowledged reality by announcing that he would be stepping down.

After the transition from Turner to Chrétien, the Liberals still had other baggage to sort out before they got to the election. The decade after Turner's arrival in the leadership illustrated perfectly how pragmatic and elastic the Liberals can be when it comes to matters of political principle. This is a party whose greatest strength is its antenna for the public mood, a party whose Internet Web site devotes 25 pages to its own history and two pages to its philosophy, and of those two pages one is given over to quotations from various Liberal leaders, including the visionary Jean Chrétien. During the first years of the Turner era, the Liberal caucus veered happily and erratically to the left, as Liberals are wont to do in opposition; Turner's campaign against the free trade agreement was the last gasp of that phase, a nod to the days when Walter Gordon inspired Liberal nationalists, if not the leadership of the party, with his vision of Canada. The 1988 election brought in a new crop of MPs, many of them determined to push the party towards the right, back to its more accustomed place at the centre of the political spectrum. Leading that pack were the three men known as the Three Ms—businessman Roy MacLaren, who had been briefly a Trudeau minister, Ottawa tax lawyer John Manley, and Paul Martin.

For as long as he has been interested in politics Martin has fancied himself a Walter Gordon nationalist, but this was not the time for Walter Gordon romantics. On that the leadership of the Liberals was united. Just as the Liberals had staged a policy conference in Kingston in 1960 to chart a new generation of social reforms and a new and fresh image for the party, so they set out to stage a "thinkers" conference in Aylmer, Quebec, in the late autumn of 1991 that would embrace the new global economy. The Kingston conference was intended to present a coherent alternative to the Conservative government of John Diefenbaker. The Aylmer conference was intended to close the door on the memory of John Turner and any Liberals, such as Lloyd Axworthy and Sheila Copps, who seemed determined to carry the nationalist flag. There was no mystery about Aylmer; it was a stacked deck, designed to get the Liberals back into the corporate mainstream, away from nationalism and Turner's campaign against the free trade agreement. Martin was one of the conference organizers who stacked that deck. With an election looming, it was time to get practical. When he wrapped up the conference, Chrétien left no doubt that the deed had been done: "In the world of tomorrow, the old concepts of right and left do not mean anything. Protectionism is not left-wing or right-wing. It is simply passé. Globalization is not right-wing or left-wing. It is simply a fact of life."

After Chrétien's closing speech, MacLaren was overheard to say, "Eat your heart out, Lloyd Axworthy."

Later, at a formal party conference, the Liberals managed to negotiate themselves into a policy that would allow them to campaign against the North American Free Trade Agreement negotiated by the United States, Mexico, and the Mulroney government; they would not trash the agreement, but they would not accept it without changes. Abrogating the agreement would be "a last resort" if changes could not be negotiated. So Chrétien and Martin and the other Liberals voted against the NAFTA bill in the House of Commons, blustered about NAFTA during the election campaign, and vowed they would not approve it without substantial changes. Their calculated ambiguity was a triumph. Six weeks after the election, the new Liberal government proclaimed NAFTA without changing a word. For the Liberals, it seemed like deft politics; in retrospect, it looked as though the debate about the very nature of the country amounted to little more than any other political promise.

At Turner's behest, the Liberals had turned on a dime in 1988 on free trade, and when Turner headed out the door they turned back again. To listen these days to Liberals like Martin, it was almost as if 1988 did not really happen; or maybe, like kids in a schoolyard, they had their fingers crossed, so it didn't count: "I have always been a free trader, and I was a free trader in '88. I focused on the defects in the free trade agreement, but, I mean, I was a free trader in '88, so essentially I was more in the line of the party historically than what happened in the '88 election." As for the repeated Liberal threats to trash NAFTA if there were not changes to the agreement—and there were none—Martin is disarmingly candid. "If in 1993, when we took office, we had tried to reverse free trade, it would have had a terrible effect. Terrible. And we would have been defeated." As for discomfort among Liberals over their spectacular policy somersault, he did not really notice. To Martin the move from anti-free trade to pro-free trade was "almost a seamless transition; I didn't notice any agony." True, one-time Liberals like Mel Hurtig and Maude Barlow were no longer

Liberals, but he didn't remember any debate gripping people on the issue, didn't notice any trauma. Moments later Martin insists that he remains a Walter Gordon Liberal: "I was an economic nationalist and still am. It's just an evolution of what economic nationalism is today."

When he chose Paul Martin to be his minister of finance, Jean Chrétien was perhaps acknowledging his own vulnerability. He liked to think of himself as a numbers guy; even when Martin was at the height of his success, Chrétien got a steady stream of reports from Finance; he was always asking questions about the economy, always wondering why Finance had not reported something to him if he or an aide discovered it in *The Economist*. He was proud that he had been the first French Canadian to serve as minister of finance and he found ways of reminding people of that. But the fact of the matter is that the world of economics and finance was never Chrétien's strong suit; he has always been a fast study, but some things are too complex to reduce to one or two pages, whatever the speed of reading it. Tommy Shoyama, his deputy minister at Finance, acknowledged what other deputy ministers had been discovering since Chrétien first entered the cabinet: Chrétien, he told Lawrence Martin, Chrétien's biographer, was "not a great student of written documents."

Trudeau's opinion of Chrétien was made clear in August 1978. The heads of the G-7 industrial states had met that summer in Bonn; Chrétien had returned home after the meeting but Trudeau had stayed and gone sailing with West German chancellor Helmut Schmidt. Apparently inspired by Schmidt and by adverse opinion polls about the state of the economy when he returned to Ottawa, Trudeau undertook to administer his own economic miracle; he went on national television to announce a $2-billion cut in federal spending and some tax cuts. Chrétien did not know about it until he saw Trudeau on television. It was only the next day, when everyone had already learned of Chrétien's public humiliation, that Trudeau bothered to answer the telephone call of his aggrieved Finance minister. When Chrétien later recorded in his autobiography that "I was made to look like a fool," it was something of an understatement. Fifteen years later, when

Chrétien chose Paul Martin to be his Finance minister, it was clear from the start that there would be no such humiliation while he was in the prime minister's office. The two men disagreed frequently and sometimes heatedly in private, but until their relationship finally collapsed, Paul Martin could never accuse his prime minister of disloyalty. Chrétien did not at first understand the depth or complexity of Canada's economic problems when he moved into 24 Sussex Drive, but he knew they were serious; that was what persuaded him to pursue David Smith's advice to seek out the A-team.

The prime minister and his A-team had their first serious test a month after they were sworn into office. They had to decide whether John Crow, the governor of the Bank of Canada, would be reappointed to a second term. Both Chrétien and Martin began with serious reservations about Crow's apparent obsession with inflation and his determination to drive it to zero. Critics believed that Crow's campaign had been responsible for the recession in Canada at the end of the Mulroney era, that if he was not the cause he was at least the aggravation. It did not help Crow's case that the business community was lobbying hard for his reappointment. On the other hand, the institutional memory of Ottawa knows well the bad blood that had soured the final years of John Diefenbaker in power when his government set out to get rid of James Coyne, the governor of that era, whose tight money policies were blamed for the economic difficulties of the Diefenbaker Conservatives. The struggle to get rid of Coyne left a terrible scar on the Diefenbaker government and neither Chrétien nor Martin wanted to inherit the same kind of disaster. However, after weeks of discussions with Crow, Martin concluded that he wanted a change at the Bank and Chrétien agreed. A senior adviser who later saw the two men in less happy times said that on the fate of Crow they were absolutely in agreement. "There was no debate—but I think they both held their breath to see what the market reaction would be." As it turned out, when Martin announced that Crow's deputy, Gordon Thiessen, would become governor and that Crow was gone, the market did not react. That meant that Martin could give his full attention to his first budget.

Years later Paul Martin was not prepared to admit that the A-team failed to impress in that first attempt at budget-making. He is not a man who finds pleasure in anything less than clear and declared success, so his inclination is first to find an excuse and then to insist that things were not that bad after all: "We came in with 60 days to do the first budget. Didn't know the books, didn't know how to go about it. We did them. We basically focused on getting the budget out; that would send a signal that we were intending to deal with the deficit, but then we just didn't have the time to do anything but basically lay out a plan. And that budget was actually very well received when it came out compared to the previous budget. Subsequently people have said, well, it wasn't very well received because they compared it to the 1995 budget, which was overwhelmingly received, but it was actually not badly received at the time. We just did what we had to do. We had to do a budget with only 60 days to do it."

There was in Martin's recollection of his first budget a little bit of romance, perhaps not unlike the memory of a first date. From the day of the government's swearing-in until the budget speech there were, in fact, 110 days, not 60. As for the reception, it is only fair to say that most commentators judged the budget not for itself but for its predecessors. Typical was Peter Cook of the *Globe and Mail*, explaining sarcastically why "this imaginative budget-making process" should be regarded with skepticism: "First, mistrust Ottawa's predictions for the year being budgeted because they are, invariably, wrong by billions. Second, take absolutely no notice of what is predicted for any subsequent year because never, in a decade of drawing pretty graphs that show the deficit hurtling earthward, has a Canadian finance minister got this particular winged elephant to stop flying higher."

Even with 110 days, it was not much time to reform a sick economy. Martin did not set impossible challenges for himself. He closed military bases, reduced military personnel, and confirmed the cancellation of helicopter purchases; he cut sharply into unemployment insurance, reducing benefits and increasing the amount of time worked before benefits could be claimed; he froze transfer payments to the provinces for education and welfare; and he renewed the government's election promise to reduce the deficit to 3 per cent of gross domestic product in 1996–97. It was all part of the attempt to build "a new economy," spending on infrastructure and training and encouraging innovation, cutting back on unemployment insurance and social security. When he faced the Commons, Martin announced that "for years, governments have been promising more than they can deliver, and delivering more than they can afford. This has to end. We are doing it." Which sounded like more of Peter Cook's grim analysis of the past. The difference was that this time it turned out that the Finance minister's forecasts were right and he apparently did intend to do what he promised.

In opposition, Martin had attacked the Conservative government for trying to solve Canada's economic problems, particularly the deficit, by cutting spending on defence, unemployment insurance, and other social programs—pretty much the kind of small-l liberal attack you would expect from the son of Paul Martin Sr. In all the curiosity about the budget, nobody spent much time recalling what Martin had said in opposition and that he had done exactly what he had told the Conservatives not to do. It was only later that people began to wonder seriously what kind of Liberal Paul Martin Jr. might indeed be.

However, not long after the applause in the Commons died down, Martin was hit by a double dose of a different kind of reality, all of it beyond his immediate control. Although the economy was doing better than expected, inflation in the United States and apprehensions about the coming Quebec referendum pushed interest rates high enough to undercut much of his budget. On top of that, when he toured the world's financial capitals and the offices of the International Monetary Fund in Washington to explain the bright new dawn in Ottawa, he walked into a wall of skepticism: "I was amazed at how little credibility a Canadian Finance minister had. People just said, we've been seeing you guys coming for 25 years, saying you were going to eliminate your deficit. We don't believe you. Go away. It's very nice to talk to you and everything else, and we're delighted to sell your bonds, but we think your country is going down the tubes. The negative position, the lack of credibility in which Canada found itself, was overwhelming and I must say I was surprised by that."

All of which meant that it would be a while before the bright new dawn came to the sub-Arctic lumbering town on the Ottawa River.

CHAPTER 8

Crafting a Budget

THROUGH MOST OF CANADIAN HISTORY, indeed the history of most countries with a parliamentary system of government, the drafting of government budgets has been one of the black arts. In no other area of endeavour do those in government take themselves so seriously. Budgets are designed behind closed doors, and only insiders get to go inside; there is an aura of whispers and muttered confidences; if some in the middle ranks of the department of Finance are assigned to work on budget preparations, it is only for a limited section, for none but the most senior of bureaucrats is allowed to know the full budget. Budget documents become the responsibility of armed guards. The unauthorized revelation of a budget detail could cost the job of a bureaucrat, the Finance minister, or both. Finance ministers had always said they would like to get rid of budget secrecy, because, after all, there is really no need. But the secrecy and the self-importance endured. So, for the department of Finance, Paul Martin was a bit of a shock. His arrival had much the same effect as throwing a grenade into a glass house.

A whole mythology quickly surrounded the new minister. Nothing was more devastating than the story of the briefing book humiliation. As all government departments did for all new ministers after an election, the department of Finance had prepared three massive briefing books on the state of the economy and these they presented to Martin while he was still in Windsor where his mother lay dying. The briefing books had been something of a struggle within the department; some officials wanted to present the new minister with a harsh outline of hard choices, in effect to try to force him into a radical debt- and deficit-reduction program; others wanted a softer approach that would more accurately reflect the restrained attitude of the Liberals during the election campaign. As one official described it, when Martin first met with the senior officials in the department he was visibly angry; he leafed through the first of the briefing books as they watched him and then opened the ring binder and dumped it into a wastepaper basket, dismissing it as pabulum as he disposed of it; he did not even bother looking at the second and third volumes. That was the story; the official who told the story later admitted that he had not actually seen Martin dump the briefing book, but he had heard about it. Martin himself acknowledged that he had heard the story; in fact, there was another story that he had hurled the briefing book at his deputy minister, David Dodge. But that was not the way he remembered it, he said, because he couldn't remember either incident. "I don't think so. I don't remember doing it. I certainly remember having some very stormy meetings, and I can remember certainly saying some rather nasty things about department of Finance briefing books.... If it's a good story, I have no problem with it. I just don't remember it." The reality was apparently less dramatic. An official who was there said that in a meeting in the department of Finance boardroom the new minister slid the briefing books across the conference table to Dodge and complained that they did not sufficiently reflect the Liberal promises in the election Red Book (but this was the same minister who later would dismiss the concerns of Finance officials by telling them "Screw the Red Book"). Still, it was a good story and it became part of the mythology.

From the start Martin made it clear to the department that he would be running things his way, and that was not the way things had run before. Less than a month after he was sworn in, he went to Montreal to speak to business students at l'Ecole des Hautes Etudes Commerciales. The department did not like the idea of Martin making his first major speech in front of students; instead, the senior bureaucrats thought it would be more appropriate to make a formal economic statement to the House of Commons. Martin confided to the students: "If I may paraphrase a famous aphorism, nothing so wonderfully concentrates the mind as the feeling that the department of Finance is slowly tightening around your neck." If that was his idea of a little joke, nothing else was. He began with the succession of budgets under the Mulroney Conservatives in which the deficit had been consistently and drastically underestimated; as he spoke it appeared that the country was headed for an astonishing deficit of between $44 billion and $46 billion. Small wonder that hundreds of thousands of Canadians had withdrawn their consent to be governed because they had lost faith in their government. Senior bureaucrats were in the audience to hear Martin announce that "a team of outside specialists" would review the Finance department's forecasting methods and performance, and he promised that the report would be made public. And, above all, the secrecy that had been the Finance department's special cloak in Ottawa would be torn away. "The debate over the right mix of monetary and fiscal policies must be taken out from behind closed doors if Canadians are to have a better understanding of the options and choices available to achieve their goals." It was going to be a bad season for sacred cows.

In those early days of the Chrétien government, the Martin style was unsettling. Not everyone adapted. Some found more congenial niches in other departments, some left government altogether. Martin wanted a public debate about budget options, and public debates will probably continue for the simple reason that they make more sense, and ultimately they are a much easier way to manage public finances because change is discussed publicly rather than being handed down arbitrarily in a budget speech. But Martin's personal style meant that there would be a much broader debate within the department of Finance, a debate that would involve harsh language, hard choices, and probably blood on the floor. Looking back on the early months of Martin's arrival at Finance, those who survived and thrived seem still to carry a mixture of smugness and sheer delight, like those who have gone through a revolution and lived to tell the tale. Liberation, however, goes only so far, especially in the world of government and politics. Those who watched the process from the inside were willing to talk about the experience—discreetly—but they were not willing to be identified.

Finance had always been accustomed to genteel discussions, where positions were put forward and the minister would go away, ponder matters, and then tell the department what his decision was. In all this, one adviser said, "it would be extremely uncommon for voices to be raised or for there to be an obvious disagreement about something." Martin changed that. "That's just not his style. I mean, for example, he doesn't go away from the table to make a decision. He's got all the people around the table that he's relying on to help him come to the right conclusion. Why just ask some questions and go away? The deliberative process happens right there in the room. You get an opinion and someone says something that causes him to think about it, so he reformulates it, puts it forward and then that gets critiqued, and someone else says, well, what about this variant? It's a very iterative process that he goes through to get there."

The traditional bureaucratic style, at its most basic, was for an official to go to a minister and say, you've got two options, and the traditional minister would say, fine, let's choose the better option. Martin, perversely, would say, why choose between two bad options? Let's find a better option. Finance did not take easily to the change, but, as one adviser suggested, it seemed to bring results.

You are forcing people out of the neat boxes that they have been in. He would be frustrated by other people's attempts to put him in a box and other people would be frustrated by him forcing them to think outside their box.... I think that people around the table in the department of Finance had never seen anything like it before. I think everyone would agree that we ended up with a lot better policy. In these marathon sessions, sitting around the boardroom table in Finance, people were forced to rethink all their assumptions. There was a group of really smart people sitting around, and everybody's ideas were pushed and poked and prodded and the net result of it was that we often came away with things that had not even been considered options at the start of the discussion.

The early Martin budgets, especially the budget of 1995, involved profound and difficult decisions that implied profound and difficult changes for the country. The debate within the department enveloped everyone: Martin and deputy minister David Dodge and assistant deputy minister Don Drummond and everyone else around the table. One of those regular participants recalled:

They were the kind of decisions that people could feel passionately about. It may have surprised them the first couple of times that he yelled at them about something, but it didn't take long before Don Drummond was yelling back at him. There was no upstairs-downstairs sense around that table. It was a very egalitarian thing. You were as likely to hear somebody say to him, "What you just said makes no sense in policy terms, you cannot do that." And he would say, "Okay, tell me why that is," and if the person could convince him why that is they would move on to something else. It's not a rage in a boss-bully kind of thing. . . . What these were were extremely passionate, deeply held debates about the nature of the role the federal government was going to play in the country. He was just in it up to his elbows with everybody else. The only difference between him and everybody else is that at the end of the day he made the call. But in terms of the argument and the discussion that ensued, I don't think anybody ever felt constrained that they couldn't say anything to him.

It was all driven by a sense that there was a consensus in the country that they had to fix the problem and that there was a window to use that consensus, and the consensus would hold only if everybody felt that everybody was sharing some of the burden and that there was some fairness in the way that the burden of deficit elimination was constructed. That's why you had to get it right in the first instance. Then on budget night, everybody who was getting their ox gored had to be able to look around and say, well, actually it turns out that everybody got their ox gored. So they weren't playing favourites. That was one of the guiding principles.

You've got this lengthy deliberative process where he internalizes the arguments, thinks them through, hears all the counter-arguments back and forth. At that point he is literally agonizing about them and if you are involved in that decision you can expect to hear from him at almost any time of the day or night. He will be at home, on the road, in a hotel room somewhere, driving a car somewhere; he'll phone and say, I've been thinking about this, I've been thinking about, you know, what about if the following four things happen. But once he's made it, he moves on. He doesn't revisit it.

But it takes him longer than it takes most people to be comfortable that he's found the right answer because he's so restless that "there must be something better out there; there must be an idea that we have not yet stumbled across." He changes his mind all the time. He changes his mind more than anybody at his level that I've ever seen in my life. He's absolutely more prepared than any politician I've ever seen in my life to have his ideas be directly challenged and controverted and for him to listen to that and agree and say, "You're right, I came in here opposed but you've persuaded me." He's literally more willing to have that done than anybody, literally anybody, that I've ever seen in politics. Bureaucrats didn't actually like it all that much. Bureaucrats like a much tidier decision-making process—here are your two options, pick one of them, go away. Locking them in a room and feeding them buffet-style meals for days on end while you make them argue and argue and argue the merits of their two positions—and the four they didn't think of—as far as they're concerned, they've already done that by the time they get to you. And his view is, well, you didn't do it with me.

Before Martin invaded his department, David Dodge had fulfilled the classic role of deputy minister, more an arbiter than a participant, managing everything with enough confidence that his political masters were neither threatened nor strained. But he soon became a convert to the open debate process; he would have parallel meetings among just his own officials to road-test a lot of the ideas, so that when he got to the big table with the minister there would not be too much embarrassment. He didn't want to be caught out with options that they had not considered. But, as the official said, it was Martin who drove the process.

The reality is that a lot of smart people contribute a lot of things, but ultimately if the decision-maker isn't picking up the right ideas, you know, my view is that it doesn't matter. So it's really his. I think he was the one who kept it all together and kept moving it and kept making mini-decisions to do it.

His idea of a good time is to sit up at a table at a seven-hour meeting in front of 20 people and have the 20 people fight with each other. Joining in the fight himself, sometimes provocatively. If enough people worry a bone long enough, in his view, you will expose all of the options and all of the vulnerabilities and all of the strengths. And it was actually a pattern that persisted for nine years—it was a rolling committee, 25 people who would meet endlessly, not only on concepts and on policy but on speeches, on details. It's almost an interesting question of how you could do that as a prime minister—you'd meet every morning at six o'clock and go to bed at two in the morning and start in the next day to cover the whole range of issues. But it worked at Finance. And it was a pretty straightforward model—as much input as you could get at the front end, as much in public as possible, to desensitize it, so that options are road-tested and people understand the range of options, so there aren't any real surprises, and then active, strong, difficult debate, which is the way he thinks. He clarifies himself in oral discussion and he hears oral discussion. You'll also hear from a number of people, I think, the degree to which you can have angry debate and angry confrontation about an issue and the next morning he will have forgotten that there was any emotional tone to it whatever. He never carries a grudge because of it and he encourages that kind of stuff. That takes a lot of getting used to because everybody gets really challenged, quite directly. Everybody goes after each other's base assumptions and base ideas.

From the start it was clear that one of the major problems was that the annual budget forecasts had been disastrously wrong for so long that they had been a joke to everyone outside government. They were not a joke to Michael Wilson and Don Mazankowski, the Conservative Finance ministers who had to face superior chuckles at every budget. Finance officials still remember with some uneasiness three screaming blowouts with Mazankowski because, once more, the deficit had come in even higher than forecast, and one occasion when Wilson was so angry that he stormed out of the boardroom and slammed the door behind him, pulling it so hard that he ripped the handle off the door. Nor was it a joke when Martin spoke to the University of Montreal students, recalling that the deficit for the previous fiscal year had been $5 billion higher than forecast and warning that for the current fiscal year it looked as though the deficit was going to be $11 billion to $13 billion higher than forecast just six months previously. One official recalled Martin's insistence on the government's credibility. "He kept making analogies to business, to the fact that he couldn't have run his company that way, that erring on the side of conservatism was probably a much smarter way to go. And he was quite troubled by the degree to which he thought people were alienated from the process—public people, businessmen. That lack of credibility implied in the numbers had impact."

Small wonder that Martin did not want to end up looking as helpless as his predecessors. Small wonder that in the future he wanted the numbers fixed, and his officials remember that he spelled it out so that there could be no mistake. Martin warned them:

If there's error, there's only error in one direction, and if you need
the initial number to be higher to ensure that, go higher. I don't care
how high you go....I have spent most of my career at the Power
Corporation and my function was taking over companies that were
bankrupt or nearly bankrupt, on behalf of Power Corporation, getting
them back on their feet, increasing their value and then selling them. I
approach it the same way every time: I go to the bankers and make out

the worst possible case; it's depressing; they all lower the value of it, and they say they didn't realize it was all that bad, and two years down the road I've fixed it up—partly because it never was quite as bad as I told everybody—and it looks like I was a saviour. That's how we're going to approach this.

That part of the exercise was sheer optics, making sure that they erred on the side of conservatism, as Martin had suggested. The other part, also drawn from his days in business, was building in safety cushions, and as one official explained it, once they began thinking about it the wonder was that it had not occurred earlier.

I don't know quite how to explain it, but when you have 20 or 25 people meeting on a regular basis, all the time, heading for one single goal and working on policy, program review, mechanics, virtually everything occurs to you. All the vulnerabilities occur to you, all the obstacles occur to you, so the contingency reserve came out of having to forecast and not make net errors that put you on the wrong side of the forecast. How do you develop a cushion? Adding an additional measure of prudence was a natural fallout of that, because there are two things that can go wrong. One is that you can have economic developments that go wrong, and the other one is that you can have forecasting errors. With a $160-billion budget, you know, to make a 2 per cent error, is still a $3.5-billion mistake, right? So if you're going to be held to a standard where your error factor has to be less than 1 per cent, then you'd better have a mechanism that makes sure that you can accommodate for those errors. So they built in two levels of security, the "prudence level," with $1.5 billion or $2 billion for econometric errors, and the "contingency" to take care of economic circumstances. And that meant that would subtract $4.5 billion to $5 billion from your forecast in order to make sure that when you erred you erred on the right side.

As the years went by Martin budgets relentlessly reduced the deficit and gradually turned the corner into surplus. And every year, miracle of miracles, the final numbers turned out to be even better than the forecasts. It certainly helped to reinforce the Martin image of success. Discussing that discrepancy between cautious forecast and glowing final numbers, a senior Finance official smiled conspiratorially: "From the purists he took some flack for having a bunch of terrible forecasters, but politically it didn't do him any harm."

The chosen forum for discussion within the Finance department was an ungainly committee called a CMO. The name dates back to the 1980s when Marshall Cohen, known to everyone as Mickey, was deputy minister of finance and Cohen, the Minister, and Others would meet; those were impressive gatherings, but under Martin the CMOs (pronounced See-mo) were an institution like no other—part endurance marathon, part graduate seminar, part group therapy. The CMOs quickly became Martin's favourite process for mutual instruction and exploration; Finance officials became accustomed to the arrival of photocopied articles from the minister's office, with a note attached: "I want a CMO on this." David Dodge would be there, as would economics adviser Peter Nicholson, assistant deputy minister Don Drummond, and any other official who might have something to say about the matter at hand. And, of course, the minister, sometimes bullying, sometimes asking the damnedest questions—"He was kind of the circus master who let everyone in the rings."

You knew you were in trouble when you went to the 21st floor and the dishes were out, and you knew they were coming to serve lunch, and then you knew you were really in trouble when they came and replaced it because supper was around the table. I can't tell you the number of days that would begin at noon and end at midnight, particularly during the update and budget preparations—six to eight weeks before. It was four, five, six, seven days a week, every day.

We would have three-hour digressions. Somebody would raise an issue like consent to govern, and suddenly you would be in a graduate political science seminar. And everyone would participate to the level of their ability, and if we didn't quite get it we would bring somebody in.

He was famous for having these meetings where suddenly he would bring in a variety of experts to talk to us for a couple or three hours about the new economy, or operating in this kind of environment, and everybody went to school. We'd all go to the same graduate seminar. And some were awful and some were really stimulating. I can't remember all the people who trotted in but there were a lot of people....

He's got no ego about this. He will ask literally any question. He's never worried about appearing stupid, so he will stop the conversation and will ask sometimes absolutely bizarre questions. Like, he didn't know how RRSPs operate. Frankly, he's a very rich guy who doesn't think very much about pensions and stuff. So you'd find yourself suddenly in this kind of weird realization that the minister of finance wasn't quite sure how the pension system works. He was perfectly happy that people knew that, and he wouldn't let you proceed until he understood it. And then of course you would find out that amongst all of you a lot of people thought they knew but didn't quite know.... Paul forced that level of discussion, and there were some brilliant guys around the table and it was just this voyage of discovery all the way through it. When you have those kinds of discussions and you are all willing to take a three-hour digression into how do you forecast economic activity and how do you make the forecast better, the chances are that at the end of that it's going to be better.

From his earliest days at Finance Martin insisted constantly on the need for national consensus and he fretted about "the feeling of disconnection Canadians have from their governments." The leaders of every party in every region of the country had been reminded of the fragility of consensus the previous year, during the Charlottetown referendum, when the political elite of the country presented the people with their constitutional prescription for what ailed the country and the people said thank you, but no. Leaders may lead, but they must not lead from so far in front that those behind cannot be persuaded to follow. Charlottetown was one element of the public mood; a continuing uneasiness about the state of the economy was another. The task was clear: "Paul always felt he was in the public education business; his job was to assemble a national consensus to endorse the kind of change that was required. But the change sometimes would have to be more incremental than you would like because at a certain point people withdraw consent because they had seen so much dramatic and urgent change over the previous decade that they needed to be brought along with it."

What he talked about was the need to ensure "sufficient public acceptance." That meant telling people what the government was trying to do, winning approval for that, and then establishing public goals so that the government's performance could be measured. Part of the technique was public opinion polling but more critical was public consultation. Martin himself was forever making public speeches, but he also turned to parliamentary committees as a relatively untried device for public consultation. Instead of stewing on the backbenches, frustrated and alienated, MPs became major players in the budgetary process. The committees were made privy to details of the proposed budget; they debated ideas among themselves and with witnesses who were called to testify in groups before the committee. Not everyone was happy with the new arrangements because it meant that interest groups that had always made a privileged private appeal to the Finance minister in advance of a budget were now scrambling with other interest groups, and they were doing it in public. They no longer had their privileged access. That was what the government had intended because the idea was that everyone would understand that in hard times budget-making was a zero-sum exercise; where you add here you take away there, and everyone had a share of the responsibility. For the government it was a way of road-testing ideas at arm's-length, without committing itself to anything; it was, said one official, "a way to watch a surrogate debate about a variety of budget measures without taking ownership of them."

The process of consultation through the parliamentary committees was the final stage of a 12-month process that was set and refined during the Martin years at Finance. The first stage was in March, when

Finance officials would conduct a major evaluation of how the February budget had been received, including analysis of polling and focus groups to gauge public attitudes. In April they started the broad design of where they hoped to go in the next budget; in June the cabinet would meet to consider its political priorities for the coming year and they would see how that meshed with the final economic figures from the previous fiscal year; in July and August Larry Hagen, Martin's speech writer, would begin a series of drafts of the economic statement that Martin would deliver in October, in which he would set out in broad terms the state of the economy and where the budget would be going in February. As soon as the economic statement was done, the public consultations began, and Hagen began the first of what might end up as 35 or more drafts of the budget speech.

As a brutal work schedule, the worst of it was in the weeks immediately before the budget, but with Martin in charge there was never any guarantee of down time. His day began at 7:30 a.m. and would frequently go until 10:30 p.m. or later. On weekends he took two huge government briefcases home with him and would work through the reports, memos, and letters that he had been unable to get to during the week. From Monday to Sunday, morning, noon, or night, he always had questions and he would call anyone in the department, from the deputy minister down, to find the official most likely to know the answer.

It was, as one official said, a bit like a Jesuit academy where everyone is simply used to working seven days a week:

> You had a whole bunch of people who understood they got two weeks off a year and the rest of it they were sitting in endless meetings. And processes developed where they could produce paper overnight and you'd have a pass-through in the morning and you'd clean it up in the afternoon and Paul would be presented with it and when he was done with his comments, back it would go for reiteration, and next day it would come back and it was just an ongoing rolling iteration, and it always got better.

All of us had moments of utter despair. You know on Sunday morning you're sitting in the office doing this shit. Or we're going through yet another draft of the briefing note. I think everybody looks back at it and says, nine years and there was not a single mistake. You know, nine years and there was nothing but budgets that reached a level of public approval that had never been reached in this country. We had budgets that had majority support levels! That had never happened in this country! That was true for four, five budgets in a row. It was an astonishing achievement. But it had to do with this process, and he was the driver of the process. Without him, everybody cheerfully would have gone home and had Easter dinner with their kids. It's obsessive. I understand what it all is. But it worked.

With his father at his side, Paul Martin Jr. launches himself into politics,
acclaimed as the Liberal candidate for LaSalle-Emard, May 29, 1988.

Paul Martin Sr. is carried around the Ottawa convention hall in January 1958, during his first failed bid for the leadership of the Liberal party.

Paul Martin Jr. speaks to Toronto university students during his unsuccessful campaign for the Liberal party leadership in 1990.

Jean Chrétien and Paul Martin give a thumbs-up as they head into the House of Commons before the February 2000 budget speech.

As Jean Chrétien gestures mockingly towards the opposition MPs, Paul Martin answers questions in the House of Commons, October 2001.

Despite increasing hostility between the two men, Jean Chrétien leads a standing ovation for Paul Martin after his budget speech in December 2001.

Three weeks after Paul Martin's dismissal from the government, a poster of
Jean Chrétien was smiling; Martin was not. White Point, N.S., June 2002.

Paul Martin and his wife, Sheila, arrive for an
Ottawa news conference, June 2002.

It was a stern and unsmiling Paul Martin who answered reporters' questions at Dalhousie University, January 14, 2003.

Later that day Paul Martin was in a different mood when he was accosted by Mary Walsh and Cathy Jones from the CBC television program *This Hour Has 22 Minutes*.

Fifteen years after stepping down as head of Canada Steamship Lines, Paul Martin acknowledges he must sell his shares in CSL to avoid any conflict of interest. March 11, 2003.

In full campaign mode in April 2003, Paul Martin visits Toronto's Chinatown to show support during the SARS outbreak.

Paul Martin, Sheila Copps and John Manley during a Liberal party leadership debate in June 2003, shortly before Manley quit the campaign.

Paul Martin waves to the crowds on Montreal's St. Catherine Street as he marches in the Canada Day parade, July 1, 2003.

CHAPTER 9

A Strange Kind of Guy

W HEN HE DELIVERED THE EULOGY at his mother's funeral, Paul Martin recalled some of the burdens Nell Martin had always had to bear: "My father, as a lot of you know, was…was not easy to get along with. In fact, he was virtually unbearable. I'm told it runs in the family.…" But for the fact that it was a funeral service, a noisy chorus of agreement would no doubt have issued from those assembled in the church. Friends, relatives, government officials, political advisers, and cabinet colleagues will all testify that Paul Martin may not be unbearable all the time, but that he is certainly unbearable part of the time. Unpredictable and unsettling most of the time. In fact, by the measure of your average politician, a quite unusual man.

In the early summer of 1994, not long after the Liberals had taken over the government, Martin was fretting about how he was going to fulfil the Liberal election promise to get rid of the hated GST, the goods and services tax imposed on Canadians by the Mulroney government. They had already unsuccessfully thrashed out the problem of the GST in a number of meetings and Martin decided that perhaps a change of venue might help. He was particularly keen because he thought he might have figured out a solution to the GST conundrum. So he invited a group of Finance officials and his own advisers down to the Martin farm at Knowlton to talk about it. On that day it fell to Don Drummond, the assistant deputy minister, to explain to the minister why his idea was not terribly brilliant after all. Martin was not amused; suddenly he became visibly angry and turned on Drummond in what most of the officials regarded as an astonishing attack. Why was he so negative? Where the hell were *his* great ideas? What did *he* have to add to the discussion? Such was the explosion that the worried officials kept inching their chairs backward so they would not find themselves in the line of fire; the official who described the scene said he was convinced that one or more of the Finance bureaucrats were going to become so agitated that they would simply topple backwards off the deck. Happily, in the end, nobody tumbled to disaster. When the discussion ended, with nobody convinced of the wisdom of the minister's GST solution, Martin announced that he needed help with the barbecue and promptly nominated Drummond as his sous-chef. Five minutes later, with everyone else watching from a safe distance, Martin and Drummond were laughing and joking, and Martin at least appeared to have forgotten the argument. It was as though it had never happened.

In his determination to pursue a problem Martin could be almost perverse. Occasionally, even if everyone at a meeting was agreed on a course of action, Martin would not let the matter go. If everyone agreed, he would decide it must be wrong. He would tell one of the senior public servants—frequently the hapless Drummond—to take the counter-argument. So Drummond or whoever was nominated would have to make the case that the solution on which everyone had agreed moments earlier was in fact the wrong answer. The chosen official would then embark on the counter-argument, only to discover that Martin would be dismissing him and denouncing him and his argument as the most stupid thing he had heard in a long time. The official who related this strange scene stopped and smiled almost apologetically. That's just the way Martin was. And he didn't do that kind of thing all the time, he said; in fact, he could be immensely charming. "I thought it could be productive without some of those excesses. I survived it, but I never thought it was very pleasant. It certainly unnerved me in many cases," the official said. "Most of the time, when there was a difficult issue, he would not say, 'We'll meet on that tomorrow.' His words were 'We'll schedule a fight on that at 10 o'clock tomorrow.' That's what he wanted...."

"The characteristic about him that I thought was unique was that I've never met anybody so unwilling to accept the status quo. In nine out of ten cases, he ultimately came back and said, 'Really, having looked at it I can't see a way of making it better.' But he would never start there. Everything started with 'Let's talk about a proposal to totally change something—not just at the edges, just totally, fundamentally, turn it upside down, operate in a totally different way. The whole tax system: let's not just talk about making a marginal change to the tax system; we're not going to change an existing rate, we're going to change the whole tax system; we're not going to tax the income bases that we tax right now.' Everything started on that basis. That was always his approach—from the day he walked in."

Sometimes the debate was about the tax system, sometimes about unemployment insurance. The problem of the GST and the question of whether the government should take a bite out of pensions lasted for months. Often the result was little or no change, but the discussions always began on the understanding that the result might be quite fundamental, radical change.

"The seniors benefit, which ultimately they dropped—I couldn't tell you the number of permutations we looked at for that thing. That went on for a year. There always had to be a better way of doing it. You know, all this resistance: 'If we'd just had the smarter idea, we would have a good policy and we'd have good communications.' There was always this perspective that 'the reason we're not seeing the right way of doing this or we're getting some resistance is that we just haven't been smart enough. We're thinking too much within the box. Let's go outside the box. Let's explore out there in space.' It was a very predictable pattern with which he approached everything, which I found quite different because most people start with 'Here's the way it is right now, and here's how you can improve it on the margins.' And he started, 'Here's the way it is right now, and now let's forget about that, and let's not think about any constraints, let's not think about how you get from A to B, let's think about B to B, and then Z and everything else. Can it be made totally different and totally better? And if yes, okay; now, after we get all that laid out, let's figure how we get from here to there.' In nine out of ten cases it was 'You know what, given the objectives and what not, we just don't really see that all these other ideas are any better than where we are right now, so either we leave it alone or we'll tinker with it at the edges.' But if you started that way, you're in trouble. He never wanted to hear that from you. He wanted to be the one to ultimately say, 'You know, I've heard all your ideas but they're really not all that great'.

"I've never had anyone doing that, forcing you constantly to think harder. Because it's really easy to say, 'Here's how you can change this thing at the margins,' but to come in with a totally different way of approaching it—instead of just filling in spaces, you're sitting back and you're totally thinking of different approaches. I've never been involved in anything that had the high quality of debate that we had around issues like that. There were bad sides of it, too, that were hard to accept. The debate got pretty nasty; there were no holds barred, certainly not at his end of it. But the faint of heart faded and were never seen again.

"There were times that I did yell at him and there were a couple of times when I actually swore at him. You can't do that every day. It's very difficult if you're a bureaucrat to do that to a minister, but it's typical of that type of situation, that if you don't do it at some point then you're just going to get walked over and then ultimately get forgotten about. He had no interest in people who weren't firm in their ideas and didn't have lots of ideas. There were a couple of people in the early days who were 'yes sir, how fast can I do that.' Well, they were never seen again."

John Godfrey, the Toronto Liberal MP whose friendship with Martin goes back to the days long before either of them were involved in politics, agrees that the Martin dialectic is not for the faint of heart or the hierarchically minded: "Deference to authority doesn't get you very far. What it says to me is that he is a man who is sufficiently self-confident intellectually that he doesn't mind going at it, and his ego will not be crushed if you give a vigorous response. And I think that's how he sorts out problems."

For officials who could adapt to the dialectic, the experience was as invigorating as it was bruising: "For me and I expect for others there was a compensating factor, and that was that I have never met anybody with so many ideas, and that's kind of neat. And it's kind of neat when somebody says, 'We're not starting this debate by saying that this is out of bounds and that is out of bounds; everything is in bounds and everything is on the table.' That was kind of enjoyable to do that. He works so hard, but many people who are really hard-working are not great thinkers because the volume of the work gets in the way of the thinking process. He did both. He always knew the technical aspects of everything, but he sat and just thought big thoughts an awful lot, especially on the weekend when he went back to his farm."

The weekend seems to be Martin's time for thinking. There is always time reserved for Mass—Saturday if he is travelling, Sunday if he is at home or at the farm—but most of the remaining time is devoted to the box-like briefcases that are his weekend chore. He works his way through briefing papers or reports, annotating them as he goes and frequently telephoning the author at whatever time he happens to finish reading them. Sometimes he wants more information, sometimes he wants to argue with a conclusion, sometimes he wants to register his own latest idea so that it will already be in the thought mill on Monday morning. Even his most devoted officials hasten to explain that not all of the ideas are brilliant or even good, indeed, that a lot of them are bad. Their consolation for Sundays interrupted by inconvenient telephone calls is that even if 95 per cent of Martin's ideas are bad, the volume of ideas is such that the 5 per cent amount to a lot of good ideas.

"I've never met anybody who had so many good ideas. But, man, I've never known anybody with so many bad ideas. There's where he was really smart and I think that was his strongest thing. He knew a lot of his ideas weren't any good and he never walked into something. That's why he had all these debating sessions and that's why he had all of these fights, and that's why he had no time for anybody who said, 'Yes, you're absolutely right, how fast do you want us to do that?'

Those people were gone just like that. I think he thought, 'I am just spewing out a lot of ideas here, these are radical changes, and maybe some of them aren't that good. I want somebody to really test this thing out.' That was probably his greatest strength."

It was not just the families of officials and advisers who resented telephone calls out of the blue when the minister of finance was overcome by a curiosity or an idea. There were also times when Martin's obsession with work crossed the acceptable line in his own family. A senior official cited a call when Martin was in the Caribbean during the Christmas holidays: "I remember one time he called me and he said, 'I've only got a couple of minutes to talk because Sheila's just dived into the swimming pool, so this is going to be real fast. Don't you talk because I don't have very long.' Then he goes, 'Okay. She's out. I gotta go.' So I guess there were certain rules about not working at Christmas. He obviously did his damnedest to bend that."

Sometimes Martin's curiosity goes well beyond the bounds of his particular work agenda. John Godfrey tells of the occasion on which he was working on a book about childhood development and sent a chapter to a number of cabinet ministers in the hope that childhood development might claim a little government attention. The only minister who got back to him was Martin, and that was at 9:30 on a Sunday morning, three weeks later. Martin had read the chapter and wanted to talk about it. Godfrey was so pleased that he sent him another chapter, and Martin called again, that time on Christmas Eve. Such is the state of politics and politicians in Ottawa these days that even Godfrey, one of Martin's old friends and himself a politician, felt he must at least wonder whether something as improbably considerate and concerned as wanting to talk about the problems of children might be merely base politics. But Godfrey quickly concluded that it was not: "Even if you were a total cynic, he couldn't possibly do all of that just to gain one more MP's support, or my riding association. There's a genuine interest in ideas."

That said, a smiling Godfrey acknowledges that Martin is a restless soul, high energy and engaged. But one must not let oneself be trampled by a Martin in full flight. Godfrey says, "He's not above using cheap Jesuitical debating tricks. You know, he's a philosophy major and he occasionally invokes things like 'arguments from superior knowledge' and other things, or complete false choices. But once you get over that and you're prepared to just go for it, in a certain kind of spirit of the chase, then it's quite stimulating, although he can certainly get stuck on certain things. You will have a conversation, and then a year later you will have the same conversation, though you thought we had gotten over that. But, to his credit, he gnaws away at things."

By way of a different illustration of Martin's curiosity about the world, Godfrey cites the weekend at the end of August 2002, when the Liberal Party caucus was gathered in Chicoutimi. As it turned out, that was the meeting at which Jean Chrétien announced that he would be stepping down from the party leadership; at the time nobody knew that, but the caucus was in an angry turmoil and steaming for a fight with the prime minister. It was a time when Martin obviously had other things on his mind and other concerns to occupy his time, but he and Godfrey had had long talks about Quebec's program of heavily subsidized day care throughout the province and Godfrey was anxious to show him one particular day-care centre in Chicoutimi. To Godfrey's concern, when he got to the centre, there was no sign of Martin. Godfrey waited almost an hour and then Martin suddenly appeared with several day-care staff in tow. Martin had arrived early and began chatting with the day-care officials and asking them questions about the operation, so they decided to give him a personal guided tour of the facility. By the end he knew almost as much about day care in Chicoutimi as Godfrey.

Martin is one of those people who does not reveal all of himself at once. Richard Mahoney did not get to see the other side of Martin until after he had gone to work for him. The two men had first met in the early 1980s, when Mahoney was an eager Young Liberal and Martin was sniffing around the fringes of politics. They kept in touch and when Martin got elected to Parliament and then decided that he would run for the leadership when John Turner stepped down, he asked

Mahoney if he would be his executive assistant. Mahoney gave up his job with a Toronto law firm and moved to Ottawa. But he had one last case to clear up and he was in Toronto for that case on the day that Turner announced he would be stepping down from the Liberal leadership. Mahoney and David Herle had earlier discussed what the drill would be if Mahoney were out of town and there was some kind of announcement that would require Martin to make a statement or be available for interviews. Everything went smoothly all day until Martin was being interviewed by Barbara Frum on CBC television that evening, and he was a disaster. In his frustration over his own dreary performance, a brooding Martin decided that Mahoney was to blame.

More than a decade later the normally jovial Mahoney still shakes his head in disbelief, wide-eyed at the explosion that faced him: "We had this horrible fight. It deteriorated into a screaming match and I had never really had one before. In my family normally we swept that kind of conflict right under the carpet, so I would rarely have that kind of conflict with people." Mahoney thought about it and did the noble thing; he wrote a letter of resignation and left it for Martin to read in the morning, which led to Mahoney's second surprise: "He came in and he was completely shocked and it was clear to me at that point that we had had two totally separate experiences. He had blown off some steam about his frustration with a day that went well but had one bad moment and he needed someone to outlet on and I was that person. I thought we'd had a relationship-ending fight."

Mahoney remains one of Martin's senior advisers. He got over the Martin outburst the way other people who know him well or work for him get over such things: they yell back and shrug it off. His staff call such incidents "beatings" and they have come to the conclusion that beatings go with the turf. Even now Mahoney concedes that it took some getting used to: "One of the things about having a relationship with Paul is that he is a very strong and tough and demonstrative guy, and he loves to mix it up. He loves to mix it up. But, like that story, the next morning, for him, it was over. So I had to actually get to the point where I was comfortable with that, and the odd thing is that before that point in my life I actually didn't think that I would be as fond of, or admire, or look up to or respect, or be friends with some-one—all of those things—that I would have those fights with."

Martin's explosive temper was starting to become known within the inner rings of Ottawa's bureaucracy in the weeks and months after he became Finance minister. That was hardly surprising in the rarified world where there is no news quite as precious as the insider news about the guy who occupies the minister's office. Martin's temper was confirmed for a wider public when the story of Mahoney's short-lived resignation appeared in *Double Vision*, the book on the early years of the Chrétien government by Ed Greenspon and Anthony Wilson-Smith. The story caused some embarrassment and inspired various efforts at damage control among Martin's people, such as the one adviser who offered an elaborate shrug and a confidential explanation that "he has a temper, but I think a lot of that stuff can get overstated, about how volatile he is." Others say, oh, yeah, and move on without really engaging in the conversation.

However, for Mahoney, the beatings are an odd barometer of per-sonal relationships. He says they do not happen with anyone with whom Martin is not comfortable. So after Martin became Finance minister, when Mahoney heard that he and David Dodge, his deputy minister, were having public fights in front of their junior bureaucrats, Mahoney concluded that their relationship would be a success because it signified that Martin liked Dodge, regarded him as an equal, and enjoyed debating with him. How often does Martin explode in frus-tration and bad temper? Once a day? Once a week? Once a month? Mahoney looks startled at the question and, briefly, more uncomfort-able. His face suddenly takes on that opaque quality that you see in friends who want to be helpful, perhaps, but certainly not too helpful. Well, not once a day, he explains, but way more than once a month.

John Duffy, who began writing speeches for Martin during the 1990 leadership campaign, insists that the explosions of temper were always two-way streets, that Martin surrounds himself with people who like a good fight, many of whom are half his age but quite happy to talk back to him. Duffy had his own introduction to that side of Martin when he was trying to write speeches for a man who was still learning the basics of public speaking: "We were awful to each other. It was an awful relationship. It was two Irish tempers in a small room under pressure. And I was the most appallingly cheeky 27-year-old twit in the history of the world, and Martin was under a lot of pressure and sometimes he didn't feel like arguing, and he'd say, 'Just write this down,' and I'd say, 'You have executive secretaries, go use them,' and we'd just get going at each other. I mean, there was blood on the walls. It was really gruelling, but I think the products actually were pretty good, and the passion that went into fighting about them usually came out up on the podium."

However unpleasant the periodic explosions of temper or frustration, there are clearly compensations, although those may not be readily apparent to anyone outside. For Mahoney, "the flip side of that is that I have never actually worked with someone who is as open to an external idea that might not be his own idea, that he might actually say, what's that about?" In some measure the appeal may lie in the curiously informal, horizontal structure of the Martin office and campaign team. Mahoney calls it "a bit of a collective system, in the sense that whatever each of us was good at, we would try and make a contribution." Another adviser describes it simply as "the most collegial office staff in the history of politics. The people who were with him in '90 are still with him. There's never been a turf issue. Not that many people are allowed in; part of the way you get allowed in is your ability to work in a horizontal structure and not to impose. So there's none of this setting people off against each other. . . . I was stunned to come to an environment where everyone listened to what everyone else said and nobody's word carried more weight than anybody else's, and you were as good as your ideas. And everybody worked at that one common purpose."

A quite different perspective on Martin comes from Michael Bellamy, the former Peace Corps volunteer who met and married Mary Anne Martin not long after Paul Martin Sr. lost the race for the

Liberal leadership to Pierre Trudeau. Bellamy, a professor of English literature in St. Paul, Minnesota, says Martin's temper is very much like that of his father. He saw it most dramatically when he and Martin were playing golf and Martin became so enraged by a bad shot that he hurled his golf club into the upper branches of the nearest tree; what made things worse for Martin trying to recover his dignity was that the club stayed up in the tree and the embarrassed Martin had to return the next day to retrieve it: "His dad was the same way. He was very explosive, and then the next day if people were looking at him funny, he didn't even understand it. He was pretty stern. He would go ballistic and then an hour later, what was the problem?"

As Bellamy describes him, the man who threw his golf club into the tree brings the same kind of intensity to business or politics or driving a car. He says, "What excites Paul is challenge—whatever the game is. I think he gets bored pretty easily, to tell you the truth. He's made his trillions or whatever it is, and, you know, if it becomes automatic after a while, he's going to look around, like a lot of people like him who are gifted and interested in where the action is. So it doesn't surprise me at all. He doesn't bear fools patiently, or, at least, what he thinks of as foolish....He's pretty impatient. He really has no patience if he thinks somebody's just being dense or perverse or whatever; he doesn't fool around that way and I think that's one of the appealing things about him. You know where he stands....But, yeah, he can be rough if he thinks you're really being out of line. I've seen that fairly often....

"That sense of fun that he gets from the challenge, whether it's negotiating or whatever it is, he really likes that and even if it isn't there he'll create it in a social situation. You know, let's play a game, let's have some excitement. It's the same way he drives an automobile. It's right on the edge. I don't think he's a bad driver; he's actually very good. He's well coordinated and everything, but everything he does is fast. He's got lots of tickets and stuff, I guess, that kind of thing. But that's kind of the way he is. He does not want to be bored—that he finds almost intolerable. When I see him anyway, that's the way he is, which is, you know, fun to be around. You want to be around somebody like that and I think that's one of the leadership things he's always had. You know, there's something going on."

While Martin was still at CSL, before politics, even when the two families were in the West Indies on holiday, he would spend a lot of time on the phone to the office, to associates, or to friends. "He's the kind of person who needs to feel like he's staying in touch," explains Bellamy. "But it wasn't like he couldn't relax. When he wasn't playing golf or talking to somebody or having dinner or whatever, he would either be reading or on the phone. There wasn't much down time. That's the way he wanted it, clearly. He wanted to know what was going on. We'd be gone for two weeks and I'm sure that if you've got to be running things, even though it was a slow time, there are times when he had to know what was happening. Driven? No, I wouldn't say that. I always have the sense that he has a lot of fun; he likes doing what he's doing and he's good at it and he gets a lot of pleasure out of it. That's my sense of him particularly, as a businessman. There are parts of politics that he's not crazy about, to put it mildly, but he seems to manage."

Bellamy says he and Martin used to argue about politics all the time and they had a lot of fun; they don't talk politics now that Martin spends his life in politics—"He doesn't need to hear from me." Even in those days Martin seemed to Bellamy to be driven as much by curiosity and the hunger for challenge as any sense of mission: "When we used to argue about politics he would say, 'I want to find out how the world works and I want to get in on it'."

If Bellamy demonstrates a particular affection for Martin it may be in part a reflection of Mary Anne's devotion to him. She still says unabashedly, "I've always worshipped him. I'm his kid sister." Because he was six years older, he was always very much a bigger brother. Typically, when Mary Anne was in Chandigarh, India, in 1968, big brother weighed in with a message out of the blue that warned bluntly: "Don't bring drugs across the border." Thirty-five years later Mary Anne remained torn between amusement and exasperation: "Well, where the hell was I going to bring drugs across the border? I was young, and he was so nervous about that kind of thing. He's totally big brother." In recent years Mary Anne has had more than her share of illness and more than her share of worried phone calls from Martin. "I can always tell when I'm really sick because Paul calls me every day," she says. "When I'm not sick I have to call him and I say, you haven't called me in a week or two weeks and I'm madder than hell. So I think it kind of explains about his friendships. He's very loyal." As she told the story, she apologized for coughing and explained that she had just got over a cold. Now if Paul had known she had a cold, she said, he would have had a fit: "He's very much a big brother."

It's the kind of story that they probably would not believe in the department of Finance in Ottawa.

CHAPTER 10

Tackling the Deficit

AUL MARTIN AND THE DEPARTMENT OF FINANCE had been preparing for the 1995 budget for the better part of a year, ever since they heard the mirthless chuckles that greeted his first attempt to rescue the Canadian economy a little more than three months after the Liberals took office. The signal failure of his February 1994 budget was a source of lingering irritation; even a decade later Martin would insist a little belligerently that his first budget was not as bad as all that. But he knew that whether or not the budget really was bad, it was *seen* to be bad. The gnomes of Zurich and the guys in the red suspenders said, oh, yeah, Canada is promising once more to reduce its deficit; well, we've heard that one before. That was the world's judgment on his first budget and for Martin it was a shock: "I couldn't believe how little credibility a Canadian Finance minister had."

It is the nature of financial crises that almost always they get worse, and as time goes by they get worse faster. It was in the course of 1994 that Martin discovered the particularly murderous impact of compound interest. From his days at CSL, when he was indebted to the bank for millions, he already knew what happened to a debt if you could not start to pay it down. The difference was that Canada's problems were not millions but billions. Someone figured out that because of interest charges the federal debt—$466 billion in 1993, $508 billion in 1994—was growing at the rate of $85,000 a minute. Rising interest rates were pushing the bill even higher than before. So, as he sat down to craft his budget for 1995, Martin knew that off the top he would have to factor in interest charges of more than $6 billion. Compound interest is not ideology, he said, it's arithmetic. Later that year he would figure out how much "the cancer of compound interest" would hurt: "That is money we did not have to pay last year. It is a new charge on the future of each and every Canadian—not because of new government spending, but because of old government debt. Think of it, $6 billion in new burden in one year alone. That's the federal government's entire R&D budget. It's three times what we spend on culture. It's more than what we spend on the child tax credit. That interest is money that cannot go to social programs, cannot go to child poverty, cannot go to science and technology, cannot go to the lowering of taxes. It robs this country of its potential. It robs our children of their future."

In his effort to win public support in the fight against the deficit, Martin's great advantage was that the arithmetic of compound interest made it all visibly awful, like a nightmare unfolding in slow motion. Canadians were not eager to share his pain, but at least they understood it. When the Liberals took office in the late autumn of 1993, of every dollar collected in federal taxes 30 cents of it were going to pay interest, and if interest rates went up again it was only going to get worse: "That increase in interest rates just meant that we didn't have a penny for education, a penny for any of the things my dad believed in.... I could just see the federal government essentially becoming the tax collector on Monday so that we could pay interest costs on Tuesday, and that was going to be the end of it. And that's the way we were going."

In the spring of 1994, two months after he had presented it, Martin's budget began to unravel. For all his bold chopping of unemployment insurance and defence spending, rising interest rates in the United States were pushing up Canadian rates, and that was pushing all his budget forecasts out the window. There were fears of an approaching American recession and fears that Canada would inevitably be pulled into the vortex of any economic problems south of the border. It was, as he said, "a scenario for Argentina." His somewhat forlorn hope was that he could establish enough credibility to hold interest rates down. However, if there were going to be any credibility it would depend on the government being apparently on track to achieve its 3 per cent target—the Liberals' election promise to reduce the deficit to 3 per cent of gross domestic product in the fiscal year 1996–97. It was Martin's good fortune that Jean Chrétien was as committed to the 3 per cent target as he was—it had been one of the fundamentals of the Liberals' election Red Book—and the 3 per cent target was effective leverage to persuade their cabinet colleagues to bear with the difficult times they would all be facing. Some of them were profoundly reluctant but in the end they went along with the target that they would achieve, as Martin said, "come hell or high water."

Even as he explained it years later, Martin's elusive credibility seemed very much a matter of smoke and mirrors: "I wanted to lay out a plan, not simply make a statement, but I wanted to be able to demonstrate very clearly that all the decisions have been taken to hit that 3 per cent target and then go beyond it to eliminate the deficit. But I also had to at the same time re-establish our credibility because interest rates are set by credibility. So it wasn't enough if the plan made sense, people had to see that it made sense and understand it in order to say, hey, there really is a change in Ottawa."

Such is the perverse nature of international finance and domestic politics that Paul Martin's mission to save Canada's economy was helped immeasurably by bad news from abroad. The first was the collapse of the Mexican economy, "the peso crisis," in late December and early January. As one of Martin's senior advisers acknowledged later, the misery of Mexico had the salutary effect of demonstrating to Canadians that there really was financial disaster in the air. And then in early January, to make the point majestically unmistakable, the *Wall Street Journal* committed itself to two lofty examinations of the perilous state of the Canadian economy. The first was a broad brush of despair about the Canadian dollar and its similarities to the Mexican peso, the curse of high debt, the departure of the Bank of Canada governor John Crow, and the uncertainty overshadowing everything in view of the imminent Quebec referendum on independence. Not content with that, the voice of Wall Street followed the next day with an editorial suggesting looming national bankruptcy: "Mexico isn't the only U.S.

neighbor flirting with the financial abyss. Turn around and check out Canada, which has now become an honorary member of the Third World in the unmanageability of its debt problem.... What's clear is that Canada can no longer dawdle over its debt and tax burdens. It has lost its triple-A credit rating and can't assume that lenders will be willing to refinance its growing debt forever. Before Canada 'hits the wall' it must put on the brakes and take its government in a new direction."

In fact, Canada had not lost its triple-A credit rating, although in a month Moody's Investors Service put Canada's debt under review for a possible downgrade, and, sure enough, the triple-A rating was withdrawn two months after that. At the same time it was clear that others had been drinking from the same gloomy trough, for in mid-January, six weeks before the budget, a KPMG survey of economic expectations revealed that only one of 30 experts believed that Ottawa's budget would *ever* be balanced and they predicted that Martin's deficit targets for the following two years would be missed. And an opinion poll at about the same time revealed that two-thirds of Canadians had little confidence that Martin would manage to bring the deficit in on target.

The polls also suggested that Canadians were ready for tough measures if they were required to overcome the deficit, but it was an attitude dictated less by optimism than by despair. One Martin adviser suggested that many Canadians felt the country was just one step ahead of the Mexicans: "I think there was a feeling that we weren't too far away from the IMF having something serious to say about the Canadian economy. And we weren't too far away from having to get some help."

By the time Sheila Martin first got to hear the 1995 budget speech, it had already gone through weeks of chopping and changing, translating and retranslating, shading and emphasizing, rehearsing and rehearsing and rehearsing. Martin's obsession with getting it absolutely right had as usual afflicted the brains trust that was always there when there was work to be done—Terrie O'Leary, his executive assistant; David Herle and Elly Alboim of Earnscliffe Strategy Group, one of Ottawa's leading consulting and lobbying firms; David Dodge, the deputy minister; Don Drummond, the assistant deputy minister in charge of taxes; Peter Daniel, the assistant deputy minister in charge of communications; and Peter Nicholson, his special economics adviser. They had shared in all the heavy lifting in the previous months, and by late Saturday afternoon they had done what they could; the speech was still too long, but they sent the minister home where he would rehearse again and again, and where he would submit himself and his budget to Sheila for final approval.

At that stage, budgets were relatively new for both Martins. In time Sheila would get to know the budget speech routine only too well, but this was early days, only their second time. Their starting point was that a man in search of credibility had to make everything as clear as possible; once it was clear enough, he had to make sure he did not bore his listeners to sleep. So at this final stage, on that and every other budget, Martin would read, Sheila would listen, they would make changes, he would read, she would listen, they would make changes. "We'd go over it and over it, and I think just hearing himself out loud helped. . . . I think for him it was a way of listening to what he had writ-ten, put into words, if you know what I mean. He has a habit sometimes of making very long sentences, for instance, and I keep say-ing, cut it down, because he'll run out of breath. Everybody's always told him that."

Sheila's final duty was to head for the House of Commons on Monday afternoon to hear the finished product: "I knew the budgets. I mean, I could give you the budget speech! And then I had to go and listen to it in the House! I could lip-read it."

Martin's budget speech that Monday afternoon was as harsh as the news could get for Canadians because his gamble was that only real harshness was going to convince the skeptics. His budget had to have credibility, and it was only going to get credibility if it hurt, and that it did. It hurt more than anyone expected. Government spending would drop by $25 billion over the following three years and in the process program spending would be reduced to a lower level than at any time since 1951. Ottawa, the government town, was losing 45,000 jobs, a 14 per cent reduction in the public service—so much for the promised "drive for jobs and growth." Subsidies to business were reduced; government activities would be put on a commercial basis; CN, the skeletal remains of the massive railway system created by the government 75 years before, would be sold, as would the government's majority holding in Petro-Canada; air traffic control would be privatized; the Crow Rate, the subsidy on which western farmers had relied for more than a century to get their grain to market, was terminated; Canadian foreign aid and contributions to international institutions such as the United Nations and the World Bank would be reduced; people from distant lands who wanted to make Canada their home would have to pay $975 to buy an application form to immigrate. Every government department except Indian and Northern Affairs had its budget cut, some by as much as 50 per cent. The Liberals' former environment critic, who had denounced the Conservative government of the day for neglecting the environment, cut the department of the Environment budget by 30 per cent. Child care, which had ranked high on the Liberals' election platform and had rated a pledge of $360 million in the 1994 budget, disappeared entirely from the government's agenda.

Perhaps most devastating for the shape and texture of the country, Martin slashed $7 billion in the federal government's transfers to the provinces for the following two years, that on top of a $1.5-billion cut in his first budget. Federal transfers to the provinces were customarily targeted for health, welfare, and postsecondary education, with the money allocated for particular programs. Henceforth the money would be transferred to each province as a lump sum, its allocation for the provinces to decide. The Canada Assistance Plan, under which Ottawa provided half the financing for welfare payments across the country, would cease to exist; the federal government would no longer have an active responsibility for Canadian citizens on welfare.

Martin made sure that everyone got the message: "Our reductions in government expenditure are unprecedented in modern Canadian history.... We are bringing government's size and structure into line with what we can afford.... This budget overhauls not only how government works but what government does."

And in a particular message that he hoped would be heard by Moody's and other guys in red suspenders: "It doesn't take a stroke of genius to understand that we have broken the back of the deficit and, in fact, that the rating agencies should have no concern."

The budget had been framed with the caution that became the watchword of the Martin era—under-promise and over-perform. His good news on that day was that for all the scorn heaped on his budget of the previous year, everything had worked out much better than expected and the deficit was not going to be nearly as bad as he feared; the deficit would be a startling $4.4 billion below the forecast. It was not a balanced budget, but it was the kind of good news that gives the process a bit of credibility.

It was only later that senior Finance officials would explain how Martin persuaded the department to provide the kind of forecasts that would help in under-promising and over-performing. The rule was that if you are preparing a forecast on economic growth, you assume the worst; if you are preparing a forecast on the size of the deficit, you assume the worst: "He would say, 'If I put a gun to your head and I say I'm going to pull the trigger'—it was an expression he used all the time—'what deficit number are you going to say?' Well, if my brain's going to be blown out, I'm going to say a pretty high number. So he said, 'If we have a famine and there's a nuclear disaster and this and this, can you guarantee me that the number's not going to be higher than that?' So you add another five million after he says that." In the textbooks on economic forecasting, it's surprising that there is not more attention paid to the consequences of a gun to the head.

As an exercise in forecasting, the process was, if nothing else, creative. But it worked. After a succession of Finance ministers whose forecasts suggested they did not seem to know what they were talking about, Martin did seem to know. Peter Cook, who 12 months before had dismissed sarcastically "this imaginative budget-making process," was a man transformed by the new budget: "For nearly 10 years, this column has reserved its harshest words and biggest doubts for Ottawa's annual exercise in budgeting. Now along comes Paul Martin and after last year's false start rewrites Canada's fiscal outlook for the balance of the 1990s and does it credibly and does it as the first Finance Minister in a generation to truly take charge of his portfolio and be given a mandate to do so by the Prime Minister."

Martin's budget left virtually nobody indifferent. A random glance at various newspapers and analysts on the day after the budget revealed that even those inclined to be critical understood that it was a new day of a new government, and in some ways a new country:

"It will create a new federal government, but one that will be less important in the future lives of Canadians...."

"The Canada that we have known is no more.... This is truly an historic change that literally ends the Canada that we've known and sets us on a much meaner course...."

"This is part of the international recipe for downsizing and down-grading social programs...."

"Finance Minister Paul Martin began reinventing the government of Canada yesterday...."

"...a historic retreat in many areas of social policy...."

"Ottawa has entered its twilight years as a force for social activism...."

"It's the beginning of federalism and the end of centralism...."

"Meagre though they've been, federal standards over welfare and social services will be virtually nonexistent."

The reactions would have been no surprise to Martin because in the previous months every aspect of the budget had been road-tested on the Commons Finance committee, on Liberal MPs, on interest groups, and on focus groups. Unlike most politicians, Martin seemed to understand almost instinctively the importance of communicating to people and the importance of listening to people. He surrounded himself with people who could reinforce his own instincts. His closest advisers at Earnscliffe Strategy Group were David Herle and Elly Alboim, former CBC-TV bureau chief; both had made themselves skilled in reading the public mood. In addition to Herle and Alboim at Earnscliffe, the assistant deputy minister for communications, Peter

Daniel, was a former CBC correspondent. What Martin did not know, they could teach him.

With the eager help of Martin and his advisers, newspapers and television shows devoted numbing attention to the yawning chasm of the deficit and the curse of compound interest. "Come hell or high water" had come to seem almost a patriotic rallying cry. So it was no shock when, in the days after the budget, the polls were enthusiastic. Clearly Canadians had got the message. Although they understood that the budget would increase unemployment and diminish social programs, 69 per cent of those polled thought Martin and the government were on the right track.

When asked later whether a lot of good was not going out with the bad as a result of his hacking at government programs, Martin was ready with the perfect answer: "That's why I resent so much that this problem was not dealt with earlier."

If there were any uncertainty about the status of Paul Martin within the Chrétien cabinet, that evaporated in the months leading up to that second budget. After the prime minister, Martin was the strongman of the cabinet: Jean Chrétien understood it, his cabinet colleagues understood it, and of course Martin understood it. He redefined his job to make himself the overseer and judge of every minister in the cabinet. Those who challenged him did so at their peril; it was like going into the corner with Gordie Howe.

For Chrétien, the choice of Martin as his most important minister must have been something of a challenge. For a start, Chrétien had a lingering uneasiness about Martin personally after the 1990 leadership race; he did not like the fact that Martin had dared to challenge him— a mere rookie presuming to seek the job for which Jean Chrétien had been hungering for almost 30 years. And he certainly did not like the campaign that Martin's people ran, calling Chrétien a *vendu*, suggesting that he was a traitor to his own people.

Besides, in their skins the two men fundamentally did not really like each other. Yet one of the cabinet ministers who was close to Chrétien and who was no fan of Martin explained that, in the simplest of terms, Chrétien felt that Martin was the best guy for the job. "Jean Chrétien didn't put him in there to screw him; he put him in there because he figured he'd have the best credibility to do the job. Martin was the one that pushed the envelope on tackling the expenditures; the PM wanted to do it but was nervous that he would not get the political support he needed. Martin actually pushed the PM—but I don't think the PM resented that. I think that he was nervous about the support and it worked out well."

The test for Martin began with a single line in his first budget that had promised a broad look at the spending of all government departments, with an eye to "the elimination or reduction of low priority programs." That promise became the program review on which Martin based the spending cuts that were fundamental to his attack on the deficit and the cabinet's attempt to refine the process of government. Martin's partner in this exercise would be Marcel Massé, the minister responsible for Public Service Renewal—a newcomer to elected office but, more importantly, a man who had spent the previous quarter century in what seemed like every senior public service job in Ottawa. The scholarly 53-year-old Massé had delved deeply into everything from economics and foreign aid to federal-provincial relations. What Massé brought to the program review was an intimate knowledge of the intricacies of government—among his many jobs he had been secretary of the cabinet and Clerk of the Privy Council—and a vast appetite to make government more efficient. Reluctant cabinet ministers or bureaucrats might gamble that they could bluff or muscle either Martin or Massé; they could not handle both of them.

An outsider would have decided that the program review was doomed before it ever began. For a start, nobody could agree on what numbers they were going to use to calculate departmental spending. Three different government agencies—Finance, Treasury Board, and the individual departments—each had its own system of calculating spending and nobody knew how to reconcile the numbers. Although Martin was central to the program review process, even Finance gave an impressive show of foot-dragging; the department at first would not show its numbers to even Massé, much less show them to more junior cabinet ministers. Martin had to lecture his departmental officials about the program review, explaining that a number of cabinet ministers were going to help make the cuts in government spending and that, really, they just had to relinquish their control of the numbers; everyone had to be brought to the table if they were going to be persuaded to buy in to the harsh measures that lay ahead. In the end the Finance officials agreed but it obviously hurt their pride; never before had the cabinet shared in the making of a budget; that was the job of Finance, the responsibility that gave Esplanade Laurier its special cachet in Ottawa.

Finance certainly had its own way in deciding the size of the cuts that were going to be imposed on each department. Far from the collegial process that Martin pursued in most decision-making, the setting of expenditure targets was impressively arbitrary. One day in early July 1994, Martin called assistant deputy minister Don Drummond to his office, with orders to bring whatever numbers he had on government spending. Martin then announced that neither of them were leaving the office until they had set spending targets for every department in the government. And so it began. Drummond would suggest that such and such a department should probably have a spending cut of X; Martin would reply that the cut should be twice that. And so it went for virtually every department, and those were the numbers that stayed. The only flaw in the system, one official said later, was that the numbers on which they agreed were then handed to Marcel Massé, to be distributed to all the ministers and their deputy ministers so that they could get down to the task of deciding where the cuts should be. At the end of August it was discovered that the numbers had never left Massé's desk. The result was that unhappy ministers and deputy ministers had even less time to perform the crude surgery on their departmental budgets.

The old system of trimming budgets was that government departments got their marching orders from a committee usually made up of the Privy Council Office, Treasury Board, and Finance. The orders were how much to cut and what to cut. Martin changed that; individual departments were told how much to cut, but the departments would recommend where the cuts should be because, after all, they knew what was important and what was not. The process depended on everyone buying in; if anyone refused, the system was in peril. The most visible rebellion came from the department of Industry. The minister, John Manley, then a relative newcomer to politics, and his veteran deputy minister, Harry Swain, embarked on what used to be known in the army as dumb insolence—not a noisy defiance but a silent and sullen refusal to act. They lobbied and wheedled all the way up to the prime minister to be spared the cuts, which, they were convinced, would destroy the department. The Program Review Committee decided they were not trying hard enough, one official explained, "and it was decided they could not be allowed to get away with it, so Finance imposed cuts and made Industry an example." Other ministers took note.

Those who faced Martin head-on did not do all that much better. One minister told of being handed an order to undertake what he regarded as a staggering cut to his department. He took the dispute back to Finance and spent two hours in a bare-knuckle argument with Martin and David Dodge. At the end of it, his reward was that Martin reduced the cut by 25 per cent and told him grudgingly that "you sure as hell fight for your department." Battered and bloodied by the encounter, the unhappy minister acknowledged that "he did his homework; he was really good."

No such acknowledgment ever came from Lloyd Axworthy, the minister who suffered most severely at the hands of Paul Martin. The two men saw themselves as the tribunes of left and right, the social and business wings of the Liberal Party, and they relished arguments. Intellectually, they seemed particularly well suited to the assignments handed them by the prime minister, Martin to tackle the deficit, Axworthy to undertake a review of the gamut of government social policies and programs. Nobody doubted Axworthy's intellectual capacity, but he was singularly lacking in people skills and in the kind of focus on the job at hand that Martin had in such abundance. Those who liked Axworthy tended to describe him as a dilettante; those less fond of him tended to call him a flake. His troubles with Martin began before Martin's first budget; the Finance minister badly needed dramatic cuts in spending and the two most obvious targets were unemployment insurance and defence. With both Axworthy and David Collenette, Martin made a deal: he would take a chunk of their budgets in his 1994 budget but would leave them out of the budget-cutting exercise that was slated for 1995 and 1996. The deal seemed reasonable enough, and it was just bad luck that dropped the Canadian economy into a serious hole at the end of the year. As a consequence of the economic troubles, despite Martin's promise of a two-year holiday, both ministries lost more money. It was a particularly grievous blow for Axworthy: there was another chunk out of unemployment insurance; block funding meant that Axworthy could not use the postsecondary funding for student loans; and the end of the Canada Assistance Plan was the end of Ottawa's commitment to welfare. There was not much left of Axworthy and not much scope for a social security review. Not surprisingly, Axworthy emerged sour and bitter. True, he got no break from Martin, but he was in the wrong place at the wrong time. Insiders will assure you that Axworthy's first mistake was in failing to build any public support for the review process; indeed, people hardly knew about it. In any case, with the IMF knocking at the gates of Ottawa, it was not the occasion for a great philosophical debate about whether the soul of the Liberal Party was to be found in social policy or in pursuit of the deficit. His failure to understand seemed particularly obtuse. Less than a year after Martin's budget, the badly beaten Axworthy turned his back on his ill-fated social policy mission; Chrétien transferred him from Human Resources Development to the more comfortable pastures of Foreign Affairs. Four years later he left politics.

Long after his 1995 budget, Paul Martin would insist that the most difficult task in his years as Finance minister was his decision in that budget to slash the federal government's transfers to the provinces.

Instead of individual allocations for health, postsecondary education, and welfare there would be a lump-sum transfer. Instead of $18 billion, the new block transfer would be $11 billion for health and postsecondary education, and nothing for those on welfare. His sorrow was that the cuts were made in two areas that Martin thought incredibly important, health and education—"I did not think it was fair, but I did it."

The explanation of why those cuts had to be made that way is the same as the explanation for virtually every aspect of government policy for as long as Martin was minister of finance and as long as the Chrétien government held out "fiscal responsibility" as its priority. Think of what might have happened if the budget had not been a success. Think of what might have happened if we had stayed with the old ways.

"If we didn't demonstrate unequivocally how we were taking hold, that budget would have failed. And that budget, in my opinion, was the last chance Canada had, or we would have become Argentina Light—meaning not as bad as Argentina, but damned near. Our credibility in the world was so low that the markets were ready to absolutely kill us and drive interest rates through the roof. We could have easily found ourselves in a situation where we really couldn't borrow. We certainly would have found ourselves in a situation where interest rates were through the roof, and we would have set ourselves on a death spiral. And in the end what that would have meant was the cuts in the transfers to the provinces in terms of heath care and education, two years later, would have been so draconian that we never would have recovered. So we had to do it. But I've got to tell you, that was not an easy decision."

Martin had more personal reasons for mixed feelings about slashing the transfers to the provinces. It was the federal government, not the provinces, that created the modern liberal state, and the creation of that state was largely the work of the Liberal Party. If there was a single voice within the Liberal Party that was more dominant than others in agitating for social reform in the period after the Second World War, it was that of Martin's father, Paul Sr. The quarter century after the war saw the creation of those programs that defined the modern

Canadian state and defined the Liberal Party—pensions, family allowances, health funding, hospital insurance, medicare (the latter two, albeit, with a vigorous push from the CCF/NDP), and the Canada Assistance Plan that established a national standard of care for those in need.

The federal government said it would continue to insist on the continuation of the basic conditions of the medicare system across the country. But henceforth the national standards that Ottawa had insisted upon for social programs and for postsecondary education would be matters of the past. It was only later that someone figured out that the Chrétien government had sanctioned a measure of decentralization, of devolution of responsibility, that Chrétien himself had fought so fiercely in his opposition to the Meech Lake accord. Martin's budget guaranteed that "downloading" would enter the Canadian political lexicon, and in the process the political balance of the country had changed.

Even before Martin had been sworn in as Finance minister in early November 1993, Premier Bob Rae of Ontario had flown to Ottawa to tell him that the provincial treasuries were already in trouble as a result of cuts imposed by the Mulroney Conservative government. There was a special urgency in Rae's plea; he was 18 months away from an election and his New Democratic Party was clearly heading for disaster. Whatever his own political vulnerability, he had a clear legitimacy as a voice for the provinces because he was perhaps the wisest of the premiers and Ontario was the most economically important of the provinces. Rae wanted the new Finance minister to sit down with the provinces and talk about what he regarded as their mutual problem.

"He listened and smiled and nothing happened," Rae said. "So at the end of the day I think he made a very tough-minded political calculation that certainly we were expendable and that the provinces were going to have to wear this thing and live with it, and the feds were going to maintain taxes at a certain level and deal with the problem as quickly as possible, which is what they did. I think it was a very calculated decision that this is what was going to need to be done in order to deal with the problem. The fact of the matter is that dealing with a deficit the size that they had required either a longer time frame and a willingness to do this more gradually—or a commitment to radical surgery. And they opted for the radical surgery."

As for the shift in the federal government's role, the devolution of power away from Ottawa towards the provinces, Rae thinks Martin is quite comfortable with that, as much as anything else, because he spent more than 20 years in Quebec before entering politics and became quite comfortable with the political culture of Quebec, which is anything but eager for a federal presence. Rae never had the sense that the shift of power to the provinces was something that caused Martin any loss of sleep at night. He is sure that Martin's answer would be—as it was—that the priority concern was getting the federal finances in order as the condition of economic recovery. Rae, who left politics after his government went down to defeat in 1995, agrees that something had to be done about the deficit, but "I think the issue for me is that I don't think it had to be done as dramatically." There should have been discussions and a recognition that Canada faced a national problem, not just a federal problem.

"I think in fact if he'd done that there would have been a willingness; the provinces would have had to respond and I think there would have been a commitment to doing it over a period of time," he says. "As it was, there's no basis in our system for that kind of consultation and it just didn't happen. Basically we were just told, this is what's going to happen, and I think we saw, particularly with respect to health care, that the provinces then said, well if that's going to be the position, if that's where we're at, then we have no option but to do X, Y, and Z. And the result was pretty brutal."

Martin does not deny Rae's complaints about the cut in transfer payments, particularly that they were "reasonably unilateral" and caused the provinces a lot of problems. That said, he is not prepared to concede that he could have or should have done anything differently: "I mean, our backs were so much to the wall that I couldn't have engaged in five years' worth of discussion."

Whatever the discomfort for the provinces, Martin shrugs with at least a show of sympathy, but that does not mean there was any regret for his drastic measures in 1995: "It was the right decision. It was the right decision. If we hadn't done it in '95, Canada would have had to do it twice as much in '96 or '98. We would have had to do it twice as much and we probably even then would not have succeeded. There comes a point where if you don't do it, you can never recoup, and we might have been in that situation. So, no regrets."

Without regrets, perhaps, but there were certainly apprehensions. That's why, as he closed his budget speech, Martin called on his personal heavy armour, the words of his father from almost 40 years before: "Government must not live in the past.... Every day there are new needs to be met. If inflation is to be fought, unemployment countered, and something done, and soon, to get Canadian prosperity back into its stride, the government must begin to plan ahead—not timidly, not tentatively—but boldly, imaginatively, and courageously."

The implication, of course, was that his father would have understood and sympathized with the difficulties he faced and would have agreed that it was too bad about some of the things he had to do, but the times called for actions that were bold, imaginative, and courageous. But would he really have said that, for example, about the changes imposed on the unemployment insurance system? That was a cause that was dear to the heart of his father, who over the years had learned a thing or two about unemployment and the misery of those with no work and no money. Nobody was surprised that Martin wanted to change the unemployment insurance system that collected about $19 billion a year. The Conservatives had started trimming the system, and David Dodge, the deputy minister of finance, had been casting covetous eyes at unemployment insurance for more than a decade, since he was at Canada Employment and Immigration. Martin took a couple of bites at the changes in unemployment insurance, and he bit with surgical precision. The benefits paid out to the unemployed were cut drastically by narrowing eligibility and reducing the period in which benefits were paid. All of a sudden, instead of being roughly in balance, unemployment insurance was running a sur-plus—a very healthy surplus that went into general government revenues, helping to balance the budget and helping to pay down the debt. With the Liberals nine years in office in 2003, the cumulative surplus had reached an astonishing $43 billion; the fund had got to the point that the auditor general, Sheila Fraser, wondered whether that was not breaking the rules. When the Liberals took power, more than two-thirds of the unemployed got unemployment insurance benefits; nine years later the system had been squeezed to the point that only a third of the unemployed got unemployment insurance. Kevin Hayes of the Canadian Labour Congress observed that "it's fairly bewildering how you can have an unemployment insurance system that becomes the cash cow for financing the government."

The good fortune of Paul Martin was that almost every criticism of his performance as Finance minister could be answered by a variation on the theme of, yeah, but think how awful it might have been if we hadn't done what we did: "If we had not dealt with the deficit we would be Argentina, or a form thereof. And under those circumstances the situation for children, for the handicapped, for everybody, would have been much, much worse...." Really, really nasty medicine, but, you know, otherwise you might have died!

None of the members of the Chrétien government, minister or backbencher, had a real taste for Martin's medicine. The ministers had suffered harsh cuts to their own budgets, and the small-l liberals such as Sheila Copps, Lloyd Axworthy, David Collenette, and others were grieving about the effect of a diminished government on the social landscape of the country, especially on the poor, the homeless, the ill. The cuts went too far, too fast, and if there was justice in the process it was too rough to see. The typical voice of the backbenchers was that of Toronto MP Dennis Mills: "Do we need to eliminate the deficit a year and a half before the deadline he promised? There were a lot of things on which that money could have been spent. The money should have been used to relieve people's pain." Various ministers anonymously echoed that view: "If you look at it, we adopted Preston

Manning's fiscal agenda, even more so. We were more ruthless than Reform was advocating.... Historians will have to decide whether or not the dismemberment of the health care system, the urban chaos that we have, the homelessness—whether it was worth the price.... If you are comfortably middle class it was worth the price because Canada is in a good position; but if you are somebody who can't feed your family, if you're living in the streets or you've been thrown out of your house, or if you're in an ambulance and you have to go to five hospitals in Toronto before an emergency department will take you in, you have a different perspective." But they too knew the numbers from the Finance department, and they knew the numbers from the polls that suggested that most Canadians approved of what Martin was doing. They were strange times, when a Liberal Finance minister could slash and chop at the programs by which Liberals were defined in their own eyes and in the eyes of the country and they all emerged from the process more popular than ever. It was not until after they had turned the corner on the deficit, when modest surpluses were beginning to appear in Martin's budgets, that the social Liberals dared to speak out and suggest that it was time to start worrying about Canada's social deficit.

Aside from the grumbles of his colleagues, Martin had a comparatively easy ride. The Bloc Québécois, the official opposition, was new to politics and did not much care for anything beyond Quebec's borders. Reform had been outflanked on the right by the deficit-cutting Liberals, and the New Democrats were so few in number that their voice was hardly heard. What criticism there was came from the outside, and those critics discovered that it was not always easy to quarrel with Martin and his budgets.

Typical of those lonely outside critics was Jim Stanford, who had finished his doctorate in the United States in 1994 and joined the Canadian Auto Workers as an economist just in time to begin working on the Alternative Federal Budget before Martin's 1995 budget. The Alternative Federal Budget was a project coordinated by the Canadian Centre for Policy Alternatives to provide a leftish view of a rightish world. Stanford worked to help provide that alternative budget perspective to every one of Martin's subsequent budgets, to the point that he could describe the Finance minister as "my alter ego." He remains a bit awed at the presumption of it: "With our Alternative Federal Budget we were a group of 15 overworked people trying to find a little bit of time, trying to do this on the side as a volunteer group, thinking, what message would work well, how would we position ourselves? Then you can just imagine Martin and his Finance department sponsoring focus groups across the country to test a whole series of carefully calculated messages and judging people's reactions and then fine-tuning the budget accordingly. You know, we felt overwhelmed at times. But you have to give him credit."

For the group that produced the Alternative Federal Budget, the starting point was the same as Martin's—the fiscal situation, with large deficits every year, was unsustainable. Too much money was being spent on debt servicing, squeezing program spending. So budgets had to be balanced: "The question was how are you going to do it and what kind of society are you going to have left when the balancing was over?" They wanted to preserve the effectiveness of social programs, including unemployment insurance, but those were the programs that Martin cut. Stanford says, "I think that revealed some of what their priorities were. These were things that business and business-friendly governments wanted to do anyway, whether we had a deficit crisis or not. We never argued that the deficit was a myth; we accepted that it was a real problem, but how you dealt with the problem would reflect your priorities."

What is unique about Stanford is not his economic and fiscal analysis of Martin but his admiration for him "despite opposing virtually everything he did as Finance minister."

He says, "If you want to have a case study of how to effect change and lead change, I think the way that Martin managed that process politically was extremely, extremely effective. Before then it was hard to imagine a politician doing that and coming out more popular than he went in. But the way that he did it reflected an incredible political skill and incredible deliberateness and incredible determination to meet those goals, and an incredible sort of savvy about how to do it in a way that messages well with the public. . . .

"I'm very ambivalent on him. Absolutely. I respect him as a politician. I admire and could learn a lot from his political and leadership skills, how he identified a challenge and put it out there for the country and made the country feel that sort of leadership quality, that if it was directed to good instead of evil, if you like, that is, to a goal that I would feel is more constructive than just slashing your way to a balanced budget, I think it would make us much stronger as a country. On the other hand, I disagree philosophically and politically and economically with the fiscal direction that he took, and I'm very bitter about the unnecessary economic and social hardship that he imposed because of the choices he made."

Stanford continues to believe those choices were regrettable and unnecessary. He traces federal cutbacks, including the cuts in transfer payments to the provinces, to health care problems, school closings, the misery resulting in unemployment insurance cuts, and infrastructure problems.

"He didn't have to make those choices, especially as a Liberal . . . So the federal government solved its fiscal deficit quickly and effectively, far in advance of its own hell or high water timetable, and that looks great. But it just disguised and relocated the problem, and the problem is one we still face. We are a wealthy, advanced, productive, civilized country and we can't pay for schools in the middle of one of our richest cities. My daughter goes to a school where the walls are crumbling and the cockroaches are all over the place and they want to close the scrappy little pool they've got in the basement, just at the moment when everyone's concerned that kids aren't getting enough physical exercise, right? How do you explain that? Paul Martin's whole approach directly contributed to that crisis and certainly established the ideological space in which allowing your schools to crumble in the middle of all this prosperity is something that is tolerated and even celebrated."

For an outsider coming to judge Paul Martin, the curse of the task is that he is a palpably nice, bright, curious man. For his officials and his staff, he may explode in frightening, frothing rages, but to outsiders he is charming and disarming. He is as likely to ask a question as to answer one. He smiles and laughs easily, he puts his feet up on a settee or a coffee table, and sometimes he will take a very long time to begin to answer a question, a flattering indication that he is actually thinking about what to say—not necessarily a common characteristic among politicians.

When Marvyn Novick first met Martin he had not expected to be particularly impressed. A professor of social policy at Ryerson University, Novick was seeing Martin as part of a delegation of Campaign 2000, an organization on child poverty of which he was co-founder and policy adviser. They were discussing a long report that, as he said, sought to make child poverty an issue of what kind of country Canada was rather than just about unfortunate kids. What astonished him was that Martin had read the report from cover to cover, and much of it was annotated; he had specific questions and he brought an extraordinary intelligence to the discussion. The meeting was supposed to last 30 or 40 minutes; it lasted for an hour and a half.

"When you meet with ministers, some of them have facades, so you never know who you're talking to or what's behind the facade," Novick says. "With Mr. Martin you had the sense that you were going beyond the facade; there was a kind of directness that was quite engaging. He brought a passion to this issue. He talked about how his father had played such a central role in building a social security system for seniors, and he talked about his father as one of the architects of medicare. There was a huge picture of his father, and you had the sense that there was this ancestral presence in the discussion. You had a sense of somebody who saw a family legacy in social development in Canada and saw in child poverty a key way to contribute to that social legacy.

"It was a glimpse of a person who was his father's son. There was a clear sense of a social connection with his father....And I was impressed by a minister who was fundamentally literate. This was not just a numbers guy. He understood what some of the key dynamics were."

Martin saw the representatives of Campaign 2000 on three other occasions; in those meetings he was more guarded than he had been at first. Novick's conclusion is that Martin knew that he was going to disappoint them because when the budget was finally balanced the focus would be on tax cuts rather than on public investments. In getting to the balanced budget, the federal government had abandoned poor people, social housing, and the unemployed: "He broke the deficit spiral by basically gutting the federal transfer spending and by severely curtailing social programs." The government did bring in the National Child Benefit, an income supplement for families in need; that was welcome but the amount was too low to have a major impact.

Told of Novick's judgment, Martin nodded wearily and said that many of the government's plans had been thrown off track following the terrorist attacks in the United States on September 11, 2001. He responds, "So I guess my answer to Marvyn would be, yeah, you're right, I wish to hell we had done a lot more and I really do intend to do a lot more. That's it."

Novick was disappointed but still impressed by his four meetings with Martin. At the final meeting he told Martin that "you're not going to build a social legacy in Canada on tax cuts." Martin did not answer.

"So that's who he is. An intriguing person. A joy to think sometimes for a brief moment that his sense of legacy was children. And quite decisive around his spending cuts and around his tax cuts. Very decisive. An ability to be decisive and to not lose credibility with a significant portion of the electorate and his Liberal caucus. Somehow people are willing to suspend critical views of Mr. Martin because he conveys an extraordinary grasp and insight, in ways that are very unusual."

It is not as though Paul Martin does not know the perils of rash deficit reduction. Consider this warning:

"The deficit is a problem and it is a very real one, but its solution does not lie in taking a broad axe to our social safety net. Canada has created a network of social programs of which we can be proud. We do not turn our backs on the sick. We do not walk away from the poor. Now, however, the Canadian commitment to social justice is coming under attack. Our universities and our health care system are under attack, as are our senior citizens.... Deficit reduction, yes! But not at any cost, and certainly not without reflection...."

The speaker was Paul Martin. It was his maiden speech in the House of Commons in 1989, and he was warning the Conservative government of the day of the dangers of going too far, too fast, in its pursuit of deficit reduction.

CHAPTER 11

The Grand Alliance

S ENATOR DAVID SMITH ONCE DESCRIBED the relationship
between Jean Chrétien and Paul Martin: "They were kind of like
Batman and Robin in terms of being very, very successful. They
weren't buddies, but they were successful. And that's fine. They didn't
have to be buddies." Neither one of them would be flattered by that
description. But they were extraordinarily successful. And even at the
best of times they certainly weren't buddies. It was the success part that
mattered to Canadians, so that in the summer of the year 2002 when
their partnership collapsed finally and irrevocably after a run of almost
nine years, it was a shock to the country; after the Mulroney years
Canada had come to rely for a certain level of comfort on the comparatively calm governance of Batman and Robin.

There are various theories as to why and when the relationship
between Chrétien and Martin began to go sour. It could have happened at almost any time in the more than 30 years they had known
each other. Probably the best guess is that the relationship never had
a hope of being entirely comfortable from the day that each acknowledged his interest in the leadership of the Liberal Party. Even after
the leadership was settled in 1990, Chrétien resented Martin's presumption in challenging him, and Martin resented Chrétien's victory
because, victory or not, Martin still wanted to be leader. Still, in
those early days it was Chrétien who went more than halfway. He
made Martin environment critic when he wanted to be environment
critic, and then at Martin's request he made him co-chair of the policy committee that hammered out the election platform, the famous

Red Book, that set out the path towards the Liberal victory in 1993.

And then Chrétien chose his former rival for the most important and difficult job in the new government, cleaning up the disaster that was the Canadian economy. Terrie O'Leary, who was Martin's executive assistant during the hard years of the deficit battles, insists that the partnership and the personal credibility that Chrétien brought to the task was fundamental to their eventual success: "Quite frankly, I don't believe Paul would have been able to do that without somebody like the prime minister. Canadians never questioned the values he brought to the exercise. They were comforted by his values. They didn't know Paul, but they knew Jean Chrétien, and Jean Chrétien brought a set of values to the exercise that allowed Paul to do the job that he did. I think that was integral to the success of the deficit fight." Even after everything had gone disastrously sour, Martin was quick to admit that Jean Chrétien did not let him down: "He was very supportive. I can't argue at all. He supported me. But, boy, I'll tell you that the battles to get there were pretty tough. Very tough."

The battles began as soon as it was clear to both of them and everyone else that Martin's first budget had not gone far enough or fast enough. Martin had been battered and bruised when he visited the financial capitals and discovered a wall of mocking incredulity wherever he went; then he became convinced there was a real danger of an American recession. If he was going to get ahead of the curve he had to move quickly, but the cautious Chrétien did not see the need for such urgency. They first butted heads on Martin's demand for a freeze on new government spending in the spring of 1994; Chrétien thought a freeze was unnecessary, but when Martin insisted, the prime minister supported his Finance minister completely—both at cabinet level and when individual ministers tried to do an end run around Martin by personal private appeals to Chrétien.

The next battle, on the issue of pension reform, was far more serious. Most Canadians were hardly aware that there was a conflict, but those who lived through it in the weeks before the 1995 budget still shake their heads at how two stubborn men—as they said of each other—came so close to disaster. Martin and the officials at Finance wanted to cut back on some of the $20 billion that was being paid out in Old Age Security every year; the plan was to reduce pension benefits for those who were comparatively better off, particularly couples who received two pensions, with a modest increase for those who were not. The left-wingers in the cabinet were horrified, as were those whose political antennae told them that messing with pensions was politically stupid, especially with a Quebec referendum on the horizon. In that latter group was Jean Chrétien. As a Chrétien adviser said later, "It didn't smell good." Chrétien repeatedly told Martin he did not think that pension reform was a good idea—in fact, that it was a bad idea—and Martin simply ignored the message. Martin kept saying that without a reduced seniors benefit the budget might fail, and that would have disastrous consequences in Quebec at referendum time; Chrétien kept saying that there was already enough structural change in the budget, that pension reform might be the straw that broke the camel's back, causing a huge backlash and horrific consequences in Quebec.

"So they both had exactly the same objective. The one thought, I have to do it because without it we're going to have a big problem, and the other said, you can't do it because if you do it we're going to have a big problem. Well, that's a very fair public policy debate. That had nothing to do with personalities." That was the charitable reading of a senior official. A less charitable reading would be that two grown men got themselves into a schoolyard squabble and could not get themselves out. At several stages Martin muttered to those who would listen that he might resign if he did not get his way. In the end Eddie Goldenberg, Chrétien's policy adviser and the most trusted mediator in Chrétien's Ottawa, was called in to negotiate a compromise. Such was Goldenberg's skill and the trust he had won that he would negotiate differences between the two for every subsequent budget because, as Martin confessed of his relations with Chrétien, "we were a little bit oil and water dealing with each other." That first compromise was that if there were going to be changes to the seniors benefit they would be delayed until the next budget. That averted the problem and much later Martin conceded that Chrétien had been right on the pension dispute.

There were other disputes at other times, sometimes surprising. Chrétien wanted to cut the capital gains tax and wanted to cut corporate taxes, but although tax cutting was certainly on Martin's agenda he thought those cuts at that time would make it seem like a rich man's budget. Such disputes did not often escalate to the level that they had to be handled by Martin and Chrétien personally. Most of the time they were hammered out by Goldenberg and either Martin or David Dodge, or by Goldenberg and Terrie O'Leary, who was as trusted and invaluable for the Finance minister as Goldenberg was for Chrétien. The reliance on mediators meant that meetings between Martin and Chrétien were not aggravated by the attempts to mix oil and water. In light of the later falling out between the two men, it is difficult to be entirely certain of their relationship. By the description of those who witnessed most of their meetings, the chemistry was always good; sometimes there was debate on issues, but there was always bantering and joking between them, the conversation moving easily back and forth between English and French, tending more towards English if it got into the subtleties of economics and finance. If there was disagreement they would usually work out a consensus, but if a consensus eluded them they would agree to think about it and return to the discussion later. Even towards the end of their relationship there was a comfortable level of confidence—at least professional, if not personal. The story is told that in late 2001 Martin wanted an early budget, and he and Chrétien scheduled a meeting at 24 Sussex Drive with senior bureaucrats. Martin arrived early, and he and Chrétien sat down for a drink of good Scotch. After a brief conversation they agreed on an early budget and settled the question before the bureaucrats arrived. It was a bureaucrat's nightmare—two politicians sitting down and settling a problem before the bureaucrats get there to manage things.

There was always some element of rivalry. Right from the days before Martin's first budget, Chrétien quarrelled with the economic forecasts that Finance was using. Martin, of course, was already engaged in his formula of under-promising and over-performing. Frustrated, Chrétien would arrive at meetings with his own forecast of how the economy was doing and would offer to bet Martin $100 as to whose forecast was closer to the final result at the end of the year. Chrétien was always closer and it got to the point after a succession of these debates that, as one official related the scene, Chrétien turned to Martin and said, "Paul, you owe me $500. Quite frankly, I don't know why you aren't paying me because I have no intention of cashing your cheque because I'm going to frame it and put it on my wall." It was a joke, of course, but it was not said entirely in a joking way, the official said; there was an edge to it.

Edge or not, even Martin loyalists like Mike Robinson, the manager of his first leadership campaign and a senior adviser since then, is prepared to acknowledge that "certainly Paul could not have done what he did without the prime minister. I think he owes Chrétien a huge debt for being able to do what he was able to do, and, you know, when the people who were with Mr. Chrétien who were in the cabinet came to him and said, 'Paul's not giving me any money, you'd better help me out,' he would never once undermine Paul in all the time he was there. So on a professional level they were very effective. I'd go further and say Paul had better budgets because of the prime minister, because when the prime minister did choose to intervene he was as often right as he was not, and there was no question that the prime minister deserves a lot more credit than he gets for that, in my view."

Ed Lumley, an old friend of both men, believes that the conflict between them was just one of those things that happen in politics for which there is no solution. "With politicians, I think that one of the worst habits we have as a profession is that we almost never forget," he says. "Sometimes walls are put up because you take positions, but then they become personalized; instead of forgetting and getting on with the next. The walls become almost insurmountable because other people build on it. But the wall is never torn down. If anything it gets reinforced over a period of time. I think Chrétien did a hell of a job as prime minister; the deficit reduction never would have worked without the two of them working in tandem. You can't do a budget without the full support of the prime minister, or you can't do the kind of things Paul did. So I don't think that Jean got his full credit from the media or anyone else for what Paul did in terms of fighting the deficit. Paul understands that. In the same way I don't think Paul got his full credit for the last election. . . .

"Over a period of time I think walls get reinforced. This gets added, that gets added, and before you know it you've got a situation, a gap that nobody can close, no matter how well you know both of them."

And large walls are sometimes made of small stones. You don't have to go far in Ottawa to find Martin loyalists who complain that Chrétien neglected Martin people; except for Ralph Goodale, no Martin supporter got into the cabinet at first; Martin supporters were not chosen for government jobs; hell, they didn't even get invited to big dinners where they could feel part of Ottawa's social life and not just Ottawa's working world. On the other side, Chrétien and his loyalists were uneasy and sometimes angry that all the credit for whatever good the Chrétien government did went to Martin. As one Chrétien friend said: "I've never heard of a case of Paul being confronted by that from somebody and saying, no, that's not fair, you know, you're not giving Chrétien credit. And I think that to the extent that he encouraged that kind of talk or didn't discourage that kind of positioning, which after all is in Paul's interest, I think Chrétien probably felt hurt by that."

BY ANY MEASURE, JEAN CHRÉTIEN was a surprising choice as prime minister. He was not lacking for experience; when he took office in 1993 he had been in politics for all but four of the previous 30 years. Except for the 1984 Liberal leadership race, he had never been defeated in a vote and he had occupied 11 different ministerial portfolios. However, he had always suffered from a reputation as a lightweight—clever, but a lightweight. He was a fast brief, but he was reluctant to read more than a page of briefing notes, two if the subject was really important. He had arrived in Ottawa, rawboned and gangly, knowing no English but eager to learn, and he was transparently ambitious. Immediately he adopted the pose of "the little guy from Shawinigan." The pose may have been partly his response to feeling isolated in the nation's capital by his lack of English, partly self-consciousness about his working-class background, partly his response to having grown up with a partial facial paralysis as the result of a childhood illness. When he ran against Turner for the leadership in 1984, the little guy from Shawinigan found expression in his appeal for a leader from "Main Street, not Bay Street." The pose became his persona and remained long after he had become a millionaire and prime minister, long after he began living and acting like a guy from Bay Street. It was the pose that Dalton Camp was writing about when he described Chrétien as the guy who drove the getaway car.

In time Chrétien became apparently totally comfortable in English but spoke with a heavy accent and occasionally bizarre syntax. In his early years in government he won great popularity, particularly in western Canada, with his passionate pan-Canadian patriotism. The fractured English established him as a straightforward, ordinary kind of guy, not complicated and elusive like Pierre Trudeau, Gerard Pelletier, and those other Quebec Liberals who usually baffled English Canada; Chrétien simply announced that he loved Canada, that all of Canada was his Canada, and for English Canada that was comforting. It was anything but comforting to Quebec. Even Quebec nationalists took a certain satisfaction in Trudeau and his colleagues, whom they regarded at least as worthy Quebeckers; they regarded Chrétien as a boob who consciously played the role of the boob to flatter English Canada. He fared just as badly for his performance in Quebec; he was pilloried for the lamentable quality of his French but he was unrepentant because "the crowds loved to hear a politician who didn't talk down to them; but I had to take a great deal of abuse from the intellectuals. Many of them were separatists, of course." That did him no harm in English Canada. When Chrétien challenged John Turner for the leadership, as Ron Graham wrote, affection was not enough to make him leader: "While his style may have struck a chord in the hearts of Canadians, many of whom shared his rawness and felt his sense of inferiority, many Liberals preferred to see themselves as they often were: winners, intellectuals, sophisticates. They talked a great deal and in glowing terms about the common people, but they weren't sure they wanted to be led by one of them. (It was a discrepancy that went to the centre of the general perception of the Liberal party as hypocritical, opportunist, and fraudulent. Many voters would soon punish them for just that discrepancy.)"

Although Liberals turned their backs on Chrétien for leader, he retained an extraordinary popularity in the country, perhaps because he had been beaten by the Liberal establishment. At the convention, when party president Iona Campagnolo pronounced that Chrétien was "number one in our hearts," it was vaguely insulting to both winner and loser, but it did not hurt Chrétien's reputation. The loss seemed to confirm his place as the little guy from Shawinigan. In the months after his defeat, Chrétien became an electric presence wherever he went; walking through a normally indifferent world, like Pearson airport in Toronto, was a revelation; heads snapped in sudden recognition and almost invariably there was a complicit smile; the bolder of the smilers would go over to shake his hand and assure him that he was a great guy and that he should hang in there. When his autobiography, *Straight from the Heart*, appeared in October 1985, there were long lineups at book signings in stores across the country; it became a phenomenal bestseller, with more than 125,000 copies sold.

The puzzle about Chrétien is that with the exception of his love for the country and his commitment to keep Quebec within Canada, he has no apparent political vision. He was elected to the House of Commons at the age of 29 and has had little life beyond politics since then; he left politics briefly in 1986 but in the succeeding four years spent much of his time plotting the downfall of John Turner. For Chrétien politics is about winning, and beyond that there seems scant purpose. If there is a single monument from his era it will be a balanced budget—a significant achievement but more to the credit of Paul Martin than his prime minister. The target of reducing the deficit to 3 per cent of gross domestic product was an idea that Chrétien had picked up from *The Economist*; Martin had wanted the party to commit itself to a more dramatic reduction of the deficit but Chrétien insisted on a more modest target. In the end, the 1995 budget was so successful in setting benchmarks for the government that the 3 per cent target was met ahead of schedule and then a balanced budget almost fell into their laps. Chrétien's caution in setting a deficit target was very much his style; he is reluctant to commit himself to a broad plan, preferring instead careful small steps, cautious incrementalism. In *Double Vision*, their study of the early years of the Chrétien government, Edward Greenspon and Anthony Wilson-Smith had a felicitous description of the prime minister's approach to government: "Chrétien loved the middle of the road, the dry ground away from the puddles." Martin, by contrast, "was a doer and a risk-taker, an entrepreneurial politician who would undertake ten tasks in the hope that nine of them would succeed. On the other hand, Chrétien's inclination, in the words of a senior government official, was to do no things and get none wrong." Occasionally other instincts were in conflict within Chrétien. He loves to make decisions; he is visceral, not intellectual. Unlike Martin, who obsessively debates options like a dog worrying a bone, Chrétien hears the issues at hand and decides, bang, bang, bang, without much debate and sometimes without much thought. At the first cabinet meeting of the Chrétien government, it was a little of the bang-bang show-off instinct that prompted Chrétien to cancel the purchase of a new fleet of military helicopters and to block the privatization of Pearson airport in Toronto. Nobody had really thought about the implications, least of all the legal consequences. The embarrassment over the airport deal was at least comparatively short-lived; the shameful helicopter fiasco dragged on for 10 years. And the rashness of both decisions cost Canadian taxpayers more than $1 billion, all quite needlessly.

The single cause to which Chrétien tied his standard was national unity, the survival of the country, and he came within a whisker of losing that, with a public performance during the 1995 Quebec referendum campaign that was as embarrassing as it was ineffectual.

Instead of rising to the occasion as Pierre Trudeau had done at the Paul Sauvé Arena in the 1980 referendum, Chrétien was obviously overwhelmed. However, although the federal side came perilously close to disaster, by the margin of a few thousand votes, the No side did win and the result was constitutional peace. And in contrast to the previous three decades, that is not to be underrated, although it is by no means clear whether Chrétien can claim any of the credit. Small wonder that in the leaders' debate during the 1997 general election, Reform's Preston Manning turned on Chrétien for his performance: "You almost blew it.... You do not deserve another chance."

Almost blew it, but not quite. Chrétien and the Liberals did get another chance. Indeed they got two more chances, two more elections, and they won them both. The bottom line is that Jean Chrétien was still prime minister when Preston Manning rode off into the sunset of early retirement. He was still prime minister when Manning's successor was shunted aside, and when both the New Democrats and the Conservatives had to find new leaders. He was the right man at the right time, or he was lucky, or he was both.

Darrell Bricker, president of public affairs for the polling firm Ipsos-Reid, got his first good look at Chrétien in 1990, just after he had won the leadership of the Liberal Party. In those days Bricker was director of research in the office of the prime minister, when the prime minister was Brian Mulroney. Armed with video clips of both Chrétien and Mulroney, Bricker went to focus groups across the country to see how people reacted to the new Liberal leader and the then established prime minister. The judgment on Mulroney he expected: people were tired of him, they hated him. They did not hate Chrétien but he did not appear to be a leader; Chrétien fared particularly badly in Quebec, where he was regarded as laughable. When Bricker reported his findings to Conservative organizers, they were delighted; they were amazed that the Liberals had been so stupid as to elect Chrétien leader; they were convinced that he would be their ticket to winning the next election.

Bricker is prepared to concede that at least part of the Liberals' victory in the 1993 election was due to Chrétien; he was particularly effective when he responded to the Conservative television commercials that mocked him for his facial distortion: "It's true that I have a physical defect. God gave it to me. When I was a kid, people were laughing at me. But I accepted that because God gave me other qualities and I'm grateful." But the election was not the result of a great public love affair with Chrétien. Rather, the Liberal victory was largely the work of the Conservatives themselves; they were profoundly unpopular after the Mulroney years, the Conservative campaign collapsed in a dozen ways, and, as Bricker says, "what they did was they spawned their own demise through the creation of the Bloc, which came out of the Tory party and the Reform, which came out of the Tory party."

Worse than that for the self-esteem of Chrétien, Bricker regards him as almost an accidental prime minister. He says, "The thing to know about Chrétien is that I think if you take him out of the current political context, he's not possible. If you take him out of the peculiar set of circumstances that you find in Canada during the 1990s, his leadership is really not possible. It's basically people saying 'Unless I've got something else to vote for, I guess I like him, I guess he's okay, I guess he's acceptable' because there's really nothing else to vote for.... If not for Mulroney, and if not for the destruction of the Progressive Conservative Party, Jean Chrétien would not be in office. That normal cycle that we have, where people kind of fall in love with governments and fall out of love with governments and go for other options, hasn't existed. It's the peculiar nature of the structure of the opposition parties that's basically made Chrétien possible."

Polling over the years reveals no evidence of a national infatuation with Chrétien. Early on, Canadians came to see him as "one click on the dial" away from being laughable and a goof, Bricker says, but he was seen at the same time as an honest and decent guy who would be comfortable sitting down in your house for dinner. Yet voters did not hate Chrétien, and even if he seemed at times clownish, "people were prepared to forgive him that because they thought fundamentally, at his core, he was an honest, good guy. He was the anti-Mulroney."

Five years after he became prime minister, about halfway through his tenure at 24 Sussex Drive, two-thirds of those questioned in an Angus Reid poll said bluntly that Chrétien should step down before another election. More than half of those who wanted Chrétien out were Liberal voters. Oddly, the country at that point seemed happy enough with the record of the Chrétien government; 50 per cent of those polled said they would vote for the Liberals. With Paul Martin and others already pawing the earth in their eagerness for a change of leadership, what must have given Chrétien heart was that although two-thirds of the country wanted him to resign, a full 38 per cent said they would vote for the Liberals if he decided to stay.

CHAPTER 12

The Partnership Crumbles

THE PROBLEM IS THAT OTTAWA can be such a bitchy town. All is well as long as you live your life as a butcher or a baker or a candlestick-maker, and in doing so you consort only with others of your ilk. Indeed, for those whose interests embrace the world of butchering and baking and candlestick-making, Ottawa is a quite beautiful community with long, cold, glorious winters and short, hot, glorious summers. But the tone of the place is set by the minority population for whom Ottawa is a company town. They are the people whose lives depend directly or indirectly on the federal government, and they define their existence by their relationship to a cabinet minister, or to the largest corner office in whatever anonymous government tower they work, to a senior bureaucrat, to a junior bureaucrat, to some backbench member of Parliament, or even to a government policy. They are themselves politicians, bureaucrats, consultants, lobbyists, and journalists or their various employees, dependents, friends, and acolytes. And they all get trapped by Ottawa's narcotic, which is power, because power is what politics and government are all about. Power is at the core of it all—those who have it and those who don't, those who fear losing it and those who are eager to get it—and, sooner or later, in the promise of its arrival or in the threat of its departure, power makes everyone a little bitchy.

John Godfrey, who is more thoughtful than is usually regarded as seemly in a member of Parliament, talks of how the passage of time corrodes the dignity of MPs who have not been chosen for the cabinet. The more time elapses, the more they feel they are losing any hope of making it into those lofty ranks, and that is where they want to be because in politics a cabinet job is the measure of success. So when cabinets are shuffled and they are not included, they become frustrated and jaded at the thought that success in their political life has passed them by.

Godfrey says, "My own feeling is that you have to tell yourself intellectually that this is a very foolish thing to aspire to, simply because if you don't tell yourself that, then you are always in a mode of self-censorship and sucking up. You keep second-guessing yourself because it might possibly have some impact on the likelihood of your being chosen. And it would be equally true of people who say, 'I've got to get another guy in there who's going to put me in,' because there's no guarantee of course that that's going to happen to anybody, and you can drive yourself just as crazy waiting for the next guy as being mad at the current guy because there are only so many places. I suspect that Mr. Martin will have a pretty big cabinet one way or another, but even then there will be a number of people out to kill him because they're not in it. That's the way these things go. I think that passage of time has, combined with frustrated ambitions, been a factor in all of this and I think that's something that goes beyond the two men. I think that would have happened in any government...."

It became hard to believe that Jean Chrétien and Paul Martin had ever coexisted except in an atmosphere of cold hostility. But they did, with a dazzling success that made their later estrangement that much more painful for their friends and colleagues. Canadian voters were blissfully unaware of rivalry; in fact, at the start, Paul Martin was riding on Jean Chrétien's coattails, as even Martin's people were prepared to admit. Insofar as he was known, Martin was the guy who always talked about the deficit and the need to balance the budget—not the kind of concern that customarily grabs a lot of attention. Chrétien had been around a long time and enjoyed a certain public confidence; as one Martin adviser acknowledged, "They did not believe that Chrétien would allow Martin to eviscerate the federal government or give away the store or be totally business-focused or become obsessed about just balancing the books."

But within the limits of political Ottawa, the bitchiness began not long after the Liberals swept to power in the late autumn of 1993. After nine years in the wilderness of the opposition benches, the Liberals might have been expected to take a certain satisfaction in their return to government. But the sense of Ins and Outs within the Liberal Party was already acute, and the Outs made it clear from the start that there was no time to waste. The rivalry was the counterpoint to everything else going on in Ottawa: their cabinet colleagues, backbenchers, senior bureaucrats, at parties involving even the people on the fringes of government and politics, everybody knew about the rivalry and talked about it. One private sector consultant who was known as an outspoken critic of the government admitted that he was actually shocked that nobody seemed to care that he was there, as Martin sympathizers traded jokes about embarrassments and indiscretions involving either Prime Minister Chrétien or his ministers or his devotees. He was a constant eavesdropper as they exchanged their jibes at winter cocktail parties, at autumn dinners, and at summer barbecues:

"It was an open secret in cloistered Ottawa that most of the Martin people considered Chrétien to be an intellectual midget, incapable of keeping Quebec in the country, incapable even of holding the Liberal Party together without the acquiescence of the Martin people. If you went to a social event that was predominantly Martin people, but not exclusively Martin people, there was a steady stream of banter, kidding around, and Chrétien was always the butt of that humour. It was quite amazing for me how readily and overtly anti-Chrétien it was. Whether there were journalists at these things, people from other factions in the Liberal Party and very senior people working throughout the government who would sit around, endure, tolerate, and sometimes contribute to jokes about Chrétien and Chrétien's people, and, you know, a lot of tongue-clucking about the scandal of the moment, or a trip to somewhere. These things all became highly coloured objects of levity. And that was steady all the way through from '93. I found it surprising."

The politics of the Liberal leadership was not just snide jokes in indiscreet circumstances. For a time the Martin supporters stopped shooting, but they never disarmed. Not long after the Chrétien government was sworn into office, there were Martin supporters who were quietly beating the bushes on Parliament Hill in pursuit of political staff who might play a role at some future leadership convention. One ministerial assistant said the pressure seemed to begin in 1994, less than a year into power, and the pitch was hardly subtle: "We're going to be the winners; if you don't sign up with us now, you're out, you'll never be in. So don't dig your grave, you'd better come with us." Although Martin loyalists were more aggressive, Chrétien supporters were eager participants in the contest of identifying friends and foes. The two sides realized that, in spite of it all, they had to coexist and they did so, but they did not really get along. The same assistant says, "There was never a misunderstanding that they liked each other. They knew they had to work together but they didn't like each other. The bad blood was there." Almost a decade after he was first bruised by the Liberal Party's internal struggles, one former ministerial assistant still resents Martin's repeated insistence that he "can't control these people" because they are, after all, just friends and supporters, not his employees. "Well, if you want to be prime minister, you've got to learn how to control those people. I don't believe it for a second. He knows what's going on. And senior people in his organization sure know what's going on."

On such questions Paul Martin claims innocence. In those early days of government, being minister of finance was a 25-hour a day job; he did not think about the leadership. "If you say to me, yes, but you kept all your friends together—I did, absolutely. These are my political friends. So I kept all my political friends together because if somebody goes through a leadership with you, you form a very close bond. As a candidate, you owe these people an enormous amount because what you're dealing with is the people who have given up an enormous amount of their time to help you. I mean, some people after leadership races, the friendships all disappear and they go away. But I really, personally, I really like these people and I was in politics and they were friends. And a lot of them knew more about politics than I ever did." He mentions particularly Terrie O'Leary, David

Herle, and Michael Robinson, all of whom were central to his organization in 1990 and who never left him (although O'Leary spent four years in Washington at the World Bank, rejoining Martin's inner circle when she returned to Ottawa). There were no paid organizers, he insists. There were lots of people who were politically involved, people who thought about leadership, people who thought about getting ready for organization—but being ready to organize is not the same as being organized.

Even some senior Chrétien supporters are prepared to acknowledge that Martin himself may not have been always active in pushing his interest, but they insist that Martin must have been aware of the activities of his friends. As one Chrétien adviser said, "It happened over a period of time, but there was absolutely no question that Martin wanted to be prime minister. It goes back a long way, and he didn't hide it. There were also a lot of people around him who wanted him to be prime minister—maybe even more than he wanted to be prime minister. So there was a lot of stuff out there that made the relationship more complicated." That particular adviser suggested that there were Martin supporters who began working for their man's renewed leadership campaign on the day after his first defeat. He was one of several Chrétien people who cited the long struggle between British prime minister Tony Blair and his old rival, Gordon Brown, Chancellor of the Exchequer; it was not that Blair and Brown hated each other, it was said, but that they had designated haters to do their hating for them—"and I think there was a bit of that here."

Occasionally, inevitably, the struggle slipped past the designated haters to the principal combatants, with predictable results. The adviser says, "I don't think any prime minister likes it when he hears that one of his ministers is trying to replace him, and I don't think he [Chrétien] made any secret of not liking it, and Martin would hear that the prime minister was not making any secret of not liking it and he would be angry with the prime minister for being angry at him, who would be angry at him for being angry at him.... You know what I mean? It was a vicious circle."

Unlike his father, who had the support of only two or three members of Parliament when he sought the party leadership in 1968, Martin won broad support within the caucus from the early days of the Chrétien government. Partly that support was the result of his friendly and gregarious nature, partly a relentless instinct to win friends and supporters. Before parliamentary reform became an element of his leadership program Martin was actually practising it, consulting constantly with MPs, formally in committees or informally over dinner. MPs who made strong speeches in caucus meetings would get telephone calls from Martin or from one of his assistants: Did he have a copy of that very interesting intervention? Might he be available to talk about it to the minister? When it came time for constituency nominating meetings across the country, Martin was always available, and apart from the prime minister himself Martin was the brightest star that an MP could hope to attract. One of his critics conceded ruefully that Martin had probably visited more constituencies than all of his cabinet colleagues together. Martin was so successful in winning the support of Italian-Canadian MPs, most of them from the Toronto area, that it became a joke in Ottawa that there would be more Italians in Martin's cabinet than Italian prime minister Silvio Berlusconi had in his cabinet. (The *Globe and Mail* unaccountably entered into the spirit of such matters in an article about Martin's leadership campaign in which it identified International Finance Minister Maurizio Bevilacqua as "liaison to the spaghetti caucus"—a reference it acknowledged with obvious embarrassment the next day as "inappropriate.")

From the earliest days there was a sense of inevitability about Martin's progress towards Sussex Drive. In discussions of the leadership there was always the suggestion that it was just a question of time, that it would be "Paul's turn," and that he was putting in loyal service until Chrétien departed. As an old friend said, there was a sense of entitlement, of something close to divine right, in Martin's quest: "There seems to have been always the sense that this was his due, that the longer the other guy held the office, the more Paul was being cheated. There's a certain group around Paul that always questioned

Chrétien's legitimacy, that always questioned Chrétien's authority, that always worked at undermining him, even though his authority within the party and his mandate within the party and with the electorate were actually pretty robust."

Whatever his problems with Martin's irregulars, Chrétien began to run into some problems with the electorate—not enough to jeopardize his majority in Parliament, but enough to remind him that fewer and fewer Canadians were enchanted by the pose of the little guy from Shawinigan. The focus of public grumbling was the goods and services tax that had been brought in by the Conservatives and that the Liberals had vowed to abolish. The 7 per cent GST was there every day every voter bought something; the GST was always right there, terribly visible. So for the Liberals it must have seemed like good politics to promise to get rid of it. But it was bad politics, as Martin would soon discover when he sat down with the Finance department and told his officials to come up with an alternative. They were difficult and occasionally ugly sessions. They explored, by Martin's account, 20 different options, but none of them worked as well as the tax they were seeking to replace. In April 1996, two and a half years after the Liberals took office, Martin told the House of Commons there would be no abolition of the GST: "We made a mistake. It was an honest mistake. It was a mistake in thinking we could bring in a completely different tax without undue economic distortion and within a reasonable time period." Martin's people were surprised that Chrétien said nothing at the time, for there had been an agreement that at the same time Chrétien would also acknowledge an honest mistake. Instead, it was Martin who bore the brunt of the initial reaction. The immediate result was that Sheila Copps resigned her seat in the Commons because she had said during the election campaign that she would resign if the GST were not abolished. She ran for the seat again in the subsequent by-election and won handily, but there was bitterness that somehow Martin had been responsible for her embarrassment; the prime minister, for one, told the Liberal caucus that the Finance minister had gone too far in his apology. For Martin, public attitudes on the GST question took on a different shading in the months to come; Martin's staff reported that people would accost him in airports across the country, telling him that the failure to keep the GST promise was a really shitty thing to have done, but at least he had said he was sorry.

The GST chickens came home to roost eight months later when Chrétien appeared at a CBC town hall meeting and was questioned by a young woman about the promise to get rid of the tax; he replied that he had never said any such thing. Defenders of Mr. Chrétien later explained that he appeared in the town hall after flying directly from Japan, that he was jet-lagged, that he was exhausted and distracted after his Japanese trip. Perhaps. That is one of those subtleties that gets lost in politics. But after the town hall show the CBC in particular had a field day in showing Chrétien's denial that he had ever made the promise, and then showing the promise as he made it. For the better part of the subsequent week Chrétien tried to explain and evade and shade and modify. At the end of it he said that "if I and others left the impression with anyone that we would be able to do away with the tax without a replacement, I want to tell them I am sorry." It was at best a mitigated apology. Such as it was, it came too late and too grudgingly to convince anyone he was really sorry; more bitter for Chrétien, it failed to assuage Quebec's columnists and editorial writers who took the view that the prime minister's performance proved what they had always said about him. Typically, in the *Journal de Montreal* Michel C. Auger wrote that "Quebeckers have long known that Jean Chrétien was capable of ignoring facts. His natural instinct, when confronted with a problem that is beyond him or that he doesn't want to deal with, has always been to say that it doesn't exist. This is a side of him that other Canadians are just discovering." Chrétien's performance over the GST still rankled 18 months later when the *Globe and Mail* complained that "all this stubborn avoidance of apology is becoming tiresome and predictable. It's the rule of the playground, where bullies insist that only losers and weaklings say they're sorry."

There are some in the Chrétien camp who believe the CBC town hall and the reaction to it was the turning point in the prime minister's relationship to his Liberal caucus and to the Canadian public. Things after that were never quite as good for Jean Chrétien. Opinion polls showed that Chrétien's popularity dropped in the month after the town hall fiasco. In the federal election six months later the Liberals were returned to power with just 38 per cent of the vote compared to 41 per cent in 1993. With regard to personal popularity, an Angus Reid poll on the eve of the vote registered 32 per cent of the voters who regarded Chrétien as the best choice for prime minister, whereas Jean Charest, who went into the election with a total caucus of two MPs, was first choice of 36 per cent of the voters. One year after the election 58 per cent of voters thought Chrétien should "step aside so someone else can lead the country." It was not an auspicious start for his second mandate.

IT TOOK A WHILE TO REGISTER, but one year after that election saw a change in Martin's office that probably doomed the Chrétien-Martin relationship. Terrie O'Leary, who had been Martin's executive assistant for almost a decade, from the first days of the leadership campaign until the balancing of the budget in early 1998, left Ottawa for Washington. After almost a decade of managing the tempestuous Martin, it was burnout time, and a grateful Martin nominated her to be Canada's representative to the World Bank. It was the kind of move that had little impact for anyone beyond shouting distance from Parliament Hill, but those who saw the dynamic of the Chrétien-Martin partnership from the inside soon understood its significance; they knew there was too much suspicion and too much ego for the relationship to continue for long, and the departure of O'Leary guaranteed that there was not even a distant hope.

O'Leary had been part of the magic glue that held them together for the first five years of government. On the Chrétien side there was Peter Donolo, the affable director of communications who had been with O'Leary and Alf Apps when they first went down to Montreal in 1981 to persuade the unknown Paul Martin to talk about politics to Young Liberals. And there was Eddie Goldenberg. When there was a problem between Chrétien and Martin, Donolo and O'Leary could usually handle it. When there was a serious problem, Goldenberg and O'Leary could usually handle it. When it was a really serious problem, Goldenberg would do his own variation of shuttle diplomacy between the prime minister and the Finance minister, and for a long time it worked.

Goldenberg was vital to the Chrétien-Martin process, as he was vital to almost every other aspect of the prime minister's job. He was ostensibly the policy adviser to Chrétien but the reality was that the whole process of government and politics ultimately was filtered through Goldenberg. He had gone to work for Chrétien when he was a summer intern in 1973; even when Chrétien was out of politics, he and Goldenberg both worked at Lang Michener, making money and waiting impatiently for John Turner to leave. Goldenberg long ago reached that status in Ottawa where nobody ever refers to him as Goldenberg; they call him simply Eddie, and if you don't know Eddie, or at least know who Eddie is, you don't understand enough about Ottawa to have things explained to you. He had arrived in Ottawa with a golden name; his father was Senator H. Carl Goldenberg, a distinguished labour lawyer and mediator, and it was evident early on that Eddie had many of the same negotiating skills. His special advantage was that he had known Paul Martin for many years; Martin was far more relaxed with Goldenberg than he ever was with Chrétien, so there were problems that could be solved with Goldenberg that never could have been solved with Chrétien. With the exception of one occasion when he was out of town, Goldenberg sat in on every meeting between the two men from the time they were sworn into government until Martin was pushed out of the cabinet in June 2002.

O'Leary had the same confident relationship with Martin that Goldenberg had with Chrétien. The difference was that if O'Leary thought Martin was being stupid, she told him so, in terms that were loud, explicit, and sometimes profane. For the fiery O'Leary nothing was sacred, certainly not her employer. From the first meetings after the change of government O'Leary would appall senior bureaucrats by her lack of reverence for the Finance minister. That was O'Leary's style, as it was Martin's. One Finance official said the five-foot-tall O'Leary would occasionally become so agitated that it seemed she might simply explode. At the same time, when committee meetings became so noisy and unruly that Martin and Finance officials would be yelling senselessly at each other, the one person who had the authority to end the meeting there and then was O'Leary—and she did it, sometimes over the protests of her boss. O'Leary was responsible for politics as well as policy, and part of her job description was the exercise of gentle diplomacy between Martin and the bureaucrats with whom he would often argue. Martin calls her "probably the best political judge, or certainly one of the best political judges and analysts, in the country." It is worth noting that nobody from either side of the Chrétien-Martin dispute speaks ill of either Goldenberg or O'Leary; it is also worthy of note that nobody ever refers to her as O'Leary. She is Terrie, like Goldenberg is Eddie, and no other description is needed.

The third member of the triumvirate that held the peace between Chrétien and the Finance minister was Peter Donolo, who always managed to seem more cheerful and agreeable than the communications director of any prime minister has a right to be. Although he was known as a friend of O'Leary, part of the mediation process between Chrétien and Martin, the importance of Donolo was recognized most acutely after he left Ottawa in 1999 to become Canadian consul in Milan. With his departure, the prime minister's office immediately became more adversarial. His replacement was Françoise Ducros, an outspoken Chrétien loyalist whose first major chore as director of communications was to spin reporters an interpretation of a cabinet shuffle; the message from the prime minister's office was that Chrétien arranged the shuffle to put Paul Martin in his place, and that was more or less the message for the next three years. From then on nobody tried to pretend there was a normal relationship between Chrétien and Martin, and that certainly helped to reinforce the lack of normalcy. Ducros left the prime minister's office after a journalist reported that she had described U.S. president George W. Bush as a moron. That was the Ducros style. As for Bush, matters were not really helped when Chrétien explained that "he is not a moron. He is my friend."

It was the arrival of Ducros on the scene and her interpretation of the 1999 cabinet shuffle that prompted David Herle to observe that there was "a lack of adult supervision" in the prime minister's office. As it was intended to do, Herle's remark upset the prime minister's office. A partner in the Earnscliffe Strategy Group, Herle is adviser and friend to Martin in matters political as well as governmental. Although the Martin organization is always described as "horizontal," Herle is effectively the top gun. He is also generally described as the Enforcer of the Martin gang, but that comes not from an organization chart but a style of politics. The soft side of Herle is evident in a wall of his office that majestically overlooks Confederation Square; the entire wall is filled by a giant photograph of the Saskatchewan Roughriders; pride of place on his desk is a photograph of Guy Lafleur of the old Montreal Canadiens and along another wall is a pair of folding seats from the old Montreal Forum. A bit like the Roughriders and the Canadiens of old, the burly, goateed Herle is thoughtful, sharp, and shrewd, and his reputation is that he takes no prisoners. In 1990, when it was clear Martin had no chance of beating Chrétien, Herle was one of those who kept pushing for every last vote and every last elbow in the ribs, whether or not the ribs belonged to a fellow Liberal, because, in politics as in those games you play only to win, there are no Marquis of Queensberry rules. In contrast, Terrie O'Leary—the volatile and explosive Terrie O'Leary, the political operative who became a policy wonk—defines politics quite differently: "At the end of the day politics has to be about having a lot of fun. You spend so much time with these people that you're working with, that it has to be something you feel energized about." What is interesting about all this is that since Martin's 1990 leadership campaign, O'Leary and Herle have been what their friends and colleagues describe in a slightly dated Ottawa way as "an item."

On March 10, 2000, a Friday, O'Leary was in Washington, attending to the business of the World Bank, and David Herle was in an airport hotel—the Regal Constellation—in Toronto, attending to the business of Paul Martin. Whether the meeting in the Regal Constellation that day was a preparation for war or a preparation for peace is in dispute. What is beyond dispute is that after the Regal Constellation, the relationship between Martin and Chrétien could never be put back together. That was the Humpty Dumpty event. Even Martin, who would not like to be thought of as party to treachery, is prepared to concede that "ever since then, the relationship became a little more distant, a bit more correct." Considering that the relationship had been becoming more distant and more correct since 1990, that seems a bit of a stretch; an even greater stretch was his further assurance that "we still worked well together."

The Regal Constellation meeting took place a week before the Liberal Party's biennial convention in Ottawa. There were perhaps 20 or 25 Liberal MPs at the meeting, all of them known as eager supporters of whatever plan might be afloat to push Jean Chrétien out the door of 24 Sussex Drive and replace him as prime minister with Paul Martin. The leadership that Friday came from Herle and three other Martin stalwarts: Ottawa lawyer Richard Mahoney, Toronto campaign organizer John Webster, and communications adviser Scott Reid. The later explanation of Martin and his people was that the meeting was called to calm things down, to tell the hotheads who were after Jean Chrétien's head that they should back off.

All might have passed unnoticed and unknown if word of the meeting had not leaked as the full Liberal convention was gathered a week later in Ottawa, at the very moment that Martin was leaving a session of the Liberals' women's association. The word among Chrétien's advisers and loyalists was that the Regal Constellation cabal had been plotting insurrection. Television cameras caught the normally composed and prepared Finance minister as he was heading down an escalator, and they continued catching him as he protested lamely that he did not know what had gone on in the meeting. He had the confused and embarrassed look of a small boy who has suddenly realized that the teacher is not going to believe the story about the dog eating his homework. Whatever the Martin gang had been talking about at the Regal Constellation, there was going to be no insurrection any time soon. The only explosion that day took place at 24 Sussex Drive, where Chrétien invited his closest and most trusted advisers for lunch, and the prime minister was angrier than they had ever seen him.

Seven months later Chrétien called an election. By any measure it was premature. The guessing was that either he was trying to catch the Canadian Alliance and its new leader, Stockwell Day, off balance or he was trying to strike quickly before Paul Martin ignited the incipient revolt in the ranks of his Liberal Party.

For those around Jean Chrétien, the 2000 federal election was, or should have been, a warning signal. The Liberals were returned to power comfortably. But it was clear that the government and more particularly the man who led it were continuing on sufferance. The bloom was off the Chrétien rose and had been for some time. The prime minister had survived, indeed thrived, for years on his beguiling mixture of candour and vulnerability and his awkward passion about the country. That was the complex that had prompted Iona Campagnolo to call him "number one in our hearts." But the longer he remained in office the more he assumed that arrogance that seems to be power's inevitable companion. He seemed to spend a lot of time on expensive golf courses with wealthy men. He had no tolerance for critics: he distinguished himself by choking a protester just because he got in the way; when he was challenged for intervening to promote the commercial interests of friends, he dismissed it all without a flicker of embarrassment; his was a government that boasted of puritan rigour in cutting back government services in the interest of saving taxpayer dollars, yet the astonishing spending customs of the department of Human Resources Development never apparently troubled his sleep. He seemed as disinterested in human rights in Vancouver as in Somalia. Increasingly and most damagingly, Chrétien was seen to be holding on to power as an end in itself, for the sake of power. He got into politics to be a politician, and it was impressive that such a limited vision had sustained him for almost four decades; however, voters seldom find it flattering to be asked merely to feed a hunger for power. Not long after he became prime minister he was asked what was most important for him and he replied it was to re-establish the credibility of government with the Canadian people, a credibility lost during the Mulroney years; he suggested to the Liberal caucus that he would put up a billboard in the caucus room to list the Liberals' election promises and to check off those that had been accomplished; the billboard idea went the way of election promises.

Cruelly but not unfairly, author Stephen Clarkson observed that "Jean Chrétien's governing style seemed inspired less by the big vision model of Pierre Trudeau than by the cautious formula practised with even greater success by William Lyon Mackenzie King: all in good time." In fairness to King, Clarkson might have conceded that King's vision, smaller and more cautious though it may have been, was at least larger and clearer than anything to which Chrétien committed himself.

It was certainly no help to Chrétien that Pierre Trudeau had died just three and a half weeks before the election was called. It was not that Trudeau was lacking in arrogance when he was in power, but even to a country that probably respected him more than loved him, it was an arrogance that seemed at least to have some justification. The country was flattered and even awed that such an exotic creature was Canada's. So, in a particularly sweet autumn, the country drew a certain comfort from the extravagance of the long public mourning in the full glare of television. In the wake of his death, there had been occasional furtive speculation as to whether the Liberals might perhaps benefit immensely from this resurrection of happier days of Liberalism, but that was to misread things, for the recollection of Trudeau seemed to play badly for the prime minister. By the measure of every picture of Trudeau on television, Jean Chrétien seemed at best terribly ordinary.

The town of Orangeville, an easy 75-minute drive through the rolling Caledon Hills northwest of Toronto, is the kind of place that political strategists watch with special attention in the course of election campaigns. Comfortably middle class, far enough from Toronto to be free of the curse of the big city but close enough to feel in touch, Orangeville and its 25,000 residents are steady. The town is not going to go crazy in the polling booths on election day. So, for strategists and reporters, places like Orangeville, like it or not, suddenly become barometers by which the mood of the nation can be judged. As Orangeville goes, if your barometric judgment is correct, so goes the province, so goes the nation. Traditionally the area around Orangeville has been Conservative territory, but like virtually every Conservative territory in the country, everything collapsed after Brian Mulroney. When Preston Manning led his Reform Party eastwards to Ontario in 1993 to gather up what remained of the conservative vote, Orangeville set a pattern for the province. The conservative vote fractured and a Liberal squeaked up the middle. It happened in 1993, when the Liberals attracted 45 per cent of the vote, and again in 1997, when they got 42 per cent. The combined Conservative and Reform vote amounted to between 48 and 52 per cent. If there had only been one small-c conservative party in the election, the bare numbers suggested that the Liberals would have been beaten quite handily. That was always the mystery that confounded Manning and his followers: why couldn't those wretched people from Ontario realize that instead of wasting their votes on the Conservatives, what they should do is vote for a real conservative party, Reform, and get the Liberal scoundrels out of there? The abstract logic of politics may be as wondrously simple as a jigsaw puzzle, but the practicalities of the business are not so convenient.

Those who judge the practicalities of Canadian politics would have observed that few if any governments have been so aided by the incompetence of their critics as the Chrétien Liberal government has been. The good fortune of the Liberals began with the 1993 election that returned them to power after nine years in opposition. At the same time unhappy voters in Quebec sent 54 members of the separatist Bloc Québécois to Ottawa and equally unhappy voters in the west gave the new Reform Party 52 MPs, virtually all of them from Alberta and British Columbia. The results meant that the official opposition in Ottawa was anchored inextricably in Quebec politics. The Bloc knew nothing of what was going on in the other three-quarters of the country and, obviously, did not care: they wanted Quebec out of Canada, and the sooner the better. The two parties could never make common cause, so in a matter of months the Liberals were once more reassured that they were indeed the government that God had always intended. With the New Democrats collapsed to nine seats and the Conservatives with just two, whatever might be the theory of parliamentary democracy, there was no sign anywhere of a government-in-waiting.

Half the secret of the Chrétien government was that those fundamentals did not change essentially in the next seven years. Jean Charest left the leadership of the Conservatives and assumed the leadership of the provincial Liberal Party in Quebec City, there to conduct noble battle for the forces of federalism. In his place in Ottawa came Joe Clark, 20 years after he had first won the leadership of the federal Conservatives. Unlike his former rival Brian Mulroney, Clark had been unable to walk from government into the plush comforts of the boardrooms of capitalism. The return to private life had been less rewarding than he had hoped; he tried consulting in Calgary and then drifted back to Ottawa to work and live, and then to the vacant leadership of the almost moribund Conservative Party. He was better at the politics of Parliament than anyone else on the opposition benches, but that was not enough to revive his party or to excite the electorate or to ruffle the feathers of a contented and self-satisfied government.

Farther along the opposition benches the picture was equally uninspiring. For a time during the late 1980s Ed Broadbent looked as though he was going to pitchfork the New Democratic Party into serious contention, if not into power. Against Brian Mulroney and John Turner, Broadbent seemed an attractive and sensible alternative. But that did not last. By the time the 1993 election was called, all three leaders had departed: Mulroney succeeded by Kim Campbell, Turner by Chrétien, and Broadbent by Audrey McLaughlin. On election day the political face of the country was transformed. With the memory of Mulroney still fresh in their minds, when the Canadian voters decided to get rid of the Conservatives they were not in a mood for subtleties. The Conservatives dropped to just two seats. The surprise was the collapse of the New Democrats; their vote dropped from 20 per cent in

1988 to just 7 per cent in 1993 and, like the Tories, the party lost its official status in Parliament. There would be nothing from the NDP to disturb the government's comfort in its own rectitude. Nor could much be expected of the Bloc; for the Liberals they were an occasional embarrassment, even an annoyance, but not a threat.

If there were going to be a change, it was going to be a result of the fledgling Reform Party finding its wings and finding a message that would fly equally in the west and at least as far east as Ontario. The man who would bear the message was Preston Manning, who had grown up in the Christian evangelical tradition that swept Social Credit to power in 1935 and continued to rule the province for more than three decades. His father had been the premier of Alberta, and the younger Manning had spent most of his adult life on the fringes of politics, absorbed by the continuing alienation of Alberta and the other western provinces from the rest of Canada. When Manning created the Reform Party he was riding a century of discontent; his message did not have to be explained twice in the west. Whether it was freight rates, oil prices, high tariffs, bilingualism, wheat marketing, or economic development, it was an article of faith in the west that the country was governed by and for the interests of central Canada. Ontario and Quebec had the population and therefore the political power, so it was inevitable that, whatever government was in power in Ottawa, it would see the country through a central Canadian prism. That was the way it had been under the Liberals; that was the way it had been under the Conservatives; that was the way it had always been. The founding cry of Reform had been that The West Wants In—into the old Canada with sufficient power to change the prism, to enlarge the country beyond the limits of that comfortable compact of Upper and Lower Canada. In the west, the impact of Manning and his supporters was electric; from the west coast to the Manitoba border Reform took 51 seats in the 1993 election. In the rest of the country, Reform took just one seat. Four years later Reform took 60 seats in the west—enough to give the party the status of official opposition in Parliament—but no seats east of the Manitoba border. However hard

Manning tried to bridge the gulf between east and west with broadly "national" policies, his party remained a creature of the west.

The solution was a reconfiguration; no longer would it be Reform, the voice of the west, but a new party that would unite the right, bringing together the Conservatives and Reformers of east and west in a United Alternative so that in future the conservative vote would not be split. Manning successfully steered Reform's transformation into the new Canadian Alliance, but it was essentially the old party with a new name because few Conservatives joined the cause. For Manning personally it was a pyrrhic victory. Three months later the members of the new Canadian Alliance turned their backs on Manning and elected Stockwell Day, a 14-year veteran of Ralph Klein's Alberta government, as their new leader.

Day was certainly no Preston Manning. He was good looking and vigorous, glib and untroubled by either modesty or second thoughts. From the moment he demonstrated a barefooted karate kick at an Ottawa convention until he arrived on a jet-ski for his first press conference as an MP, he was showboat politics. In time he would seem foolishly headstrong, at once brittle and impulsive; but at first, as he swept past Manning and headed towards Ottawa, for an electorate wearied of Liberals, Day was impressive. From March to October when the election was called, the polls showed a steady decline, from 60 per cent to 52 per cent, for Jean Chrétien. During that same period the standing of Stockwell Day rose from 42 to 53 per cent. Because the last election had been in the spring of 1997, the Liberal government could have waited another 18 months before calling the election. For the Liberals, one virtue of an early election would be catching the Alliance off balance. The prime minister was taking a chance. One poll, taken after the election was called, showed that half the electorate regarded the Liberals as arrogant and corrupt, including even a quarter of the Liberals questioned. A majority of the country thought Chrétien did not have what it takes to govern; sharing that view were 28 per cent of the Liberals polled.

If Chrétien had found himself in Orangeville on the day the election was called he would not have been flattered; but, cagey political animal that he is, he might have concluded that his Liberals would survive. On that day and until the eve of the election, the citizens on the streets of Orangeville held onto a handful of views that did not much change. They thought that calling the election so early was shabby and cynical politics; they were uncertain and uneasy about Stockwell Day; they no longer liked Jean Chrétien and they really wished that Paul Martin were the leader of the Liberal Party. The unhappy division of the electorate was there on the doorstep of a tax accounting firm on Orangeville's main street. Kathryn Hollands shrugged off the cynicism of the early election call because "there's nothing that surprises me about politicians." Ms. Hollands wished that Paul Martin were leading the Liberals, but better the Liberals, even with Chrétien, than the Alliance and Stockwell Day's secret right-wing agenda. Her boss, Jim Gateman, would be voting Alliance because Chrétien and the Liberals who throw public money around so casually had simply been around too long. The tie-breaker was James Woods, a driver of the Orangeville municipal bus service, on the grounds that he always gets to listen to a lot of people talking a lot of politics. People didn't really like either Chrétien or Day, he reported, but they would be sticking with Chrétien because they liked Paul Martin. On voting day, that was how it all worked out in Orangeville and in the country; the Liberals stayed Liberal and the small-c conservatives divided their loyalties between the Alliance and the Conservatives. Months later, as he came under increasing pressure from his caucus, the prime minister would snap at his unruly MPs that he, Jean Chrétien, had won a third straight election in 2000. That is not how it seemed on the streets of Orangeville, or anywhere else in the country.

The star of the campaign was Paul Martin, just as he had been the star of the Liberal government since it came to power in 1993. People who couldn't tell the difference between a debt and a deficit knew that Martin had done what other Finance ministers failed to do; he was not spending more money than he was collecting. No longer were there sneering jibes from south of the border about the northern peso or the hand-wringing of the *Wall Street Journal* about Canada becoming an honorary member of the Third World. True, there had been pain, but it was no longer pain followed by nothing but more pain. Perhaps it was an illusion but the national finances at last seemed to make sense, and the guy responsible was Martin.

The burden of his campaign, of course, was not the Liberals but the Alliance, playing on the electorate's uncertainty and even suspicion about Stockwell Day. There was nothing subtle about it, but it was good swingeing politics, suggesting over and over again that Day had a secret plan, a secret agenda: "Say what you mean. Mean what you say. Tell Canadians what your real plan is." He did not say that it was a plan or an agenda concocted by right-wing Christian fundamentalists, but by that stage he did not have to be so crass; most of his audience had their own suspicions.

After the public adoration, the curious result of the Martin campaign was that, intentionally or not, he seemed to change his political coloration. For seven years he had been the scourge of the spending instincts of the Liberal Party. He cut programs and he cut spending, and if at the end of the year he had an extra dime or an extra billion dollars, it went to pay down the debt. After his first two budgets there were Conservatives who allowed themselves to wonder aloud whether the Liberal Finance minister might not be happier in the ranks of the Conservatives where he could be, after all, the leader. But on the campaign trail, at least, as he sought to draw a clear line between the Alliance and its "narrow vision of the role of government," he began to sound like an old-fashioned Liberal. In particular he clawed apart the Alliance promise to cut $19 billion from government spending: "I know these numbers, and you can't take $19 billion out of our spending without touching health care or without touching old age pensions. And we won't allow them to do that. . . . Let us understand that we must protect the most vulnerable among us so that we can build the society of tomorrow. . . . You cannot build a country if the haves grow more rich while the have-nots grow more numerous." It was the kind of stuff his father would have said.

So when Martin travelled through southwestern Ontario halfway through the campaign, his progress was triumphal. He reminded them all of how, when he was a small boy, he used to come through these same towns, indeed these same halls, with his father, so many years ago. They crowded in to touch him and he in turn shook hands and hugged and laughed. At every stop he would single out the local MPs and the great work they were doing in Ottawa for the country and for the party. For the average MP, such praise from the star of the government is heady stuff, the kind of attention that is likely to be remembered when votes are cast for the future leadership of the party. Wherever he went, sooner or later, someone would ask Paul Martin when he was going to take over as the leader of the party, and he always slipped the question and talked of the Liberal team and its triumphs. Only the alert would notice that he never mentioned the name of the team captain.

CHAPTER 13

The Sale of CSL

IT WAS JULIUS CAESAR WHO SET the standard for such matters. "I wish my wife to be not so much as suspected," he said. For all his other faults, Caesar understood the vulnerability of those who strut the public stage. The merest whiff of suspicion, the hint of a doubt, can be corrosive. That is why, with uneven success, those in public life are expected to adhere to the standard that Caesar set for his wife—not only to behave appropriately at all times but to be seen to so behave. To be, in other words, above and beyond suspicion.

For a time it was clear that Paul Martin understood what Caesar was saying and shared his view. When he began his political life in 1988, Martin went far beyond what was expected of an ordinary member of Parliament. To the Clerk of the House of Commons he submitted a 58-page report in which he set down in detail the extent of his considerable wealth. It was the action of a man who clearly understood the nature of suspicion about those in public life. He had been, after all, a captain of industry, with holdings that were vast and varied, and he knew that he could not afford any suggestion that his public life was somehow serving his private interests—not when he was an opposition MP, not when he went into government as Jean Chrétien's minister of finance. Martin and his friends would argue that the solution was transparency, that there could be nothing untoward because everyone who cared knew the name and function of each of his individual companies. Indeed, even when extensive holdings were discussed, even his critics were quick to observe that there was no evidence that Martin ever intervened in favour of his own interests; he was not so much as suspected.

One of the puzzling aspects of the Chrétien Liberals was their insensitivity on the broad question of conflict of interest once they got into government. This was not their posture in opposition, not their stance in the 1993 election campaign when they promised to restore "public trust and confidence" in government. One of their commitments was the appointment by Parliament of an ethics commissioner who would report to Parliament and would answer to Parliament rather than to the prime minister's office. Martin appeared personally before a joint parliamentary committee in 1992 urging the creation of an independent ethics commissioner as an officer of Parliament. Yet when the Liberals got to power that never happened, and for at least his final years as prime minister Chrétien was the particular victim of his own failure to fulfil his campaign promise. Instead there was an ethics counsellor, Howard Wilson, who was held up by Chrétien as an arbiter of right and wrong but who was, at the end of the day, an appointee of the prime minister and his political adviser on how to handle questions of conflict. Whether it was about his own indiscretions or the indiscretions of various of his cabinet ministers—and there was an embarrassing succession—Chrétien should have been able to turn to someone with an element of independence as an adjudicator; instead he had only the man he appointed.

People seemed to like and respect Howard Wilson personally, but he had been put in an unenviable position. An impossible position. Perhaps if he had been a servant of Parliament, rather than of the prime minister, he might have cast a more skeptical eye on the blind management agreement that he presented to Paul Martin for signature after he became minister of finance in December 1993. It was not a blind trust in which Martin's financial and business interests would be managed without his knowledge or direction. Instead it removed the minister from normal management and day-to-day decision-making. But, Wilson said, "in exceptional circumstances, a public office holder may need to be informed about a business situation under a blind management agreement." Not just any old circumstance, mind you, but one in which the counsellor's office is convinced "that the situation has very significant consequences for the business, generally involving a high degree of risk."

Caesar would never have allowed his wife to go anywhere near such an agreement. As Conservative leader Joe Clark said, "This is a blind trust with a seeing-eye dog that has unusual capacities to smell, to hear, and to hold meetings." In another flight of humour Clark described the blind management agreement as a "venetian blind."

Four months after Jean Chrétien announced that he would be stepping down as prime minister and leader of the Liberal Party, in January 2003, Martin spoke to Howard Wilson "to seek his advice on what measures might be required to uphold the public interest if I were to become prime minister." The two men agreed that there would be broad consultations undertaken, and the two experts they chose to consult were impressive indeed: Coulter Osborne, Ontario's Integrity Commissioner, a former Associate Chief Justice of the Court of Appeal of Ontario, and Ted Hughes, Conflict of Interest Commissioner for the Northwest Territories, who was also a former judge and, among other roles, Conflict of Interest Commissioner in British Columbia and the Yukon.

As Martin reported later, "When I met them, I asked for their unvarnished advice and the unanimous view expressed to me that day was that sale of the company was not required."

The conclusion that perhaps even Martin might draw in retrospect is that you don't ask a lawyer, indeed a former judge, about public behaviour unless you want an answer that tells you what the law is or is not. On matters of public behaviour you might better ask Caesar, or perhaps even his wife. The same fine distinction was underlined by President George W. Bush during the swearing-in of his White House aides on his first day in office. He said that he expected every member of his administration to behave legally and ethically, adding that "this means avoiding even the appearance of problems."

To satisfy his own standards, Bush and his vice president, Dick Cheney, both sold their principal holdings before they took office, and Bush insisted that the members of his cabinet do the same. His first secretary of the treasury, Paul O'Neill (coincidentally a pal of Paul Martin at international meetings such as the G-7 and G-20), had to sell an estimated $100 million in stock and options in Alcoa, where he had been chief executive. O'Neill's successor, John W. Snow, had to sell $80 million in stock, options, and retirement compensation. Defense Secretary Donald Rumsfeld had to liquidate stocks valued at about the same as those of O'Neill. And so it went right through Bush's cabinet; of the 15 people chosen for his cabinet, 10 were millionaires, but "avoiding even the appearance of problems" was the price that had to be paid for high public office.

That kind of conflict of interest intrudes less in Canadian public life than in the United States, where cabinet members are unelected and usually plucked from the world of business. In Canada's parliamentary system, those who are the obvious candidates for cabinet office tend to be people who have spent a good deal of time in the political system; where others are out in the world of business and industry, the politically ambitious are in the House of Commons, making not much more than they need to live. True, some of the country's prime ministers in recent times have been wealthy men—Pierre Trudeau, Brian Mulroney, Jean Chrétien—but politics is not usually regarded as the sport of the rich. That was one of the reasons why, from the first day he was in politics, Martin stood out. But, standing out as much as he did, it seemed odd in retrospect that it was not a matter of concern to him and to his colleagues in government.

In the end, of course, something did seem odd at least to Martin— or he realized that it might seem odd to others. That was when he went to see Howard Wilson in January 2003, to inquire about what he might have to do if he became prime minister. Considering that he had first declared his eagerness for the prime minister's job a full 14 years earlier, it did seem almost a last-minute afterthought. However, the answer he got was reassuring: the sale of CSL was not required.

What followed a few weeks later was one of those unexpected political eruptions that send shock waves far beyond the limits of what seems reasonable. On an inside page of the *National Post*, on February

17, appeared a story that said "Paul Martin's shipping company has business ties to a controversial power project partially owned by the son of former Indonesian president Mohamed Suharto, the dictator who enriched himself and his family in a 32-year reign of corruption and nepotism." The rest of the story did not live up to the breathless promise of that first paragraph. But after an almost incomprehensible sortie into the arcanum of Indonesian politics and economics, the story noted that Martin was supposed to stay uninvolved in the operations of his company but was well aware of the Indonesian contract. Indeed, Howard Wilson was at a meeting in which he was told about the contract.

For years Martin had seemed unassailable. As a politician he led a charmed and painless life. Reporters and opposition critics had tried at various times to prod him, but even when they seemed to make contact they failed to make him squeal. He was challenged periodically about the foreign registration of CSL vessels, a process that began after he stepped out of the company, when the company's international commitments increased dramatically. There is no mystery about foreign flagging and Martin is blunt about it: "It was either you do that or you wouldn't be in business." One of the facts of life, he would say, is that there is a cost differential between a Canadian and a Ukrainian crew: "You can't pay Canadian wages when someone else is paying Ukrainian wages. It's as simple as that." No hand-wringing liberalism on that one.

In the wake of the *National Post* story, those on the trail of Martin thought they had a stick sharp enough to do the job. Their cries were not about Indonesia, of course, but about the blind trust that wasn't. A leaky blind trust, said the *Globe and Mail*. A blind trust with a seeing-eye dog, said Joe Clark. Stephen Harper of the Canadian Alliance harrumphed that a blind trust should be a deaf and dumb trust. But of course Martin did not have his CSL holdings in a blind trust and never had. Howard Wilson had told him to sign a blind management agreement, which was quite different. He could be informed "in exceptional circumstances" about a business situation. As well, as Martin said later, he had the right to instruct the company what to do in these exceptional circumstances but never did.

The first point to note in all this was that there was nothing new about Martin's blind management agreement; for nine years it had been a matter of public record, spelled out on the ethics counsellor's Web site. Reporters and politicians had never bothered to check. After all, everyone knew that Martin's holdings were in a blind trust, and that was the end of it. More important, whether it was new or not, whether it had anything to do with Indonesia or not, whether there was or was not the slightest whiff of impropriety, the stick was indeed sharp enough to make Martin wiggle, if not squeal. People started asking whether he was going to sell Canada Steamship Lines. If not, why not.

When he went to see Howard Wilson in January, Martin was playing smart politics. He wanted to handle the problem of his wealth before it became a matter of public debate. What better solution than a blue-ribbon panel of experts who could present Wilson and Martin and the country with a neatly packaged set of recommendations, all carefully considered and weighed? This would not be one of those rambling public discussions on questions of public policy that he so loved to unleash when he was running the department of Finance. No, he wanted something more discreet. The peril of public debates about things like personal wealth is that they are vulnerable to the variable winds of populism; they are apt to get out of control. And that, of course, is exactly what happened, and, try as he might, Martin could not get things back under control.

His first line of attack was to say he would not sell his shipping interests if he became prime minister because there would be no need; there would be different structures to cover his role as prime minister and those structures would be monitored by an independent ethics commissioner who would report to Parliament. As he explained in an interview that appeared on the front page of the *Globe and Mail*: "I think the question that has to be asked is, 'Do we want, in this kind of economy, to essentially say to entrepreneurs or people who have built things that there is no role for them in public life?' I believe that the focus ought to be putting in place the structures that would be required to give the public full confidence."

As evidence of his own good faith on the question Martin pointed to his declaration of his assets when he entered Parliament: "I think that I should be judged by my history and by my behaviour....I walked the extra mile. I went far beyond what was the requirement at that time."

The next day Martin upped the ante, telling reporters that he would step aside from some government decisions if he were a prime minister faced with a conflict of interest. Then it would be up to the ethics commissioner to decide who would take his place as prime minister while the discussions were underway. The former Finance minister, normally unflappable, was beginning to seem like a man who has discovered the ground slipping away from under his feet.

The third line of attack two days later was more emotional, a 1,300-word front-page interview in the *National Post* that lacked only swelling violins: "Paul Martin says he will not sell his beloved Canada Steamship Lines because it would be turning 'a dream into a nightmare'—for himself, for his three sons and for all those who believe that strong Canadian companies should stay in Canada."

"I don't want to sell the company because I've had this love affair with ships since I was five years old. I don't want to sell this company because I had this dream to build a multinational and I did it," he told the *Post*. He must remain the owner of CSL, he said, because he feared that if the company were put up for sale it would end up in foreign hands: "I just couldn't live with myself if this dream was turned over to another country....That would be a dream turned into a nightmare."

Ten days later it was clear that Martin had not succeeded in getting the debate about CSL under control. The genie was out of the bottle and raising hell, so the task was to get rid of the genie. He called a press conference at the National Press Theatre, across Wellington Street from Parliament Hill, to announce that he was turning CSL over to his three sons, Paul, 36, Jamie, 33, and David, 28. The three already technically owned CSL because they held all the common shares, but Martin would be turning over the special class of voting shares that allowed him to maintain theoretical control, although, he said, he had not exercised that control since entering the cabinet. He said he had always intended to pass control to the three sons some day and he would be doing that whether or not he won the leadership. The bottom line would be that he would sever all ties with CSL and he would relinquish any future claim to reacquire control after he leaves public life.

Afterwards, the curiosity was why he had not done it earlier. Once he had made the announcement, it seemed so simple. He had been lusting after the prime minister's job since before he entered politics, and his instincts told him right from the start that he would be vulnerable on questions about his wealth if he were not candid about it. In fairness, he could not have handed over his shipping empire to his three sons when he first went into politics; two of them were in their teens and the other was barely in his twenties. There was also obviously confusion in his own mind and he was not really prepared to deal with that confusion. His explanation is that when he went into politics he did not intend to spend the rest of his life in politics; he always had it in the back of his mind that he would eventually go back to CSL. That, as he came to admit, was not realistic. The company had operated happily without him for 15 years and did not need him back; anyway, he was out of touch and no longer knew anybody in the industry; he didn't even know the CSL customer list anymore.

Even the understanding that he really had no future role in CSL did not persuade him that he should sever the remaining links that were bound eventually to cause him political discomfort and perhaps acute embarrassment. It was one of those curious blind spots that were not supposed to be part of the persona of Paul Martin. "To be quite honest, it was sort of hard to let go," he said. "Just totally psychologically."

Sort of hard to let go? Caesar would have sneered.

CHAPTER 14

Open Warfare

CONSIDERING THE SEETHING HOSTILITY between them, for both Paul Martin and Jean Chrétien it was cold comfort that they complemented each other—one a comparatively unknown businessman, not an obvious candidate for public affection, the other a familiar figure on the political landscape who for a time really was immensely popular. So they fitted together and they carried a whole government between them, and it was the comfort of that fit that made their later estrangement that much more painful for their friends and colleagues.

The comfort of the fit was at least in part an illusion. It has since become clear they were never as comfortable with each other as they seemed or as illusion dictated. Both men fancied they had wounds to heal—to avenge, perhaps—after the 1990 leadership fight, and both men had long memories of friendships and betrayal. Even alert public servants believed for years that they could apply a 1990 test to government decisions. One senior official shrugged and said: "Everything divides in that government according to who you supported in 1990. You can look at any single issue, any decision in budget of who got the money. Martin will deny that until the end of the world, and everybody else will deny that but I can tell you that there's a 95 per cent correlation. . . . I don't care what the idea is; you tell me who's proposing it and I'll tell you whether it will go through or not. Some real turkeys from certain quarters will go through and some brilliant ideas from others never got one second of debate."

The illusion of a happy partnership was finally shattered in the days after the meeting at the Regal Constellation hotel in 2000. However much Martin insisted that the meeting was to cool things down, not to heat things up, Chrétien did not buy it. Martin's ambition to succeed to the Liberal leadership had never been a secret, but a meeting of a couple of dozen MPs in an airport hotel smelled like sedition. A year later Chrétien's chief of staff, Jean Pelletier, said that the prime minister would have stepped down before the next election if he had not found himself being pushed aside by Martin's followers in an attempted putsch, which the usually discreet Pelletier described as disgusting. Chrétien himself confirmed Pelletier's comment, explaining that he had said he would step down if people were "nice" to him; but he was still in office, leading to the conclusion that people had not been nice to him.

What was left of the Chrétien-Martin relationship was not helped by the prime minister's increasing tendency in any conversation to launch into a long monologue. Whatever the subject, Chrétien usually could answer with an anecdote that allowed him to monopolize the conversation. This was not something directed exclusively at Martin; it happened with everyone. One of the urban legends in Ottawa is that when Chrétien met a senior Japanese cabinet minister he startled the visitor by reciting the name of every Japanese finance minister for the previous 25 years. As even an old friend observed, "He tends more to talk than to listen." It was one extra burden for an already failing relationship, according to someone who has known both men for years: "[Chrétien] does not have a Receive button and hasn't for years. He's just on Send. So trying to have a conversation with Chrétien is an enormous frustration for anybody. You can't have a conversation with him for more than five minutes before he goes into a monologue about something from his past, or some anecdote, or some opinion. I don't know at what point he concluded that he had all the wisdom that he needed, but it was some time ago—that basically he could operate using the intellectual capital he had accumulated over the years.

"So trying to engage him in a discussion about policy issues was an enormously frustrating experience for Paul. When they actually tried in the early years to have bilaterals, when they would talk about these issues, Paul would, as he would for anything like that, he'd be full of ideas, he'd have a list of things he wanted to discuss, a list of things he wanted the prime minister to sign off on, and would never get past item one on the agenda, when the PM would start giving him these bromides of his experience over the years. They just weren't two personalities who thought the same way, who had the same value system. It was just like oil and water. I don't think it was fatal to their ability to function in the roles they played, but it led to the personal distance which has been so obvious in recent months. . . .

"It was an evolution that had its antecedents in the leadership, which brought them to where they ended up. And I place the responsibility for that on their inability to get beyond the professional relationship, which was a particularly strong one. And that's something I'm sure both of them would be prepared in a moment of honest reflection to admit was a damned good partnership for all those years."

By the spring of 2000, in the wake of the Regal Constellation debacle, it was too late even to think of getting beyond a professional relationship. Nobody tried to cling any longer to the illusion of a happy partnership. An old friend of Chrétien arrived at 24 Sussex Drive to discover a prime minister obsessed. He had concerns of his own that he wanted to discuss but he found that Chrétien had just one thing on his mind. No matter the topic, the prime minister returned to his obsession, over and over again: "That fucking Paul Martin."

That summer Paul Martin began to wonder seriously whether he should remain in politics. Relations with the prime minister were becoming increasingly difficult and there was no sign that Chrétien might be thinking of stepping down. As for Chrétien, a number of the prime minister's old friends had counselled him not to push his luck, to be content with being the first Liberal prime minister since Mackenzie King to win two majorities in a row. At least some of Martin's advisers had expected that Chrétien would step down; they had thought of challenging Chrétien in the Liberal party's 1998 review but resisted the temptation because that might persuade him to stay.

For Martin, the political road seemed blocked for a while. There was the possibility of a major job at either the World Bank or the International Monetary Fund and a number of friends and advisers were suggesting he walk away from Ottawa. He thought about making such a change because by then he had been in politics for a dozen years "and Sheila is not overwhelmed by the whole concept."

When word got out that Martin might be quitting, the Liberal caucus bombarded him with calls, imploring him not to leave because his departure would doom their chances of re-election. Eddie Goldenberg was in the Eastern Townships that summer and he dropped in to the Martin farm and added his own encouragement, but there was no suggestion that he was acting as an emissary of the prime minister. In the end, Martin said he decided to stay because of his Liberal colleagues. They had helped him to sell his budgets, he said, and he was not prepared to leave them in the lurch.

And what about the other side? Should Jean Chrétien have walked away from the job just because Paul Martin wanted to walk in? Even one of Martin's most trusted advisers concedes that people don't just walk away. When they go, they are either defeated or forced out when they are facing imminent defeat; they don't walk away from apparently strong political circumstances, and Chrétien, for one, wasn't going to go: "It's a cautionary tale for anyone who's involved in politics, because Jean Chrétien was not long ago one of the most popular people who had ever been involved in politics, and he led an absurdly popular government. The fact that that is not how he will be remembered—that he will be remembered as a guy who tried desperately to hang on—is a really sad and cautionary tale."

Is it really all just vile politics, or is it perhaps human frailty? Consider the judgment of John Godfrey, a close friend and admirer of Paul Martin. Godfrey suggests that Chrétien's determination to hang on is understandably human. "I think that basically people like that job, and if they're good at it, they enjoy the power, they enjoy the perks, they enjoy the travel, they enjoy meeting people. And who wouldn't? And what are you going to do afterwards, play golf? I think it's completely human to want to keep on doing it as long as you can if you're enjoying it, if you're having a good time and it seems to be working. Goodness me, if you've just had three elections and you won a majority, so to have somebody kind of breathing down your neck, I could imagine that it would take a very magnanimous personality.... I mean, these are very competitive people. You don't get to be prime minister of Canada without being competitive. That would not be in the nature of things."

There is more. Godfrey used the word "competitive" but that is perhaps a euphemism. Prime ministers are also selfish; they rarely feel beholden to the political parties that chose them as leader and maintained them in power. They stay on, clutching at power and privilege. Over the past half century which prime ministers did not overstay their welcome: St. Laurent? Trudeau? Mulroney? St. Laurent hung on until he was defeated and his party stumbled into disaster; Trudeau and Mulroney left just before they got splattered by the blood of their slaughtered colleagues. John Diefenbaker held on until his party brought him down by a humiliating rebellion. Clark, Turner, and Campbell were dead before they had a chance to live. Only Lester Pearson chose the moment of his going. But the best of politics is counter-intuitive; Pearson was prime minister for just five years and those years will always be recorded as a time of minority government, of vicious, destructive, corrosive politics. But those five years fundamentally changed Canada—they saw the introduction of universal health care, a national public contributory pension plan, a supplementary pension system for those in need, a national welfare system; the acknowledgment of Quebec as a presence distinct and apart; the cautious embrace of bilingualism; and after almost 100 years the adoption of a Canadian flag. Pearson left a massive legacy and without much apparent ego, a combination quite uncommon.

QUITE APART FROM HIS RELATIONSHIP with his Finance minister, Chrétien did not have an entirely easy time. From the start, a succession of troubles raised serious questions about the competence of those running the government. The Liberals' troubles, such as they were, were of their own making, beginning with the Pearson airport sale, the cancellation of the helicopter purchases, and the quite shocking public pursuit of Brian Mulroney over the Airbus deal. It was not a time of particularly horrendous scandals, but there was too often a greasy abuse of power, the mark of a political party more satisfied with itself than concerned about its public responsibilities. Before he became prime minister, Chrétien had said he wanted to re-establish the credibility of government in the minds of the Canadian people, and he had told a Liberal convention that "I cannot deliver perfection, but I can deliver what is needed for this country. I can deliver honesty to Canada again." Even with a discount for political rhetoric in quest of power, such an assurance from Chrétien did suggest a certain attitude. But when the Liberals settled into power there did not seem much evidence of that attitude. There was instead an apparent disdain—jokes about pepper-spraying protesters; the cancellation of an embarrassing public inquiry; the grudging compensation for the victims of tainted blood; a sweetheart contract for a cabinet minister's former girlfriend; for another cabinet minister who was bounced from the cabinet after allegations about public works contracts, a soft landing at the Canadian embassy in Copenhagen; and a billion-dollar gun registry that became an embarrassment to anyone who believes in public institutions. As for a prime minister who lobbies the head of the Business Development Bank, effectively his employee, to lend money to an inn—a prime minister who first denies it, then admits it— onlookers can only conclude that this falls into Chrétien's category of "cannot deliver perfection."

Chrétien's good fortune was that from the time he became prime minister his political opposition was singularly ineffective. The only sustained, indeed relentless, criticism came from the *National Post*, and on his gloomier days Chrétien must have thought that having the *Post* delivered to his desk every day was a bit like sleeping with a rabid terrier. The *Post* was launched by Conrad Black in October 1998 to challenge the *Globe and Mail*'s status as Canada's national newspaper.

On the *Post*'s good days it was an excellent newspaper; on its bad days it was embarrassing. In its news pages as enthusiastically as in its opinion columns the *Post* embraced the views of its proprietor, who seems to regard Canada as a silly little backwater, guided by policies devised by cringing lefties who are intent on frustrating the country's continental destiny. The *Post* was tireless in its dislike of Chrétien. The prime minister got some of his own back when the British Conservative party leader, the now forgotten William Hague, nominated Black to the House of Lords. Chrétien blocked Black's peerage on the grounds that Canadians are not supposed to have foreign titles. It was a questionable but not unpopular move in a land where the yokels have scant patience for those who seek honours in another land. For Chrétien it was a sweet, if vindictive, victory. The self-satisfied Black professed no interest: "Whether I'm a member of the House of Lords is of no interest to anybody and not, frankly, of overwhelming interest to me." The suspicion was that Black was exaggerating his lack of interest. At about the same time *The Times* quoted him as saying "By the time I've finished with Chrétien, you'll be able to squeeze him through an eye-dropper." There was never evidence of an eye-dropper large enough, and a short time later Black sold the money-losing *Post* and his other newspaper interests in Canada and renounced his Canadian citizenship so that he could claim the peerage that was not of overwhelming interest.

MARTIN AND HIS ADVISERS BEGAN to notice a change in the Ottawa climate not long after the terrorist attacks on the United States on September 11, 2001; those terrible events were not the cause of changes in Ottawa but they were a convenient line of demarcation. It was after September 11 that Jean Chrétien moved to clip the wings of his Finance minister—or that was how matters were seen by the Martin people. A succession of incidents seemed to fit into a pattern.

In the hours after the attacks, Martin was on the phone to the finance ministers of the G-7 leading industrial countries and they agreed that there should be a statement saying they had confidence in the world's financial system; the statement was duly drafted in the

Finance department at Esplanade Laurier. But the prime minister's office suddenly announced that Martin would not be speaking on such matters, so the statement drafted in Ottawa was issued in Italy.

In the weeks after the shock of the terrorist attacks, Martin thought the date of the budget should be advanced from February to December; the PMO finally agreed but only after a long struggle.

In early January Martin and Chrétien found themselves butting heads over federal-provincial relations. The auditor general discovered that the federal government had handed four provinces more than $3 billion in overpayment; Martin said that in view of the fact it was Ottawa's error, some way should be found to lighten the burden of repayment and part of the amount simply should be forgiven; Chrétien said it was Ottawa's money and the provinces should repay the whole amount. Martin suggested the whole cabinet should look at the problem because of the political ramifications; Chrétien refused to take it to cabinet. (In the end John Manley, who followed Martin in Finance, took the hard Chrétien approach but six months later Manley backed down and wrote off most of the overpayment.)

Other issues were not even discussed. For example, the prime minister decided the government should buy two Challenger executive jets for the use of the prime minister, other ministers, and government officials; neither the Finance minister nor the full cabinet were consulted about the expenditure of $101 million. When Chrétien went to the UN Conference on Financing for Development, he promised that Canada's development assistance budget, then $2.4 billion, would be increased annually by 8 per cent. This came as a surprise to the Finance minister and his officials.

To Martin and his staff the pattern seemed unmistakable. They concluded that, gradually, the Finance minister's ability to control the finances of the country was being limited: "What was happening was that the prime minister was no longer saying 'You decide and I'll support you'. The prime minister was saying 'I'm going to decide'."

Not surprisingly the winter and spring of 2002 were not happy times for either Chrétien or Martin. Stan Keyes, a Liberal MP who was outspoken in his hostility to Chrétien, was elected chairman of the national Liberal caucus; Chrétien was said to have gone white at the news. Typical of the sour mood on the other side, the Martin staff began referring to the prime minister's office and the Privy Council Office as "the centre," thereby endowing it with a mixture of anonymity, menace, and distance. One reporter who had particularly good contacts in the prime minister's office was dismissed by Martin staff as "the *Pravda* of the PMO." For those with a taste for irony, good news came in early May when Moody's Investor Service upgraded Canada's credit rating to triple-A, the first return to that exalted status since Moody's withdrew the top rating a few weeks after Martin's 1995 budget. That was a brief blip; the Chrétien-Martin rivalry remained the leitmotiv of government gossip and newspaper leaks. Yet the end, when it happened, came with a speed that shocked everyone.

On the morning of May 30, a Thursday, Chrétien walked into a meeting of his cabinet and confronted his ministers with something approaching a declaration of war. There was a clear suggestion later that the principal target of his anger was his Finance minister but the prime minister did not actually name names in the meeting. Chrétien, who had given his ministers permission to begin campaigning for an eventual leadership election, told them to shut down their campaigns immediately. He also told them to shut down their fund-raising activities. He said he would serve out his mandate, theoretically any time up to the autumn of 2005. His sharpest words were delivered on the subject of cabinet loyalty; he said he believed embarrassing leaks about the activities of some ministers were a result of the undeclared leadership race—in other words, that ministers sympathetic to the prime minister had been made victims so that the government would be discredited. In demanding the support and loyalty of the cabinet, Chrétien, according to CTV news that evening, stared at Martin. An hour later, when Martin assembled his key advisers he was in no doubt that he had been the specific target of the prime minister's attack. Even when he talked later to reporters, an obviously angry Chrétien mentioned no minister in particular, but he challenged reporters to identify those who had leaked embarrassing information: "If you want to have a good story, give me the names of the guys who are leaking to you and you will have a great story. So, if you are lacking things for your headlines, give me the names. You will have a lot of fireworks and you will have very easy stories for many months to come. And you know me, I love fights. And I would like to have the name of the people who are, you know, double-crossing the rest of the caucus and the cabinet."

A different kind of head-butting had already engaged Martin's staff and the prime minister's office. The PMO had demanded a copy of the speech Martin would be delivering on Friday morning, the day after Chrétien's ultimatum, to the Federation of Canadian Municipalities. The PMO did not normally check speeches by Martin or other ministers but Martin's executive assistant, Tim Murphy, had lunch with Paul Genest, a senior policy adviser in the PMO, to explain roughly what Martin would be saying; a day later, that was not enough; the PMO wanted to see a copy of the speech. After the speech was sent over, the PMO demanded the removal of Martin's phrase "a new deal for cities." In the end Martin delivered the speech as written and even the title boasted of a new deal for cities.

As Martin was meeting with his staff to consider the comments Chrétien had made at cabinet that morning, the prime minister's chief of staff, Percy Downe, phoned Martin's office in a state of agitation because Chrétien and Martin would both be speaking in Toronto on Friday evening. To the PMO it looked like sabotage, although Martin's speech, a fund-raiser for an Ontario MPP, had been scheduled for six weeks and the prime minister's had been arranged only recently. That set off a succession of phone calls, including one from David Smith. Not content with the suggestion that Martin would change the time of his own speech so as not to clash with the prime minister, the PMO demanded that Martin introduce the prime minister and forsake his own speech. The reply of Martin's office was that if that was Chrétien's wish, he should personally phone Martin and tell him so. Chrétien did not call.

After his speech at the fund-raising dinner, Martin talked with reporters and effectively challenged Chrétien either to back down or to fire him:

"Some time ago, the prime minister stated that it was fine for people to organize for the leadership. In fact, he even encouraged some candidates to present their candidature. Now it would appear that he has changed his mind. That's his prerogative. I just really don't know how this is going to work. I don't know what it means. Does it mean that potential candidates shouldn't go to fund-raising dinners? Does it mean that they shouldn't go to party functions? Does it mean they shouldn't go to riding meetings? These are all things I guess which will have to be determined.

"Let me just say that I'm obviously going to have to reflect on my options. But when I do so, I'm not going to do so only in the context of a leadership race. There's something far more important at issue here—that's the government, and the country.

"We have affected a remarkable turnaround as a nation in the course of the last six or seven years. We really are now at the point of takeoff. And we have some very, very important decisions and choices to make. And I must say that I have to reflect, given the events of the last couple of days, on my capacity now as a member of the cabinet, as a member of the government, to have an impact on those decisions—matters that I feel very strongly about. The question is, will my continuation in the cabinet, given these events, permit me in fact to exercise the kinds of responsibility and influence that I believe a minister of finance must?"

When he was asked if was considering resigning, he replied, "I've just said I'm going to reflect on my options...."

As Martin headed off to his farm in the Eastern Townships to consider his options, Chrétien had his own gathering with reporters and he did not sound like a man afflicted by second thoughts. If leadership contenders continued to organize and raise money, he said, "they will have plenty of time to organize because they will not be ministers anymore." As for the future, well, he might stay even longer than he had threatened the previous day: "I will stay until the end of my term, after that, whether or not I'll be a candidate for the fourth time will depend on my health, that will depend on my energy, that will depend on whether or not I want to do other things."

For the next 40 hours the future of Martin and the Chrétien government was the subject of endless consultation and negotiation, although the two principals did not speak to each other until the end of the process, and then for only a minute or two. Paul Desmarais, the father-in-law of Chrétien's daughter France and Martin's former boss, tried to mediate. Inevitably, Eddie Goldenberg tried yet another high-wire act of conciliation. The measure of their distance is their last conversation early on Sunday afternoon: Goldenberg phoned Martin to say he had Chrétien on the line; Chrétien got on the phone to say that Eddie had a letter to read to Martin; Eddie got on the phone to read the letter. The letter said that Martin was quitting because of differences over the Liberal leadership. Martin replied that he had not quit, that he was still considering his options. Martin was in his car on the way back to Ottawa when he heard on the CBC's Sunday afternoon phone-in show, "Cross Country Checkup," that John Manley had taken over as Finance minister.

ON MONDAY CHRÉTIEN RELEASED A LETTER he had sent to Martin:

Dear Paul:
It is with sadness that I confirm that you are leaving the cabinet. As I told you, I will always be grateful to you for your remarkable work as Minister of Finance. There are very few Canadians who have ever served in a cabinet with such distinction.

Together we have achieved a great deal for Canada and Canadians. The success of the government's economic policy has situated Canada very well for continued growth and prosperity. Your contribution as Minister of Finance will be a continuing source of pride for you and for me.

You and I have worked extremely well together, ever since we took office in November, 1993, on all matters relating to government policy. We have always been in full agreement on economic and fiscal policy.

But, unfortunately, matters unrelated to governing have gotten in the way of our working together on government policy. As such, we both understand, with real regret, that it is in the best interest of the government and the country that you step down from the cabinet.

As Prime Minister and on behalf of all our colleagues in cabinet, I thank you for a job very well done. Aline and I wish you and Sheila all the very best.

Sincerely yours,
Jean Chrétien

The curiosity is that two men who had known each other so long, had worked together with such brilliant success, could not talk to each other. Neither one could pick up the phone to call the other. Mike Robinson, who had watched the relationship between the two men from the privileged position as a Martin adviser for more than a dozen years, believes that such a relationship was simply not meant to be.

He says, "I don't think they ever built the kind of personal relationship that went beyond the professional respect, and I think it is because they are very different people. One's an intuitive politician, the other's an intellectual politician. They're not people who could have a social conversation and want to talk about the same things. It's very hard to get Mr. Martin to talk about politics; it's easy to get him to talk about policy. The opposite would be true with Mr. Chrétien. So they never bonded in a personal way; they never formed a friendship; they never formed a relationship that would give them something to fall back on when their paths started to go in different directions. The most notable example is during the weekend when Mr. Martin was dismissed from the cabinet. . . .

"Everybody was saying they should call each other but neither of them until the very end of the process really [felt] like they had the kind of relationship where that would be a conversation they would want to have. So that's unfortunate. I think an awful lot of the work that was

necessary to get them through the period when they were both working together was handled by intermediaries, and a lot of the dialogue
and discussion about issues was handled by intermediaries, and handled
very effectively. But they never had the personal relationship that would
have allowed them to have the kinds of conversations that would have
[avoided] some of the problems that occurred in the last while. I don't
ascribe that in unequal proportions to either of them."

Months later a senior Chrétien loyalist suggested that if there were
one event more decisive than others in deciding the fate of the Liberal
Party, it was Jean Chrétien's casual musing about the possibility of running for a fourth term in office. When that happened—whether
Chrétien was being serious or mischievous, and there were some close
to him who insist he might have been serious—it was a dead certainty
that the prospect of the prime minister heading for a fourth term
would have inspired a profoundly ugly party revolt. Yet other senior
Liberals dismiss as groundless any suggestion that Chrétien would
have run again. Before there could be any election the party constitution dictated that there would have to be a review of Chrétien's
leadership in February 2003, and the prime minister was unprepared
for such a challenge. In 1998, when there was a similar leadership
review, Chrétien had four organizers campaigning full-time for him; in
the summer of 2002, given the mood of the party, he would have
needed at least a dozen organizers but had none. The conclusion must
be that he was not going to lay his leadership on the line, that before
his term was up he was heading out the door. By mid-July, a month
after Martin was pushed out of the cabinet, it was clear to everyone
that a review would be bloody and that Chrétien would be running the
risk of a humiliating defeat. Even the Liberal president, Stephen
LeDrew, was saying that virtually nobody in the party wanted a convention. For Chrétien, the problem was that he had lost control of the
party; after years of diligent politicking he had established his control
of the party in 1990 and apparently did not think much about it after
that, on the grounds that as long as he was a winner he was in good
shape. Similarly, he had been casual about his relationship to the

parliamentary caucus. On the other hand, a lot of people had noticed that Liberals favourably disposed to Paul Martin were getting themselves elected to local party executives all across the country; Chrétien was the leader but the party apparatus was increasingly on the side of Martin, and, as always, Martin was tireless in consulting and flattering his fellow MPs.

Yet what was clear in hindsight had not always been so apparent. In February 2002, the normally astute Paul Wells assured the readers of the *National Post* that there could be no serious challenge to Chrétien at the review then scheduled a year hence: "I'm here to tell you it is lunacy to imagine Mr. Chrétien faces any serious danger in that leadership vote. Liberals value loyalty to the tribe more highly than almost any other value—except power. But loyalty to a guy who reliably delivers power is absolute. Mr. Chrétien cannot be picked off in a vote of the membership. It cannot be done. Which is why the Martin camp, as a few of them are willing to admit, won't try."

Until Martin was dumped from the cabinet in early June, the Liberals still enjoyed enough support in the country to get themselves returned to power. Almost two-thirds of those polled approved of the way Chrétien was running the country (although almost seven in ten thought he should step down before the next election). That changed on the first weekend of June. In an Ipsos-Reid poll held immediately after Martin's departure, Chrétien's approval rating dropped to 46 per cent while 78 per cent approved Martin's performance. Asked who should be the next Liberal leader, 18 per cent said Chrétien; 48 per cent chose Martin. By the end of the summer only 31 per cent of those polled by Ipsos-Reid said they had a positive impression of Chrétien; 70 per cent said the departure of Martin was a serious blow to the government.

The end of the struggle came faster than anyone could have imagined. By mid-August Liberal organizers were talking about setting up Chrétien campaign offices in preparation for the leadership review and the national Liberal caucus was getting ready to meet in Chicoutimi, Quebec. Justice Minister Martin Cauchon, a Quebecker with ambitions for the future, asked David Smith if he could meet some key

Toronto Liberals who were friendly to Chrétien; Smith and Warren Kinsella put on a dinner for Cauchon and about 35 Chrétien loyalists at the discreet and very private University Club on University Avenue. That was August 12. Four days later Smith played host at the Gentlemen's Annual Summer Soirée at his farm outside Cobourg, on Lake Ontario. By tradition Smith's soirée is a broad church event, meaning that Chrétien and Martin people are invited and are expected to behave themselves. It's the kind of occasion in which old foes gather, hands grabbing shoulders, and they say to each other that no matter what happens, remember that we're all Liberal. With the help of 50 lobsters and copious amounts of wine, Scotch, and cigars, they did behave—"Very civilized, nobody was insulting anybody," reported one participant—although Art Eggleton was still complaining that he had been kicked out of the cabinet for giving a government contract to a former girlfriend. And there was, inevitably, talk about the caucus meeting in Chicoutimi.

On the following Tuesday, August 20, Chrétien boarded a government Challenger in Toronto, where he had been making a speech. In retrospect, there was something in the prime minister's mood that suggested that he had already made up his mind before the plane took off for Chicoutimi. However, there was nothing to be divined from his speech that night. It was vigorous and forward-looking, telling Liberals they had "a responsibility to pull together, to respect the traditions of our party, to end the fighting." But one senior Liberal who prowled the corridors of the hotel, listening to their conversations, concluded that the Liberals were not in a mood to end the fighting: "You could just see how disemboweling this exercise was going to be if it proceeded."

Early next morning calls went out to the most senior Chrétien loyalists—Eddie Goldenberg, David Smith, Francie Ducros, David Collenette, John Manley, Sheila Copps. They all went to his room to hear the news from him personally. Later, with Aline at his side, he faced the full caucus and announced that after 40 years he would be leaving politics. Not right away, but in 18 months, in February 2004. His own explanation for lingering another year and a half was that he wanted to finish his mandate. The conclusion of most people was that he was staying on as long as possible to reduce Paul Martin's chances of succeeding him. In the next day's *Globe and Mail* Jeffrey Simpson warned of "the transparent venom infusing the Prime Minister's gambit...." What Chrétien was saying to the Liberal Party, Simpson said, was "let me politically castrate Paul Martin." More likely Chrétien would have described him as "that fucking Paul Martin."

CHAPTER 15

The Future

IN THE MONTHS AFTER HIS DEPARTURE from the Chrétien cabinet, Paul Martin was an oddly elusive man. He would pop up in odd places around the country where local Martin organizers had arranged for him to have lunch with the Chamber of Commerce, or the Chinese-Canadian Association, and perhaps have a chat with a couple of the store-owners on Main Street. And then he would pop up somewhere else, another town in another time zone, lunching with the retail merchants' association, or the Ukrainian-Canadian society, and then a photo-op. Canada, he would tell them, is a land of tremendous excitement and great opportunity, with a wondrous future to build, and he would shake as many hands as he could. The idea was that people would say to themselves and to their neighbours that this Paul Martin was certainly getting around. Smart guy. Probably going to be the next prime minister, they would say. Nobody would remember much of what he said in those months, and that was part of the plan.

All front-runners always suffer from the same malady. Their challenge is not to win the leadership; their challenge is not to lose it. Front-runners have no place to go but down, and for a decade Paul Martin had been so far ahead as the next leader of the Liberal Party that the very thought of how far he could fall must have been by itself enough to give him a nosebleed. So he was not going to push forward a basket of ideas that his opponents could mock or steal. Like all front-runners, he contented himself with heartwarming banalities with which opponents could not quarrel and which they would not deign to steal. Even when the actual leadership campaign got underway there was no obvious reason to change tactics when there was nowhere to go but down.

The result was that Martin set records for the ability to say little of consequence, to take no position, to take no chance. In the process, of course, he was fearless and clear-eyed—always eager to say the right thing, always anxious never to say the wrong thing, never, ever, to offend a potential voter. The health care system has always been one of the absolutes in the Martin view of the world, yet about the Romanow report on health care Martin had nothing to say. A statement from the Martin campaign proclaimed with great determination that the Romanow report "provides an opening for Canada to fix medicare in a way that enshrines values Canadians hold dear and outcomes they are demanding." The statement notes that Romanow called for an infusion of $15 billion into the system but says nothing about whether Martin thinks that it is too high, too low, or just about right. The significance of the report, Martin said, "is that it provides a starting point from which to begin fixing the health care system." Best of all: "It's time to move from debate about what needs to be done to action on what must be done." On several occasions during the campaign, Martin undertook to speak about the vexing problem of hospital waiting lists. His solution was to gather data about waiting lists, then, "engag[e] experts and patients to set maximum acceptable wait times according to the type of disease or surgical procedure."

At least in domestic policies, the leadership campaign provided few exceptions to his proffered diet of pabulum. He acknowledged that he had been skeptical about changing the funding for cities across the country, but concluded in the end that perhaps the solution was sharing the gasoline tax so that cities could have stable and predictable funding. The background of that startling reversal is that Martin had originally drafted his policy on cities with a lot of advice from Jack Layton, then the head of the Federation of Canadian Municipalities and later the leader of the New Democratic Party. On that issue at least he had stolen the initiative from Layton. Whether within your own party or among the opposition parties, neutralizing your opponents is basic politics.

There were other areas where he simply skated away from anything that looked like thin ice. Same-sex marriage was not a new arrival on the Canadian political agenda but in the spring of 2003 Martin could still excuse himself on the grounds that "it's an issue I'm wrestling with." Wrestling leaves it open and avoids offending the social conservatives in the Liberal Party and in the country. On the other hand, he did say that he would not appeal a court decision that required the government to include same-sex relationships in the definition of marriage: "We can't discriminate between Canadians; it's a question of rights." In 1990, he was personally uncomfortable about abortion but said that the state cannot prevent a woman from having an abortion if that is what she is determined to do. In the end his response was not really about abortion but about equality of opportunity: "I am not prepared to live in a state where the rich can go to New York and the poor can go to a back alley." It was more comfortable to weigh the injustice of the financial choice between a back alley and a New York abortion clinic than to argue a question of rights.

On other matters Martin demonstrated different hesitations. From his early days in Parliament there was never any doubt, for example, where he stood on the environment. He had been the Liberal environment critic; he had been to the Earth Summit in Rio de Janeiro from which came the Kyoto Protocol; there was no more eager defender of the environment. Whatever the Conservative government did on the environment, it was too little, too late, for the MP from LaSalle-Emard. He warned against the destruction of the environment merely for the sake of economic growth; he promised that a Liberal government would weigh the impact on the environment of all government policies. Where 10 years before you could not move far enough or fast enough to protect the environment, when it came to the Kyoto Protocol and the prospect of the Liberal leadership in the distance, Martin was not so sure. In the end he buckled and voted with the government to ratify the Kyoto agreement, but only after public hand-wringing because the provinces, especially the west, and industry had not been consulted. In fact, Chrétien was handing everyone a package whose consequences and costs were quite unknown. In other circumstances, if there had not been a pattern of hesitation, Martin's reluctance on Kyoto would have been understandable. But when Industry Minister Allan Rock suggested that Martin's response to any problem is to study it to death, the jibe seemed reasonable.

Yet, if Martin seemed strangely muted in the months after he left the government, in at least one area he produced an impressively radical reform package that was the result of a long process of study and consultation. His proposals on parliamentary reform would significantly reduce the power of the prime minister and his office, and at the same time would increase the power of ordinary members of Parliament. The proposals were the result of six months of study and discussion by a group of backbench MPs and outside specialists such as Patrick Monahan, a professor of law at Osgoode Hall. Monahan offered a significant judgment on Martin's methods: "My experience working with him over these past number of months has convinced me, first, that he finds debate and contrary viewpoints welcome and healthy—something to be encouraged and nourished rather than suppressed—and, second, that he believes that the first task of political leaders is to persuade others of the merits of their views rather than order the rank and file to fall into line." What was surprising was that after a lot of argument, Martin agreed that nominations to the Supreme Court should be confirmed by Parliament; that was one area where he had not been initially keen to share prime ministerial power. The interesting question about Martin's proposals to rectify the "democratic deficit" is whether he does not run the risk of handcuffing himself or any other future prime minister. Greater democracy could have been practised by any prime minister in the last 25 years under the customs of government or the standing orders of the House of Commons, but they chose not to. The uncertainty is whether, by actually institutionalizing reduced power for the executive, he does not make the whole process of governing more difficult and less effective. That said, a weakness for democracy is rarely among the sins laid at the feet of those who would be leaders.

If in the course of the Liberal leadership campaign Martin was reluctant to tie his fate to the specifics of certain policies, it was clearly not because he was lacking in passion. From the environment to housing, from child care to the disabled, from aboriginals to child poverty, there are lots of passions. And emotions that measure oddly against a minister of finance who was so driven that he could actually make the country care about the budget deficit and the GDP-to-debt ratio. What stands out was an interview that Martin gave to the *Ottawa Citizen* in January 1997 about the poverty that afflicts about one in five Canadian children:

"I believe child poverty is the great social policy challenge of this generation....

"I mean, Christ, you should say, 'What in God's name?' I think you should feel terrible about those kids. I think you should feel terrible about rising inequality. I think you should basically say to yourself: 'What kind of a society do we have when we see these gigantic salaries up here and this huge amount of poverty down there?' I think we're now reaching the point of absurdity in terms of inequalities....

"Well, Jesus Christ, that's staggering. Holy God, it's awful! There's Third World poverty in this country! It is beyond belief....

"The problem isn't that the parents will take the money and go spend it on booze. The problem is that the parents are going to deprive themselves far more, in order to provide for their children....

"Poverty begets poverty....

"If you allow 20 per cent of your society to grow up with all of the problems that poverty brings, then don't think that you're going to have a healthy society. And if you don't have a healthy society, you're going to have a rotten economy....

"How can any decent human being allow other human beings at the very beginning of their lives to lead the kind of lives that poor kids are forced to endure? That, in my opinion, is an argument that is simply unanswerable...."

(There are times when syntax deserts Martin entirely. They seem to be occasions when he is dealing with subjects that carry a certain emotional baggage, where crisp clarity succumbs to incoherent loosey-goosey. A listener who claims to understand is probably more guided by sympathy than logic. For example, in another interview, in the winter of 2003, he said, "If we don't deal with the issue of child poverty, if we don't deal with the issue of...you know, because the market economy does lead to child poverty, don't kid yourself. It leads to exacerbating the existing inequities.")

Martin continues to believe that the Child Tax Benefit, a program designed to help families with children, was the single most important program introduced by the Chrétien government. Yet that too was limited by the spectre of Canada going the way of Argentina, so people like Marvyn Novick retorted that the program was welcome but the amount of the benefits was too low to have a real impact. And to that Martin could only shrug sadly and say, "I wish to hell we had done a lot more..."

Perhaps that is one of the reasons Martin came to enjoy such wide popularity across the country. He gave heart to almost everyone, suggesting that with a little time and patience and good fortune their dreams would be fulfilled—as far as could be reasonably hoped—with a combination of Paul Martin and the Liberal Party. A few months after Martin left the government, the *Globe and Mail*'s Jeffrey Simpson described Martin's impact on Canada's varied citizenry. He wrote, "He took on a certain diaphanous quality in which people could read into him almost whatever they wanted. Quebec nationalists viewed him as more in tune with their province's specificity. Western Canadians believed him more sympathetic to their region. Business, big and small, considered him their friend. Social activists hoped that inside the former finance minister beat the heart of a social-policy reformer. Environmentalists, remembering his interest in their cause as an opposition MP, thought him a potential ally." His departure from government did not seem to diminish his lustre. In the spring of 2003 Frank Graves of Ekos Research reported that in his 25 years of looking at public opinion in Canada, he had never seen anyone who raised such expectations as Martin, who managed to be at once the darling of both small-c conservatives and small-l liberals. That blurring of traditional political loyalties was not accidental. Martin insisted that the customary left-right measure of politics no longer applied, that it was all part of a logical continuum: first get the economy on an even keel, then develop the social programs that will enable people to participate in the economy: "That's my interpretation of my job. I mean, it really isn't a right wing or a left wing, it's basically that the two have got to go together."

Paul Martin still defines himself as a Walter Gordon nationalist, and he says so quite without irony. The surprise is that most of the business class, where Martin spent the early part of his working life, regarded Walter Gordon as an embarrassment. They rejoiced in whatever protection might be available for their business, but they did not like to think of themselves as nationalist, and especially not as anti-American. Whatever his early inclinations, Martin is no longer in favour of the kind of restrictions on foreign ownership that Gordon was trying to sell the Liberal Party in the 1960s, when he thought it was reasonable that there should be at least 25 per cent Canadian ownership in any foreign company in Canada. His own solution is global, with government policies to encourage the growth of business that can take on the world on the world's terms. He does not say so, but that is essentially the gamble he took at Canada Steamship Lines—nor does he admit that Canadians who undertake that kind of gamble are lucky to emerge alive. But Martin himself is a product of the global economy. He says, "We're 30 million people. We've got to go from a standing start to having companies that are operating around the world, that they're big enough not to get taken over, and they're taking over other people. The only way you do that is if you're in every major market in the world. So government's responsibility ought to be basically out there helping Canadians export, making sure they can get access to markets and making sure that their financial structures are strong enough."

When he talks about Canada's relations with the United States, Martin does so in terms of his own upbringing across the river from Detroit—a bigger city and a bigger country. But, perversely, despite the difference in size there was a sense that you could take them on any time—"an enormous sense of confidence that we could do whatever the hell we want." Confidence is always part of the formula: "I really do believe that we are as confident a nation today as we have ever been in our history, and that we have reason for that confidence in terms of what we have accomplished and what we can accomplish, and that living side by side with the United States is not a disadvantage. It is the world's most powerful economy. It is a huge market and a great advantage for us, provided we recognize how well placed that confidence is, and provided that we understand that the way in which you exercise your sovereignty can't be protectionist, can't be the result of an inferiority complex, which is why I come back to the confidence. It has to be really placed in those areas where sovereignty really counts."

For anyone in the Chrétien government, the subject of military spending is an embarrassment. Together, Chrétien and Martin led the way in stripping a once-proud and internationally admired military. When every other spending program was up for grabs, it was inevitable that the military budget would be irresistible for a Finance minister looking to save money. Even with helicopters dropping out of the sky because they were simply too old and inadequate, the government did not seem alarmed or even aware. The terrorist attacks on New York and Washington in September 2001 changed all that. It was all very well for Canadian troops to take up duty in Afghanistan; it was odd that a country that took such pride in peacekeeping endeavours had to borrow aircraft to get the troops to their destination. After a decade of deprivation, the military, Martin eagerly agreed, would have more personnel and more equipment.

Martin's memory of the painful conflict between sovereignty and military imperatives goes back to the early 1960s when Canada was crippled by the searing debate over the deployment of U.S. nuclear weapons on Canadian soil. It was over the Bomarc missile dispute that a comparatively young Pierre Trudeau denounced Lester Pearson, the Nobel Peace Prize winner, as the unfrocked prince of peace. It was a brawl that shook a generation. Whatever might have seemed reasonable two generations ago, Martin believes that the defence of North America must fall to Canada and the United States together. He now expects a major debate about North American integration, but the starting point of that debate is that there are differences that will not change: "There's always going to be a border. There has to be a border. We are two different countries. We've got different interests and we suffer different pressures. But what we've got to do is serve our own interest. So, for the sake of discussion, it means that on the one hand it may well be that from a defence point of view we're going to need more cooperation. We want to protect North America from international terrorism. I don't think you protect North America from international terrorism by ignoring the fact that you are part of North America. So I think that's going to require greater cooperation with the Americans in terms of defence. But I would not be prepared to extend that to immigration. I mean, we will set our own immigration policy. I think it means that we have to have an even more aggressive cultural policy, basically making sure that the manifestations of our Canadian sovereignty in terms of culture are done. You know, not only do we want Canadians to hear Canadian stories, we want foreigners to hear Canadian stories. We've got to be very, very, as I say, proactive.…

"So if you're going to talk about your own national security, you'd better understand that you'd better cooperate on a North American basis because if you don't cooperate on a North American basis then our country is going to be at risk. So I don't have any difficulty saying, yeah, I really want to cooperate with the Americans. I do not want the Americans to come in here and help us. That's really important. I don't want the Americans to think they have to come in here and help us. We'll do our own thing. But that doesn't mean we shouldn't be cooperating fully with them in what they're doing and let them cooperate fully with us in what we're doing because whether they're the Americans or not, we share this particular continent."

It was not pure happenstance that in the summer of the year 2000 Paul Martin was wondering whether he should stay in politics in Canada, waiting for Jean Chrétien to leave, or whether he might better take a fling on a broader stage. Martin had already tasted the narcotic pleasures that were to be found in international politics, and he liked what he had tasted. Once he had solved the problem of Canada's deficit and set the national economy on a roll, it was increasingly the world stage that captured his attention. When he was fired from the Chrétien government, he was one of the senior statesmen of the world of finance. The problems of that world had come crashing in on him early enough. Just a year after the Chrétien government took office, the Mexican financial crisis exploded and sent shock waves everywhere. Then came Thailand and the Asian crisis, then Argentina and Korea, Brazil and Russia. Early on, as the newest finance minister of the G-7 nations, Martin took an active role in urging international supervision of financial institutions. As well as promoting help for those countries that seemed to be on the verge of collapse, Martin was pushing the International Monetary Fund and the World Bank to take the lead in creating a system of more adequate international supervision and regulation.

Martin's breakthrough came when he tried to figure out a forum that could speak with authority on international financial affairs and possibly even draw up rules for the future. The G-7, which later became the G-8 with the addition of Russia, was a perfect size—seven finance ministers plus their deputies, who all knew each other and could get down to serious discussion without the formal set-piece speeches of the United Nations to which nobody listened. But the vulnerable states with the damaged economies were not going to be interested in a new set of regulations for their financial systems if they had no part in drafting those rules. So the solution was a new organization made up of the G-7 countries plus a scattering of 11 states representing the main regions and economic groupings in the world, as well as the European Union, the European Central Bank, the World Bank, and the International Monetary Fund. It did not quite add up to 20, but G-20 seemed a catchy title. It would not be a bricks and mortar institution; there would be no permanent and implacable secretariat as there is at the United Nations; the secretariat would be whoever is chosen to be chair. Martin was selected as chair of the G-20's inaugural meeting in Berlin in 1999 and of the meetings in the following years in Montreal and Ottawa.

The G-20 is not going to save the world, and Martin admits that some of the energy within the group disappeared after the first excitement (coincidentally after his two-year stint as chair). But he sees that kind of limited grouping of countries as one of the answers to what the world needs. It is an argument that Canadians are likely to hear again from Paul Martin, and he thinks Canadians are particularly receptive. When he began talking across the country about Canada's stake in the world's financial situation, he was making an argument for international economic stability, but then he discovered his audiences were taking the argument further. He says, "That argument sold very, very well. But as I would make it to audiences, I suddenly realized that what really got them excited was me saying, 'The world's got to come to a better system of governance and Canada's going to lead the way.' And I can tell you, I didn't have to sell that. Canada's role in the world is a tremendously exciting thing to Canadians. It's a sense of purpose, it's a sense of confidence, it's a sense of belief in what we can do....

"Canada has an opportunity—not to follow the States, not to follow Europe—we have the opportunity to play the most important role in leading the world to the way in which it's going to govern itself.... And that is really going to excite Canadians.... I can tell you it really, really, really hits a resonant chord, and I believe it has to do with a sense of purpose, that the country wants to feel that it has a purpose, and it's looking for somebody to express that."

Martin became fascinated by the problems of world governance while he was still Finance minister and was still spending a lot of time with political and financial leaders from other parts of the world. He became convinced that the most important job of the current generation of political leaders will be to establish how the world is going to govern itself. By the process of elimination, he concluded that Canada was going to have to play a leading role because the Europeans are totally absorbed with how they are going to govern Europe, the

Japanese have their own financial problems, and the Americans are so dominant that they have not really thought about the problem. His pitch to the Americans is that they have to start thinking about how the world will govern itself; if they put off thinking about it, simply resting on their laurels, in 20 or 30 years the Chinese will have an economy as large as that of the Americans, and then it will be the Chinese who will want to set the rules and for the Americans it will be too late. The other argument for moving now is that the balance of power is such that nation states can still set the rules. The global threat to national sovereignty will come if nation states fail to set the rules, "because if they don't put together the rules of the game then the large multinational institutions are going to simply run rampant."

From the abstract question of governance, Martin moves smartly into the practicalities of what the nations of the world can and must do—introduce an international anti-trust law and an international bankruptcy law that would freeze national debts and allow countries to reorganize their affairs rather than suffer a massive national collapse. And why not a world welfare system? Why is the funding for AIDS so massively undersubscribed? "We within our borders recognize that we have to have a basic level of welfare for the poorest of the poor in our country. We've got to recognize sooner or later that the same thing has to apply internationally. I would like to think that we would basically recognize that we've got to help people—period—I mean, because they are people, whether they live in Africa, or whether they live in Bangladesh, or whether they live in some part of Canada.

"I guess my own belief is that at some point, 50 or 60 years from now, somebody is going to look back and say, 'I don't believe that they thought back at the turn of the 21st century that the solution to Africa's problems was some kind of public and private charity as opposed to a fundamental structuring of how the world governs itself.' I think that in 50 or 60 years they are going to look back as if we were, you know, coming out of caves."

Martin sees a fundamental conflict between the United States and the rest of the world on every issue, whether it be Osama bin Laden or an argument about an international criminal court. The United States recognizes only its own definition of the problem. He says, "It is the world saying we work through the world and the Americans saying the highest document in the world is the American Constitution. That's the conflict. I don't know whether they are acting any different than any hegemon has ever acted. But my argument to them on every single one of these issues all along has been to put together a world of laws which will limit us all but nonetheless a world that will work. We've got a window of maybe 20 or 30 years because once you're no longer the hegemon, which you're not going to be in 20 or 30 years, we're not going to be able to do this the same way. And so you've got 20 or 30 years to put this together and you should use your period of hegemony to establish the rules by which the world will govern itself. Now. Don't wait, because in 30 years you'll wish to hell you had done it and it's going to be too late."

When Paul Martin talks of the future and of what might be expected from a Martin government, he talks both of the nation state and of the world. First and overwhelmingly, the task would be to ensure that Canada has the highest living standard possible—the logical result of the struggle to balance the budget, which leads to funding social programs, job creation, dealing with the gap between rich and poor, making sure that people with disabilities have a level playing field. In more poetic terms, he says a little self-consciously, "I want this to be the place where the best and the brightest want to stay and the freshest talents want to come. If that's happening, you can solve your other problems." Fundamental is the national disgrace of aboriginal poverty. "Anybody who goes into public life and says he is not going to break the back of that problem shouldn't go into public life, in my opinion." In fact, if Canada does not deal with the aboriginal question, the fastest-growing segment of the population, the country will not make it. Similarly, if the waves of immigrants coming to the country are not helped to adjust to the society, Canada will end up with the same lack of social cohesion that now afflicts Europe. In the coming decade of change, some countries will fall by the wayside because their social structures cannot face up to the pressures of change. Ten years ago chances were that Canada would not make it through; today chances are much better, but not guaranteed.

"If we don't deal with those issues, then our society isn't going to make it. We won't have the upward mobility, and we just won't have the sense of fairness, we won't have the desire to stay together. If we don't take the position internationally and lead on it as to how the world's going to govern itself, we'll all end up being governed by the United States. And if the world ends up being governed by the United States, we're going to suffer more than anybody else because we're cheek by jowl with them. . . . So our health care system, our education system, the way we deal with child poverty, the way we deal with foreign policy, the way we deal with all of these issues, are an essential part of answering that question that historians are going to ask 50 years from now. . . .

"I want historians to look back and say that in this decade a Martin-led government essentially did what had to be done to make sure that when this huge catharsis that the world is going through was completed, Canada was one of the very few countries that came out on top."

CHAPTER 16

Martin and Martin

A N OLD FRIEND OF PAUL MARTIN'S once remarked, "The motivation that drives him is that he would never want to repeat the experience of his father; he would never want to be the person who ran and lost. That is absolutely his worst nightmare...."

For as long as he can remember, Paul Martin was aware that his father was Paul Martin. When he was a kid there would always be other kids ready to remind him that his father was some kind of politician; their parents said so. When he got older the connection would have been made more subtly, but made. The University of Toronto Liberal club insisted that, hell, the son of Paul Martin just had to become a member of the U of T Liberal club. Later, even when he buried himself in business, people always said that the son of Paul Martin must be interested in politics, must be preparing himself for a political career. And when he did run for Parliament many years later, they all said they could feel the man's ambition from the time they first met him, just like his father. He never said much about it, they said, but you could tell. His sister, Mary Anne, says she always knew: "It was sort of like one of the things that was taken for granted, that we knew Paul was going to go into politics." Even those who had never seen him except on television agreed; it was Popular Psychology (Politics) 101. Always the ambition was linked to his father; it was the loyal son avenging his father's defeats, the son carrying on his mission, the son fulfilling his father's dream. Just about everyone said so—except Paul Martin.

"I've always felt that people make far too much out of '68, or my dad's run for the leadership against Mike Pearson. This idea that I would run for the leadership because my father was denied it, and all that—that's just not there. That's a figment of somebody else's imagination."

How could so many people be so wrong?

It is not a subject that Martin enjoys. He has been put through the question—or the suggestion—since he first became remotely interested in politics, so his words come out with rehearsed earnestness, fragments of a well-worn script. Of course it's natural for people to think that he is merely trying to fulfil his father's dream, but that's not it at all. And anyway, he does not think his father's career was diminished by not being prime minister. Look at John Diefenbaker; he was prime minister but Diefenbaker marked Canadian history, he says, far less than his father did. Two of the greatest figures of the postwar era were his father and C.D. Howe, but neither of them was prime minister. The son wants to become prime minister, but not because his father never made it: "I've always thought my dad had one of the great political careers and I had no desire—maybe subconsciously, way down deep—but I can tell you, consciously, I have no desire to fulfil his dream."

Mike Robinson, who has been in the inner circle since Martin got into politics, is one of the few who insist that the question of ambition is exaggerated: "I think it would be fair to say that he doesn't have that all-consuming driving ambition that some people ascribe to him. I think a lot of people who support him have that ambition for him, but I think there were scenarios where he could have quite happily left politics after being the minister of finance without feeling that his ambition was frustrated. I think there were times when he thought seriously about whether or not in fact he wanted to make the commitment for what would obviously be another significant chunk of his life, in moving from Finance to higher office.... If scenarios had developed another way, if the prime minister had made a decision to stay, I don't think Paul would have felt that his political career or his contribution was somehow inadequate. If it had unfolded in a different way and he had left public life a year ago or two years ago, I don't think it would have been with great regret."

A different reading—or maybe just a different perspective—comes from a friend who has known Martin for more than 20 years and who was one of the original group that invited the unknown Montreal businessman to Grindstone Island: "I think he would take some satisfaction in achieving that office, and I think it would be because he would know how proud his father would be of him. His respect and affection for his father is a driving motivation in his life; absolutely, he is the most important person in Paul's life. And so I think he would like to do it for his father, more than for himself in some ways.

"The motivation that drives him is that he would never want to repeat the experience of his father; he would never want to be the person who ran and lost. That is absolutely his worst nightmare—again, as much for his father as for himself. So I think he's driven by fear of failure and I think he's driven by his desire to do something that he knows his father would have been proud of. I don't think it's a driving personal ambition that he desperately wants to be prime minister. I really don't. I think that he would have been quite comfortable personally being remembered as the guy who was the best Finance minister that the country ever had, who was instrumental in starting the G-20, who gave Canada the best decade of economic prosperity that it had had in 40 or 50 years. I think he would feel that was enough of an accomplishment personally."

But of course there was ambition. There were times when the flame of that ambition burned more brightly than others, but from the day he got into politics there was no doubting the ambition. He had an organization around him that was predicated on his eventual arrival at 24 Sussex Drive, and for that journey Finance was an impressive stepping stone. Yet when he talks of what politics should be about, what emerges is an image that runs curiously counter to what the country came to expect during his eight and a half years as minister of finance. Avenging his father's political defeat may not be his explicit goal, but he insists on his loyalty to his father's ideas and values, on the absolute dominance of social policy, especially health care—"From that point of view, sure, I regard myself as a spear carrier for his ideas." At the height of his success at Finance people talked of him as a conservative, as a blue, blue Liberal, but this is a man who in international terms talks of the inevitability and desirability of world welfare; in national terms he returns again and again to the late Tommy Douglas, who became premier of Saskatchewan in 1944, heading the first socialist government in North America. Paul Martin boasts of his father and Tommy Douglas in the same breath—"My father was out of that same generation and was of the same tendency as Tommy Douglas. He and Tommy Douglas were very, very close." Left-winger though he was, Douglas was a fiscal conservative; he always balanced Saskatchewan's books and he got himself out of the hands of the bankers, which makes him a hero in the eyes of a later federal Finance minister. Douglas was enough of a fiscal conservative that he could launch medicare in Saskatchewan as the model for the rest of the country, which again makes him a hero.

"Tommy Douglas pushed the envelope; my dad pushed the envelope. But I remember the conversations; he was also very fiscally conservative. My dad was constantly railing against Finance ministers, railing against the government because they kept holding him back. They may have been too fiscally conservative but I can tell you, my dad never would have conceived of this huge buildup of debt, I don't believe, that occurred in the 70s and 80s....

"A lot of people will tell you that the '95 budget represented a huge watershed and everything else. There was not a massive debate over the '95 budget. I wasn't conscious of engaging in a huge philosophical debate on that issue. I mean, it was 'We've got to preserve the social programs and this is what we have to do,' and there wasn't a lot of angst over it....

"I could easily describe myself as being out of the Tommy Douglas school. Tommy Douglas was obviously, in terms of social policy, considerably to the left, but he was a fiscal conservative. Tommy Douglas was essentially saying no country, no province, should ever put itself in the hands of the bankers. I happen to believe that very strongly."

With bankers pushed to one side, Martin does a quick checklist of the responsibilities of government. Education, health care, clean air, clean water, basic infrastructure, and, in a country like Canada, culture—"I don't think the role of government is to clean up its balance sheet and reduce its taxes. I think those should be given. Governments shouldn't have huge debts and our taxes should be competitive. But it shouldn't be the role of government to clean itself up. That should be a given. The role of government should be to provide public goods."

Despite his insistence on their similarities, father and son led quite different lives. The one grew up uncomfortably close to poverty, the other grew up comfortably ensconced in the middle class. One of the memorable passages of the father's memoirs was his explanation that "there were some games we did not play. I remember seeing a friend, Bob Bromley, dressed in white ducks, ambling down to have a game of tennis in the court next to the Presbyterian church. People like me did not play tennis. It was a badge of social distinction, and unless your father happened to be an accountant, a doctor or a lawyer, was a sport you had no part of." The son learned to play tennis on the private court at his mother Nell's family cottage; the only limitation on his tennis these days is a knee that he badly smashed when showing off on water skis at Bob Fung's cottage, not long after he finished law school.

Neither father nor son led a particularly opulent lifestyle; like his father, Paul Jr.'s idea of a good time is an evening of reading or talking. But they come from astonishingly different political cultures, partly a reflection of themselves, partly a reflection of the times. In his memoirs Walter Gordon painted a quite captivating picture of the bare-bones 1958 Liberal leadership campaign, when Lester Pearson beat Paul Sr. By Gordon's calculation the winning campaign cost about $3,000. He was shocked that in the next campaign, in 1968, when Paul Sr. lost to Pierre Trudeau, it was said that some candidates actually spent more than $300,000—"It must have taken experts to do that!" Little could he have known. To win the Liberal leadership in 1990 Jean Chrétien spent a little over $2.4 million and in the losing cause Paul Jr. spent a little under $2.4 million.

Throughout his life Paul Sr. had benefited from benefactors; in early life they got him through school and university; in later life people like

Paul Nathanson, head of Famous Players, gave him some legal work when he was in opposition or invited him to his Florida home for a visit. It was comfortable but hardly the High Life; he remained a man who always put aside 10 per cent of every paycheque for a rainy day. However kind his benefactors may have been, they did not make Paul Martin Sr. the kind of blue-chip candidate that his son became. In his memoirs he painstakingly charted his devotion to the United Auto Workers union, and every year he led the Labour Day parade through Windsor. It hurt him and surprised him that union voters did not always cast their ballots for him, a loyal friend of labour in the councils of the nation. His multimillionaire son's most notable attachment to labour came on an evening in September 2002, when his appearance at the hall in North Toronto of the Universal Workers Union, local 183, brought in $750,000 for the leadership campaign. The leading figure that evening was Tony Dionisio, business manager of the local, supported by Craig Dobbin, a Newfoundland businessman, and Steve Hudson, a former Toronto financier who is now a hair replacement advocate based in Florida—all of them formerly supporters of Brian Tobin who took their money and their enthusiasm for democracy to Martin as soon as Tobin saw his own cause was lost and wisely bailed out.

The sheer scale of fund-raising would have shocked Martin's father. In the first 10 months after he was fired from the Chrétien cabinet, contributions to the Martin campaign totalled $4.3 million. Most of those were $1,000 cheques but some were for far more—$100,000 from Vancouver businessman Jimmy Pattison, another $100,000 from Amadeus Capital Corp., and $75,000 from the Onex Corporation, the conglomerate controlled by Martin's chum Gerry Schwartz. On top of the $4.3 million an unknown amount of money was contributed to a blind trust set up for the Martin campaign while he was still in the government. Nor did it include fund-raising efforts for various other Liberals, whether federal or provincial, who called on the Liberal Party's number-one crowd-pleaser for help. In August 2002, for example, Albina Guarnieri, MP for Mississauga East, played host to her favourite Liberal at the championship Glen Abbey golf course. She had the help of Toronto businessman Navin Chandaria, who invited a mixture of friends and power brokers and community leaders for a day at Glen Abbey. The community leaders were there for tea and talk with the former Finance minister; the others arrived with their chequebooks and their golf clubs. Those who went just for dinner paid $1,000 for their meal; the 36 foursomes that played the Glen Abbey course and got to chat with Martin in the course of the day shelled out $10,000 for each foursome. The total take was about $450,000, which after costs worked out to a $200,000 bonus for the Mississauga East Liberal association bank account. The ebullient Chandaria, who supports the Ontario Conservatives in provincial elections, confided later that he was planning a dinner of about 20 friends at his farm for Martin; he expected that would net $500,000 for the Martin campaign.

With Martin accumulating that kind of money, it was hardly surprising that some of the other contenders in the race to succeed Jean Chrétien simply dropped by the wayside; it seemed like an invitation to spend a lot of money for no particular purpose. Martin did not like to be reminded of how he seemed to be the favourite of the rich guys because he was seen to be a Business Liberal, a right-wing Liberal. Instantly defensive and slightly huffy, he replied that John Manley, his successor as Finance minister, was regarded as substantially more to the right than he was. He continued, "I am really not a Business Liberal. If I was a Business Liberal I wouldn't have gone into politics. A sound economy is certainly a major part, but I am much more in my father's vein, both in terms of international affairs and in terms of the role of activist government than I am by what we normally connotate as a Business Liberal."

"I am much more in my father's vein...." It was the yardstick by which he measured his life. One thing that friends and acquaintances have always known about Martin is that he adored his father. Until his father's death they used to talk on the phone several times a day, sometimes in heated argument, but they would talk. He loved to quote old speeches of his father's to justify his own political performance, particularly over harsh budgets, or simply invoked his memory as a moral guarantee: "I am not only a member of Parliament myself, I am the son of a member of Parliament...." The message was that you may be uneasy about the son, but you can forgive him when you remember what a good guy his father was, a left-wing Liberal in a centre-right government, a guy who fought for health care and pensions.

The curious legacy of Paul Martin as Finance minister is that it is impossible to conclude from his time in Finance what the shape of a Paul Martin government would be. He took office with an uncertain reputation; he was both an outspoken small-l liberal, very much the son of his father, and the voice of big business. He represented the kind of ambiguity that the Liberals have always found electorally convenient. But, in office, the ministry of finance and the albatross of the deficit defined a rather different politics in which critics like the historian Desmond Morton could find little redeeming virtue. Morton says, "Political rivals, Chrétien and Paul Martin were as conservative as self-made millionaires should be. Both believed strongly that what Canada's dominant middle class wanted was for Canada's finances to be brought under control by any means short of higher taxes. It didn't matter if the poor complained; their old advocates, the NDP, had just joined the Tories in oblivion." By the measure of Martin's budgets alone, Morton is certainly not wrong. But Martin of course would reply that the times were such that there was no choice, there could be no softer options, for that was the way to Argentina. Always he insisted that things would be different when the government got its finances in order.

In the months after his 1995 budget, Martin gave two particularly interesting speeches, one to a symposium in Jackson Hole, Wyoming, the other to the Ottawa-Carleton Board of Trade. Those are the speeches to which Martin advisers refer reporters who are inquiring about what or who might be the real Paul Martin. In both speeches the Finance minister did a masterly job of treading a careful path between the ambiguities of Liberalism, trying to accommodate the imperatives of father and son, straining to maintain the ties between Martin and Martin.

"For some, smaller government is an objective in itself. But for us, it is simply a means to an end. We do believe that government should do only what it can do best—and leave the rest for those who can do better—whether business, labour, or the voluntary sectors....

"What we must still achieve at the end of the day is a government that is fully capable of assisting the disadvantaged; a government that is unequivocally committed to our publicly funded national system of health care; a government that is more adept at providing those things the private marketplace cannot—things such as strategic support for aspects of science and technology; and a government that is focused on getting the incentives right—whether to foster environmental protection, to attract footloose investment, or to spring people from the welfare trap and onto the job ladder....

"We live in a reality where the possibility of governments spending still more money is simply not on....

"The fact is chronic deficits threaten to put the social conscience of government out of business....

"Our view is straightforward, if government doesn't need to run something, it shouldn't, and in the future, it won't....

"For all our success, we cannot rest any of us as long as the level of unemployment remains what it is. We cannot rest any of us until the reality and the roots of poverty are addressed."

At that stage, Martin clearly understood the dimensions of the challenge he faced. However, actually reconciling the ambiguities of Liberalism, the conflicting imperatives of Martin and Martin, would be another matter. Martin can hardly be expected to bear the responsibility, but it is worth noting that except for the deficit (and the continuing struggle over leadership) there is little to identify the Chrétien era. Perhaps, in fairness, that is the evidence of the overwhelming impact of the deficit crisis, for the agenda spelled out by Martin in 1995 was essentially not much more than a variation on Mackenzie King: government if necessary, but not necessarily government.

As always, the touchstone is the attitude towards government. Even as he trod the delicate path, back and forth between left and right, Martin firmly included himself among "those of us who believe in a socially progressive and proactive role for government." Perhaps more intriguing was a Martin speech three years later, by which time the deficit had been conquered and he could take a little distance from the struggle that had so consumed the early years of the Liberal government. At the annual Couchiching conference he was looking to the future, to what kind of place Canada would be in the year 2026, in a thoroughly globalized world. It is a future in which there is a network of support that makes child poverty a distant memory, a social infrastructure "that is without compare in terms of progressivity," a universally accessible health care system that remains as an enduring symbol of Canadian values, and the economic and social blight that afflicts native people will have been largely replaced by optimism. He warned that there must be stronger institutions "to restrain the commercial and financial excesses of the market," and he warns also that "at the heart of globalization lies an inherent bias toward inequality." Martin calls for a strengthening and renewal of those institutions of support that define Canada as a caring society and mocks those on the far right who "trot out a series of arguments why strong social programs cannot be sustained."

But whether it is a question of stronger financial supervision internationally or the social economy in Canada, there will be a constant need to redefine the role of government. He says, "The fact is that the room for national governments has never been greater. Their role might change and the focus might shift but their fundamental obligation will remain resolute: to protect the interests of people.... The single world market does not trade in the currency of individual needs. Only governments will recognize their inherent worth. Only governments will fight on their behalf." That sketch of the Canada of the future could have been drawn by his father.

IN THE END, PAUL MARTIN IS AN ENIGMA, unknowable to others and perhaps to himself. His ambition and his desire for political success are beyond measure. He tried once for the leadership of his party and was thoroughly beaten for his efforts, but he agreed to work for the man who beat him and together they formed one of the most effective, if not the most effective, political combinations the country has ever seen. As he did so, he never for a moment relinquished his ambition for the higher post he was once denied; he waited a dozen years until the final struggle that resulted first in Martin's expulsion from the cabinet and then the collapse of Jean Chrétien in the face of an army of Martin supporters who were prepared to rise and strike him down. If the ambition is clear, the values that underlie it are less so. The success of the fight against the deficit is undisputed; to those who say, yes, but at what cost, it will always be a valid retort to observe that for too many years there had been a succession of Finance ministers who promised to do something about the deficit and all they did was let it get worse. Yet the man who includes himself among those "who believe in a socially progressive and pro-active role for government" is also the man who boasted of reducing the level of government program spending to its lowest level in 50 years; the man who says that "what we must still achieve at the end of the day is a government that is fully capable of assisting the disadvantaged" is the man who ended the federal responsibility for the most disadvantaged in Canadian society. Yes, he will say, but think of the perils of Argentina, and to that there can be no answer.

The outsider might guess that at the end of the day Martin is uncertain within himself; he has certainly not got the comfort of an ideologue who can provide a fast and satisfying response to any situation. Alternatively he may be profoundly political, taking cover behind the ambiguity that is the Liberal Party; the party and the man have suited each other perfectly. In all probability the measure of the man will not be known immediately. He must be seen as a work in progress, the nature of which can be revealed only in power. It is only if and when Martin becomes prime minister that there will be an answer to the questions that have been asked about him since he first appeared on the fringes of the Liberal Party: Does he come bearing the values of the corporate world in which he had such singular success? Or does he come as the spear carrier of the ideas of his father, from a time when the foundation of the modern Canadian state was established? Paul Martin would have us believe that he is the son of his father, for he himself believes this to be true. But that has yet to be proven.

Index

Photo Credits

1. With his father at his side, Paul Martin Jr. launches himself into politics, May 1988. (CP/Allen McInnis)
2. Paul Martin Sr. is carried around the Ottawa convention hall in January 1958. (CP)
3. Paul Martin Jr. speaks to university students in Toronto, 1990. (CP/Reg Innel)
4. Jean Chrétien and Paul Martin before the February 2000 budget speech. (CP/Tom Hanson)
5. Paul Martin answers questions in the House of Commons, October 2001. (CP/Tom Hanson)
6. Jean Chrétien leads a standing ovation for Paul Martin after his budget speech, December 2001. (CP/Tom Hanson)
7. After his dismissal from the government. White Point, N.S., June 2002. (CP/Andrew Vaughan)
8. Paul Martin and his wife, Sheila. Ottawa, June 2002. (CP/Fred Chartrand)
9. Paul Martin answering questions from reporters at Dalhousie University, January 2003. (CP/Andrew Vaughan)
10. Paul Martin with Mary Walsh and Cathy Jones from CBC's *This Hour Has 22 Minutes*, January 2003. (CP/Andrew Vaughan)
11. Paul Martin acknowledges he must sell his shares in Canada Steamship Lines to avoid conflict of interest, March 2003. (CP/Tom Hanson)
12. Paul Martin visits Toronto's Chinatown to show support during the SARS outbreak, April 2003. (CP/Globe and Mail J.P. Moczulski)
13. Paul Martin, Sheila Copps and John Manley during a Liberal party leadership debate in June 2003. (CP/Jonathan Hayward)
14. Paul Martin in the Canada Day parade, July 1, 2003. (CP/Paul Chiasson)